POSTCARD HISTORY SERIES

Mineral Point

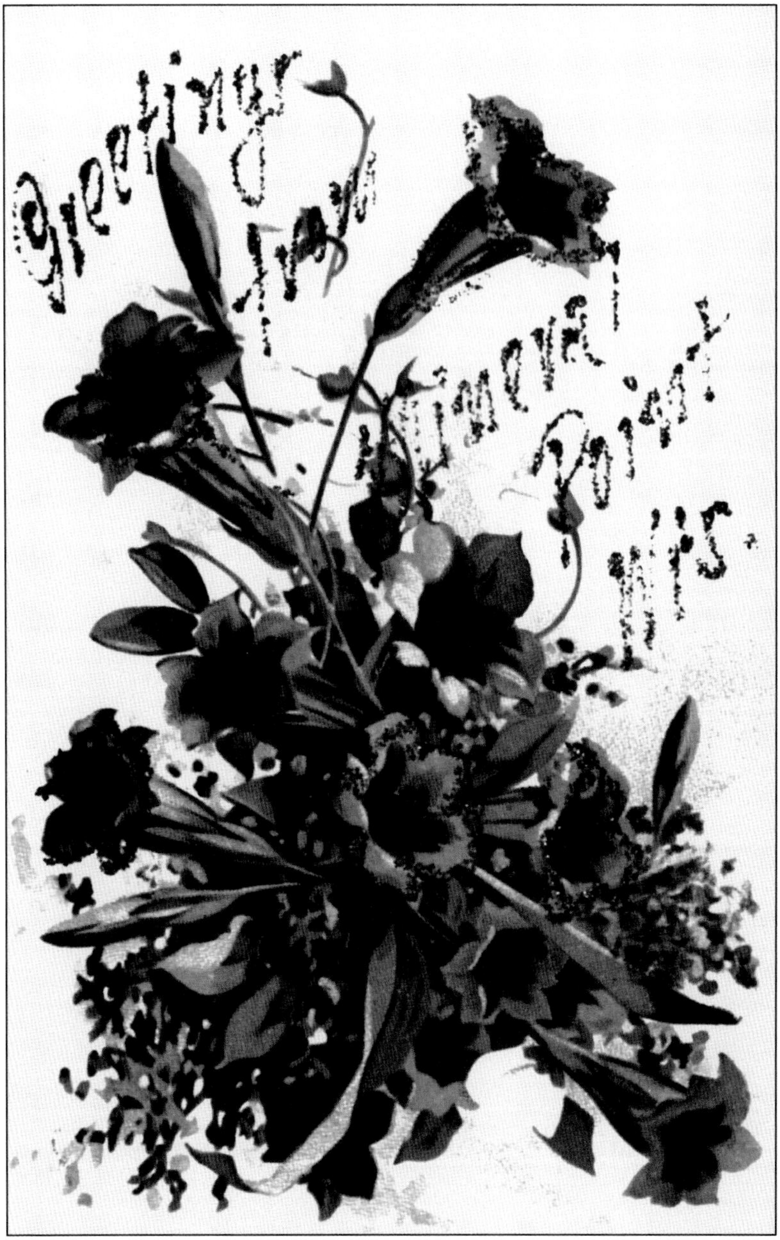

This "Greetings from Mineral Point" postcard dates from 1908.

On the front cover: Pendarvis House is a Cornish miner's house that most represents the image of the past and the present of Mineral Point. Today it is the beginning of all tours of the village. Yesterday it was where one could eat the best Cornish pasties of the area. (Photograph by Gari Walz.)

On the back cover: Called the Badger Hole or the Dugout, this is the first mining shack of the area. New arrivals wasted little time; they often dug into the side of a hill and called it home. These first settlers came to be known as "Badgers" for their likeness to the animals that lived in dens; thus Wisconsin was nicknamed the Badger State. (Photograph by Gari Walz.)

POSTCARD HISTORY SERIES

Mineral Point

Kay Price and Marian Hendricks

ARCADIA
PUBLISHING

ISBN 978-0-7385-5215-6

Published by Arcadia Publishing
Charleston SC, Chicago IL, Portsmouth NH, San Francisco CA

Printed in the United States of America

Library of Congress Catalog Card Number: 2007941890

For all general information contact Arcadia Publishing at:
Telephone 843-853-2070
Fax 843-853-0044
E-mail sales@arcadiapublishing.com
For customer service and orders:
Toll-Free 1-888-313-2665

Visit us on the Internet at www.arcadiapublishing.com

This book is dedicated to all the people who came before us to settle this rich land. They came with little to guide them, except their dreams of a better future for their children. Their work was without end. We are those children, whose lives have been better and easier because they came before us. We thank them. We remember them. We honor them.

Contents

Acknowledgments

This book could not have been written without the permission of the archives room in the Mineral Point Library. We used their postcard collection that was donated by Robert Neal. Mary Alice Moore, the curator of the archives room, was invaluable with her assistance. This book would have been much more difficult to write without her help. She gave of her time and her knowledge. She worked several 12-hour days organizing, copying, and scanning the postcards. She researched and answered any of our questions. She helped in ways too numerous to describe. We will forever be in her debt. Her friendship was an extra bonus, one that will continue long after the completion of this book.

We especially appreciate the help and assistance of the following: Barbara Polizzi, director of the Mineral Point Library, was helpful in her support and allowed us to use the scanning machine in the library. She was always available to answer a question. Joy Gieseke, executive director of the Mineral Point Chamber of Commerce, provided us with information and guidance. Jim Stroschein, president of the Mineral Point Historical Society, was most helpful in providing us with information on several historic subjects. He found articles for us that furnished us with background information. He was always pleasant and ready to assist. The Gundry House and the Mineral Point Historical Society deserve a special thanks for helping us market our book.

Pendarvis provided photographs from their collection that we appreciated. Nancy Pfotenhauer, secretary of the Mineral Point Historical Society and a frequent volunteer at the archival room, answered questions and made suggestions that were valuable.

We wish to thank the following artists for use of their postcard photographs: Gari Walz, Michael Mewis, Pat Ripp, and Betty France. We greatly appreciate your permission to use your art on these pages. Hopefully you will be happy with the end results. We appreciate the contribution of anyone we may have forgotten to mention. Sometimes it is hard to track down people. Please know that we tried.

A special thank-you goes to Bill Dyke for writing the prologue for this book. His understanding of the history of the area, combined with his own legal background as judge of Iowa County, offers a unique viewpoint.

PROLOGUE

This gathering of scenes of Mineral Point is a link to the colorful history of a unique community. Mineral Point is the place where Wisconsin began with the swearing in ceremony of Henry Dodge as the first governor of the Wisconsin Territory.

Mineral Point owes its beginnings to the hardy group of prospectors who found lead ore, known as galena, in 1827. Through the boom and bust that followed, Mineral Point held onto its identity. Today a great many of the homes and shops retain the distinct patterns of the past.

The hills and valleys of Mineral Point and the pathways that pass through them are part of this gathering of the visions of the past and the dreams that preserve them to this day.

We owe this collection to the devoted custodians of the visual and historical record. Both the volunteers in the historical society and in the Mineral Point Room carry on with the preservation of this community's memories. The individual citizens, who simply love their hometown, work in harmony with the volunteers to maintain the memories of those who came before us. Together they keep the history alive and sparkling in the sun.

Every footstep you take in Mineral Point follows a pathway of the past. As one who has traced those steps—as an admirer of Mineral Point, respecter of its heritage, and a well-wisher for the future of this one-of-a-kind community—it is a pleasure to commend this book to you.

William D. Dyke
Judge of Iowa County

Introduction

When I was growing up in Mineral Point in the 1920s, it was not unusual to see miners on High Street (the main street) returning from their day's work in the mines. Their faces were blackened from the lead ore dust, and they wore visor caps with calcium carbide lanterns attached to the front of the cap. The lanterns lit their way in tunnels as black as night in the mines. Mineral Point was established in 1827, when lead was discovered in the area. Miners from Cornwall, England, came to work in the mines. For many years Mineral Point prospered from mining lead and zinc.

My family moved to Mineral Point in 1922, when my father, Lewis Graves, a medical doctor, took over the practice of the retiring doctor. The first year we rented the second floor of the Penhallagon house on South Iowa Street. With the approach of winter, the Penhallagons made plans to spend the season in Florida. They had a separate furnace for the water heating system for their first-floor home. Before leaving, they drained the water from the pipes so there would be no danger of water freezing and breaking the pipes during the cold winter. They thought they could safely leave the furnace unused until they returned. However, the water pipes that heated our second floor home came up through the corner of each of the now unheated 12-foot-high first-floor rooms and were exposed to the freezing cold. Little heat reached our flat. Dad was warm only when he was at his office, and I when I was at school. I do not know how my mother, Mabelle, and my baby brother, Howard, survived. It was a winter to remember.

In 1923, we purchased the house at 121 Dodge Street, the second house north of the city (or water tower) park. It was a comfortable house with a large yard. There was a vegetable garden, flower gardens, and even a goldfish pond. Later the nice front yard was diminished when Highway 151, which extended along Dodge Street, was widened.

Soon after moving to Mineral Point, when I was eight years of age, I began taking piano lessons from Nettie Wallis, the sister of Mrs. Henry Bray. Nettie taught piano in the front parlor of the Bray house. When Nettie was young, she was engaged to be married. But the engagement was broken, and she continued to teach in the Bray house. Years later, when her health was failing, she divided her Haviland china bridal set among her advanced students. My place setting is displayed in my china cabinet to this day. Nettie was an excellent teacher—thorough, yet patient and kind.

In the winter, when there was a good blanket of snow, it was time to get out the skis. I had to walk only a block to where we could ski down a rather steep hill for a block, then on into a farmer's field. Of course, it was a long walk back to the top, but great fun to ski back down again. There were also plenty of hillsides for sledding.

In the summer we loved to roller-skate even though there were many inclines. If a descent became too steep, we stopped by skating onto the grass at the side. Swimming at Soldier's

Memorial Park was always fun. There were swimming lessons, which included diving. The water slide was exciting. Nearby in the park were well-used tennis courts. The swimming pool had been built in 1922, adjacent to Hoard Street (Shake Rag Street). A small stream flowed close to the street toward the Pecatonica River. The stream was dammed, and water accumulated in the excavated area to form a lake. There were bathhouses, a slide to the water, and diving boards. A large crowd gathered for the dedication. The band played and everyone was proud of the addition to the city.

During one of my father's four terms as mayor, the city celebrated the renovation of the city park at the high end of High Street. A small information center was built. The bandstand nearby was freshly painted. The band, in full-dress uniforms, played joyfully. As mayor, Dad introduced the guest speaker, the governor of Wisconsin, who had come from Madison for this outstanding event. On festive occasions the city band marched proudly up and down High Street. On special summer evenings they played in the bandstand. The delightful music wafted over the surrounding hillsides, and people gathered and milled about.

Life was simple; life was good. Then, like a streak of lightning, the Great Depression hit. Mineral Point suffered greatly. The mines and the zinc furnace closed, putting many men out of work. Many families were sorely affected. Then the bank closed, creating more disastrous problems. Debts mounted. Some bills were paid with a sack of potatoes or other produce, poultry, or eggs. There was little money for paying bills or making mortgage payments. Foreclosures were common, and everyone was hurting.

In 1935 Robert Neal, a native of Mineral Point, returned to his hometown after having studied architecture and working in New York City and London, England. He met Edgar Hellum of Stoughton, Wisconsin, who shared his interest in the old stone houses of the original miners of Mineral Point. For $15 they purchased an old, abandoned, deteriorating rock cottage on Hoard Street, commonly referred to as Shake Rag Street. It was so named because the miners' wives, reputedly, would shake white towels for the miner husbands to see when it was dinnertime. They had a lookout on top of the mine watching for the rag to wave.

Neal and Hellum named the cottage Pendarvis after an estate in Cornwall, England, in honor of Neal's Cornish heritage. Soon thereafter, they bought the second similar house next door and named it Trelawny. After considerable restoration with the help of an experienced stonemason from Cornwall, in 1940 the two men began serving a traditional Cornish tea. The menu consisted of Cornish pasty (a meat pie), plum preserves with clotted cream, saffron cake, and figgy hobbin (a rolled pastry with raisins). Later the men purchased their third house, which they named Polperro, as well as additional land and a log row house named Tamblyn's Row. It had a basement built into the hillside that housed a tiddlywink, or pub. The entire group of buildings was purchased in 1970 by the State of Wisconsin and is treasured today as a state historical site.

In 1939 an artist named Max Fernekes, with his wife and children, purchased a house near Pendarvis for their home and art studio. There was considerable interest in his work, and soon other artisans settled in Mineral Point. Today Mineral Point has a thriving community of artists, and there are gift shops and galleries on Shake Rag, Commerce, and High Streets.

Thousands of people come to Mineral Point each year to visit Pendarvis and the other historical sites, to shop for original artwork, and to enjoy a delicious Cornish pasty. Mineral Point has successfully blended the past and the present. Mineral Point is rejuvenated.

—Marian Hendricks

One

Zinc and Acid Works

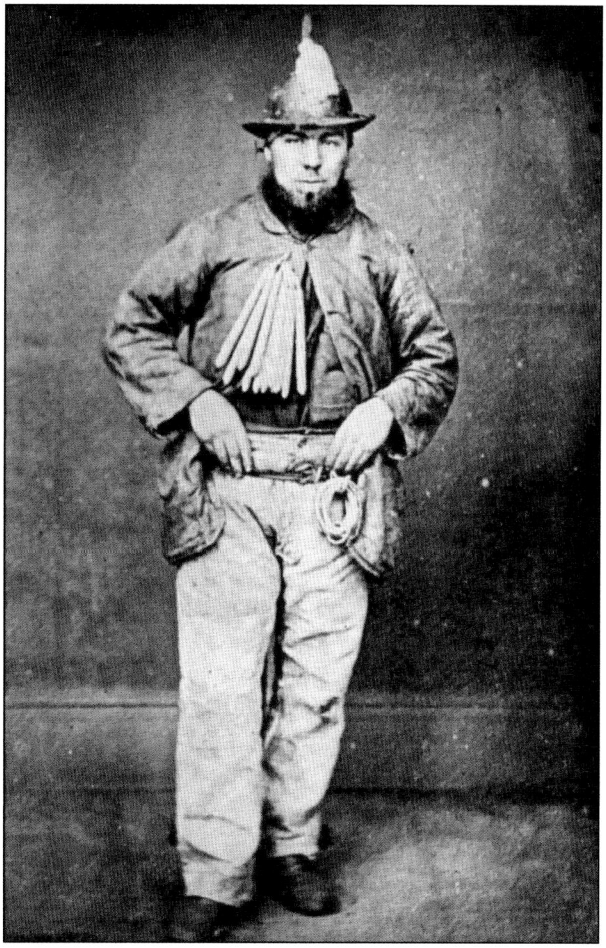

There was nothing glamorous about Wisconsin's mining era. The days were very long, and the work was extremely hard and dangerous. Poisonous gases, rock falls, and shafts collapsing, causing cave-ins, were all a part of the day-to-day dangers facing miners. With over 95 percent of the population male in the early 1820s, weekends were often spent gambling, beer drinking, and carousing. Their life expectancy was short.

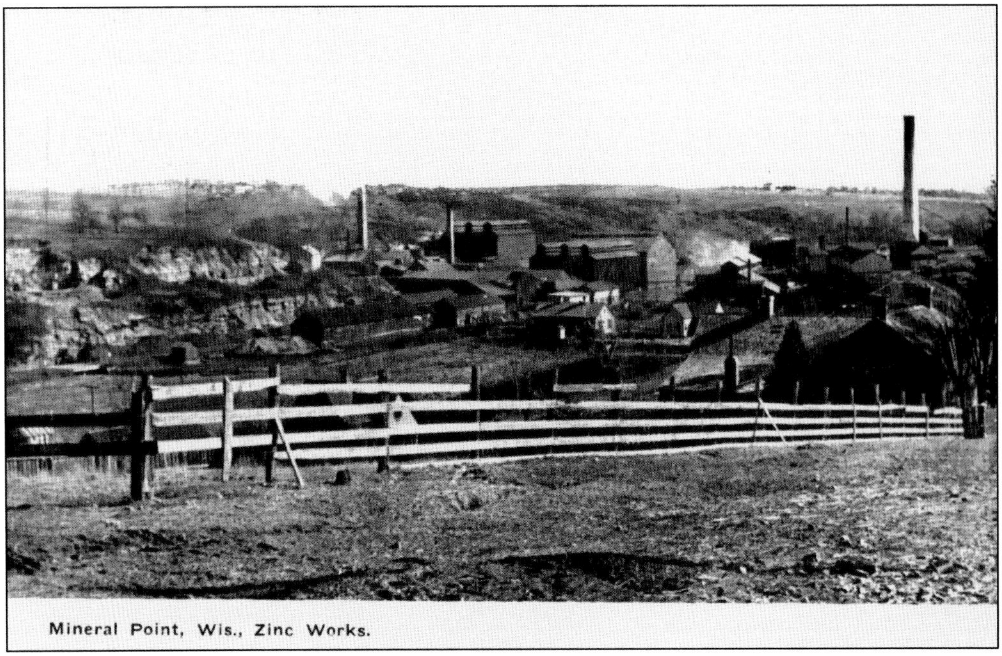

In the late 1820s, Wisconsin grew from several hundred settlers to 10,000 people in a few years. By the late 1830s, the Cornish miners immigrated to Wisconsin from Cornwall, England, settling around Mineral Point. This is regarded as the first large-group European migration to Wisconsin. These photographs show the earliest mines in the Mineral Point area.

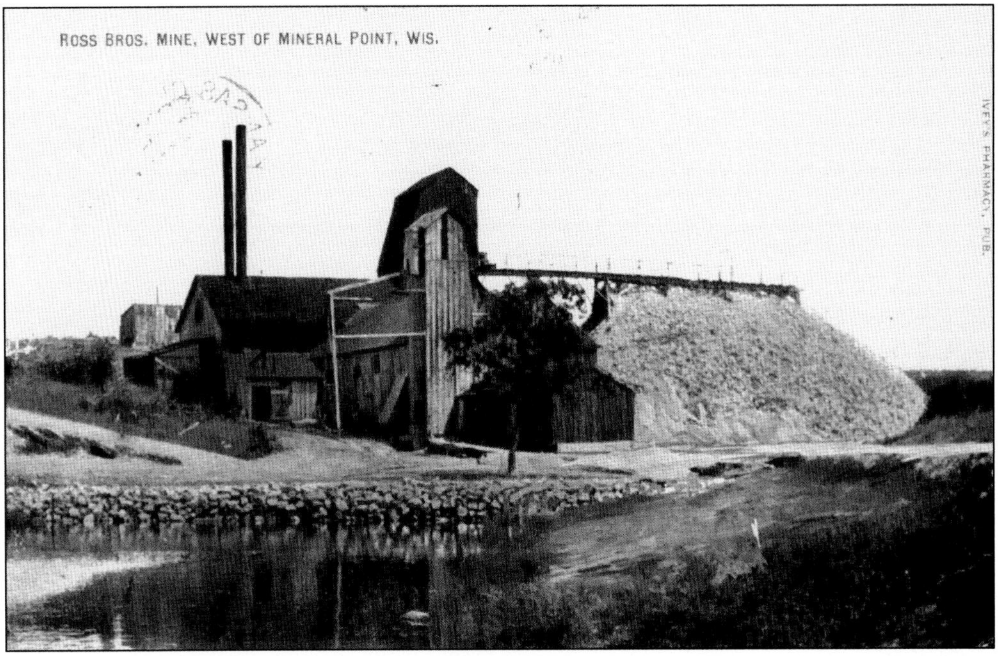

Lead was used for bullets, pewter, type, weights, pipes, and especially paint. It was soft and easy to melt and silvery grey in color. The price was good at $5 for 100 pounds. This plant would develop into a giant operation covering 52 acres and be a major influence on the economy of Mineral Point up until its closing in 1930.

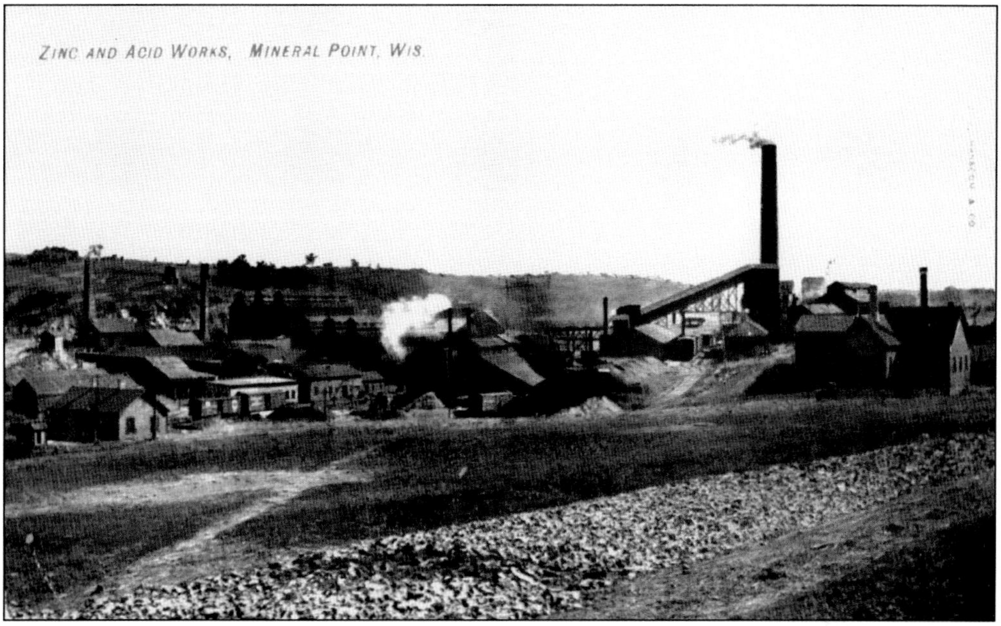

Local businessmen banded together to start the Mineral Point Zinc and Acid Works. It was a brave venture that proved to be very profitable for the whole area. This 1910 view is before the engine room was built. In the fall of 1882, the furnaces of the Mineral Point Zinc Works were fired up for the first time. By 1906 the zinc works employed 364 men at this plant. The plant developed into a giant operation until it closed in 1930.

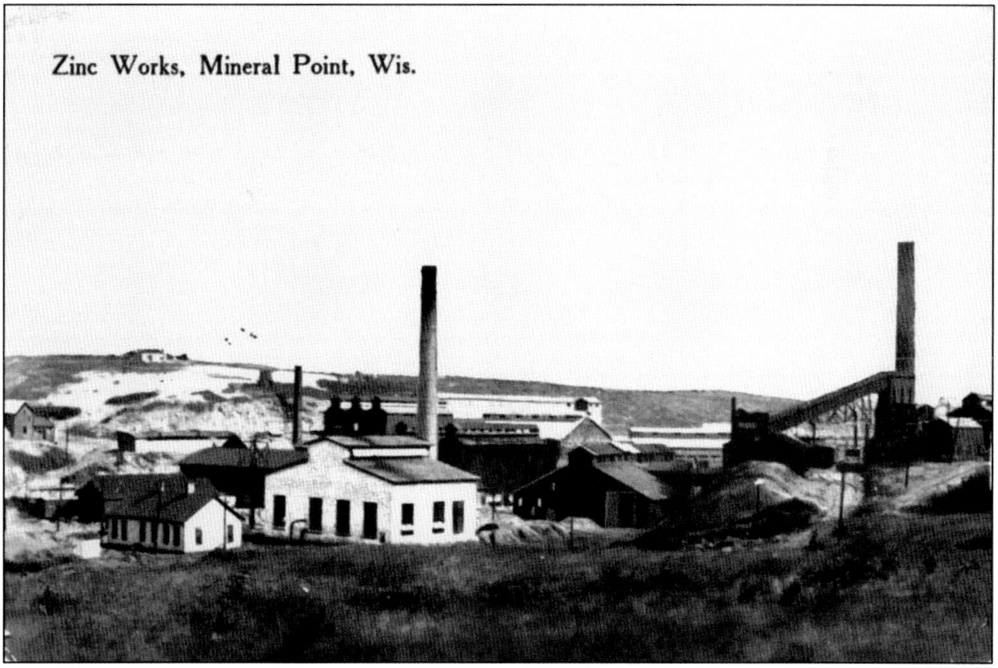

The Mineral Point Zinc Works and Acid Plant was one of the largest ore-smelting plants in the United States. Ore was shipped here from all over the country to be smelted. Here they processed lead oxide for paint, made it into pure zinc and turned the sulfur gases into sulfuric acid.

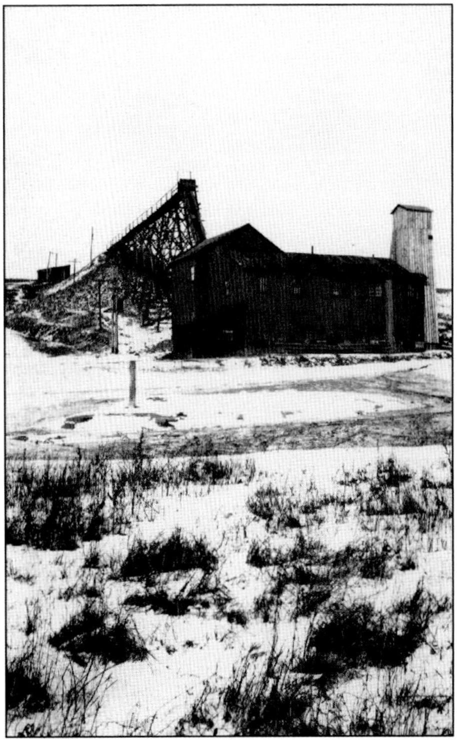

The Merry Christmas Mine was one of the Mineral Point area's larger mines. It underlies the eastern part of Mineral Point Hill where the original discovery of lead ore was made in about 1825. This mine was opened as the Merry Christmas Mine about 1906. It operated with some interruptions until 1912. It was closed, according to reports, because of a fatal rock fall. Today it is a part of the Pendarvis State Historic Site with 43 acres of restored prairie.

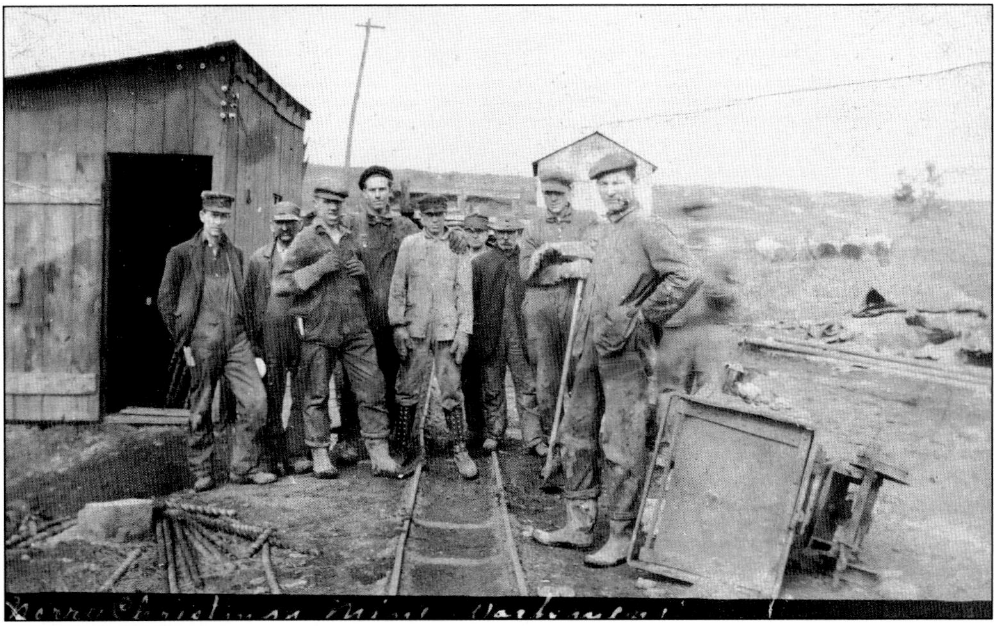

Merry Christmas Miners stand before the entrance to the mine shaft. They were a loyal bunch who watched each other's backs. They would risk their lives for each other. Prior to this more advanced way of mining, these men used wooden windlasses to carry them below. One miner would ride the bucket down, one leg in the bucket, the other dangling, entrusting his partner to safely lower or raise him. Partners would either crank up buckets of ore to the surface or fill buckets of ore down below.

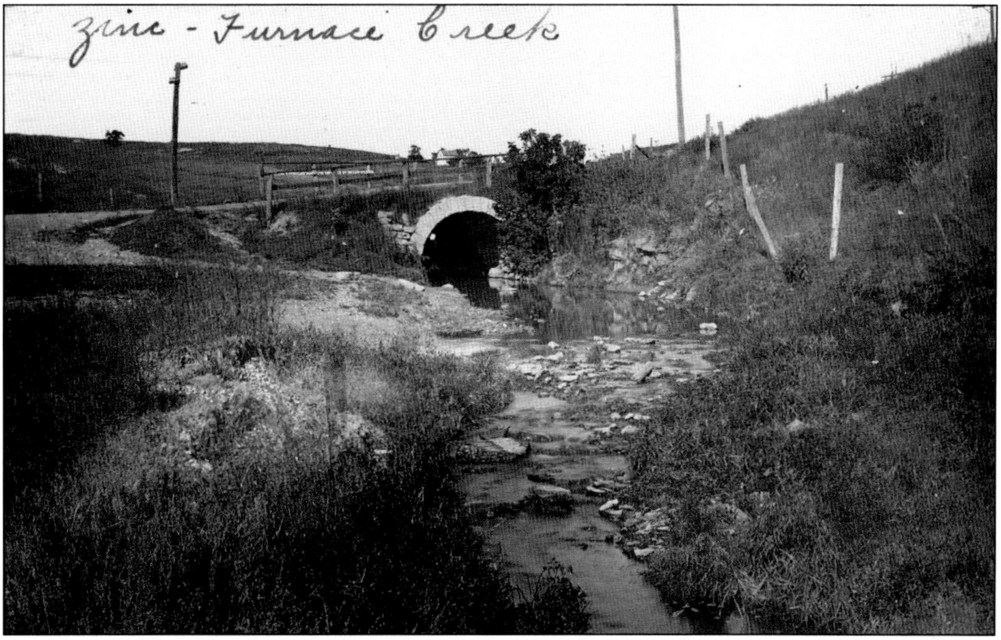

This was the Zinc Furnace Creek. Mining residue caused pollution that has only recently been cleaned up. This is now a trout stream below the Merry Christmas Mine. Previously the leaching of contaminants from the tailings or waste piles altered the soil and polluted the streams.

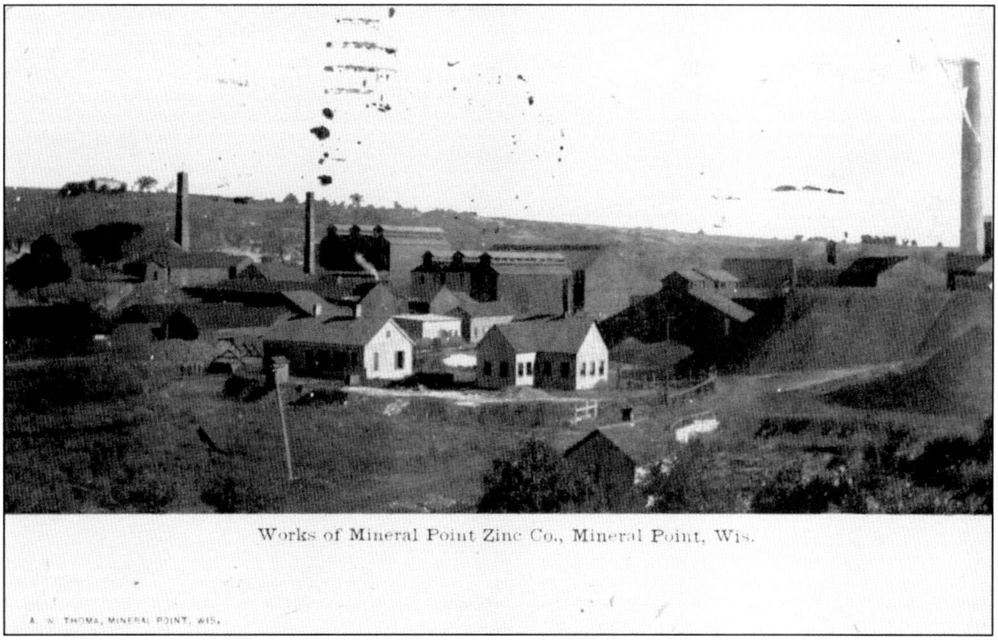

Mines sprung up all around the Mineral Point area. The first mines were lead ore mines. When the Cornish miners arrived they knew how to dig deeper; they started to mine zinc. The bedrock of the Driftless Area, a type of limestone called galena dolomite, was laid down in a shallow sea more than 400 million years ago. Lead, zinc, and copper mineral deposits filled existing crevices close to the surface of the limestone. The shallowness of the deposits meant that the minerals could be extracted readily.

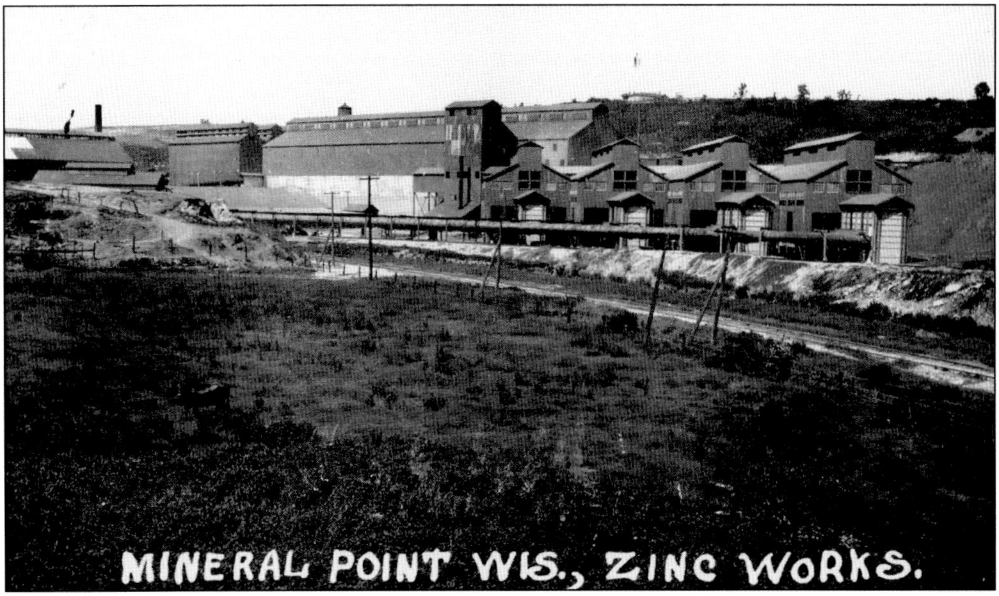

Six local businessmen joined together to start the zinc works. They hired engineers from out east to give them advice. Eventually they merged with the New Jersey Zinc Company. By 1884 the zinc works were burning up to 20 tons per day of zinc ore. It was mixed with coal screenings in the furnaces and transformed into a white powder that resembled flour. The businessmen made their fortunes here. They used some of their money to bring in the railroad to export the zinc.

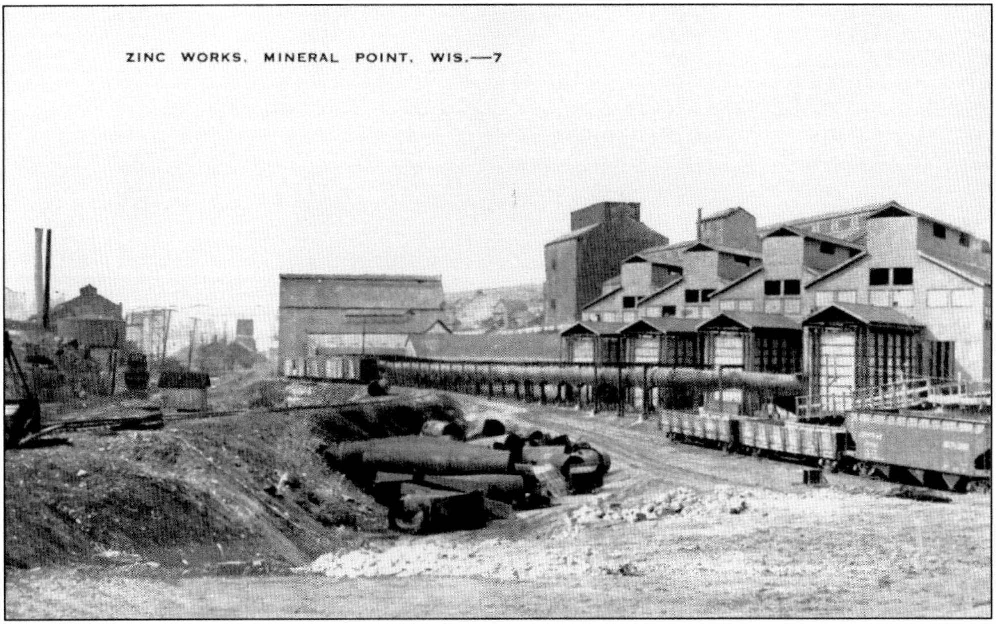

After the New Jersey Zinc Company bought into the operation, they added a sulfuric acid plant to take advantage of a by-product from the ore roasting. This allowed the utilization of the sulfur fumes at a profit, instead of allowing them to escape and be a possible nuisance.

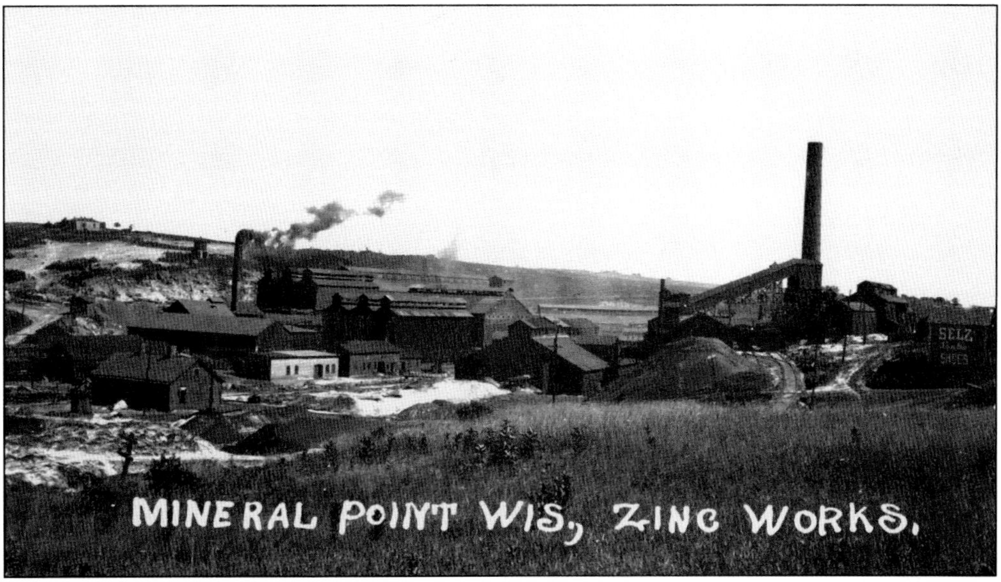

The zinc works were the largest employer of the Mineral Point area. At one point they could not get enough help. They advertised for hundreds of more workers. They needed machine men, shovelers, and common laborers. They hired 50 Mexicans in 1925.

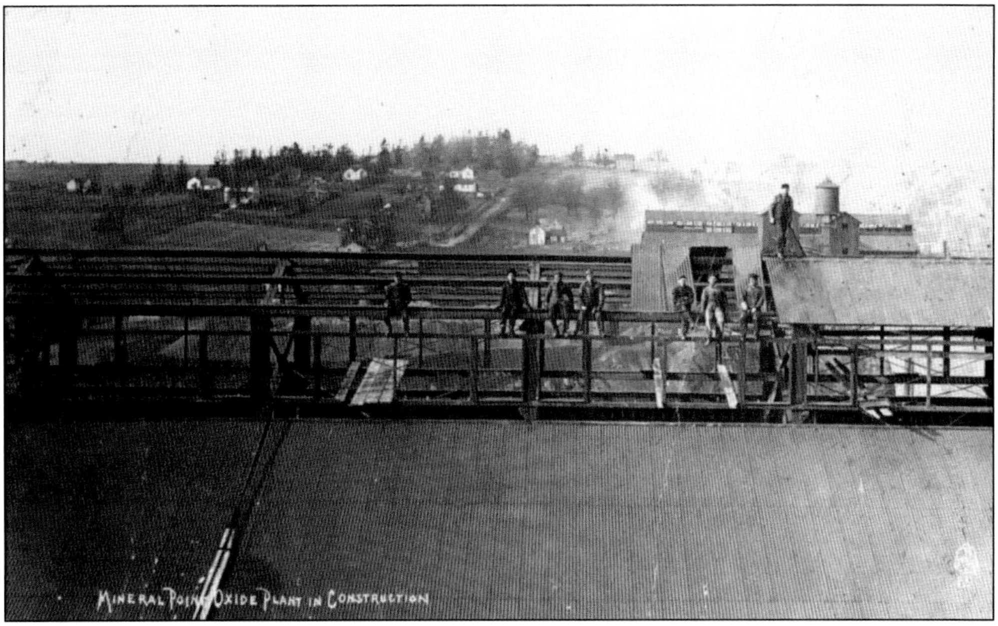

This photograph shows a zinc oxide plant under construction. As the demand for lead continued, the sophistication of the mining operation advanced. Very few shallow mines were used because of their inefficiency. But as the technology advanced, so did the cost of procurement.

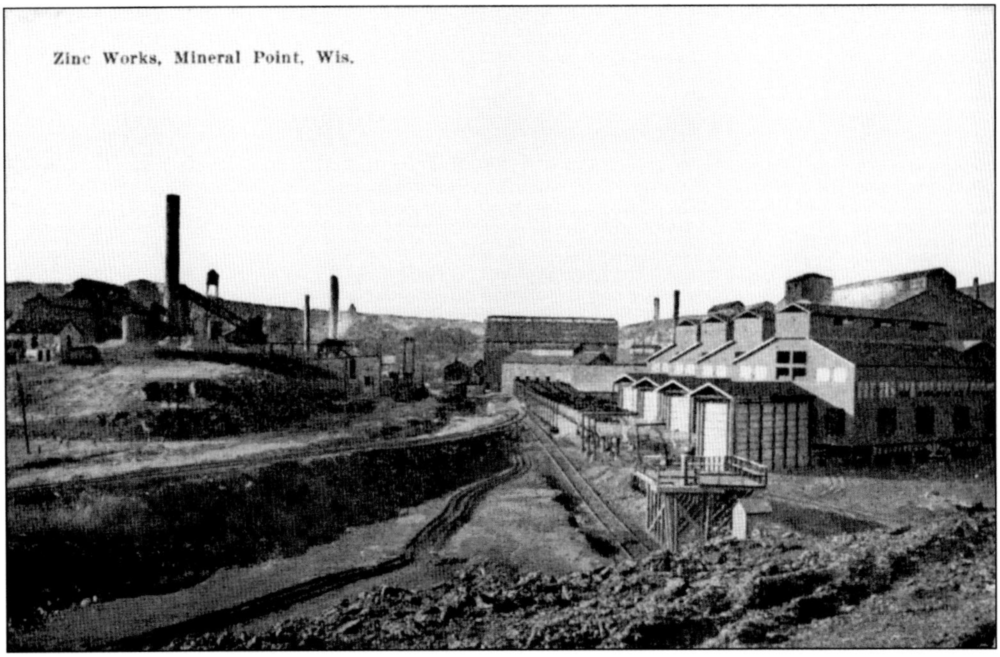

Starting in 1882, the zinc plant had one furnace. In 1894, as the plant expanded during the boom years that followed, it grew to three furnaces and a number of additional support buildings. By 1870 the output of zinc was actually greater than lead.

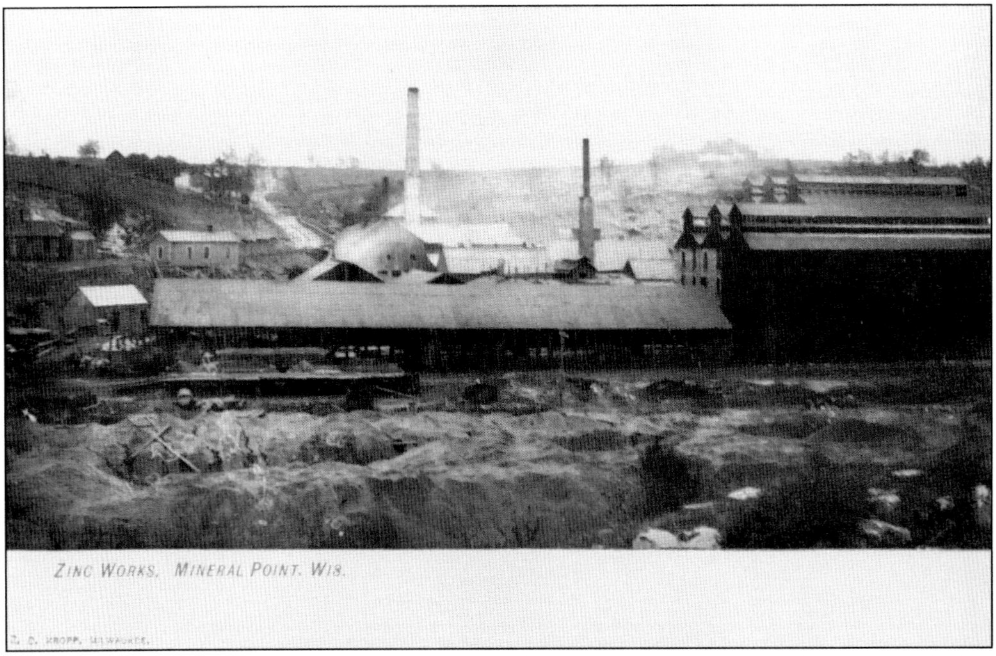

Zinc was used to galvanize pails and pipes to keep them from rusting. The explosives used during World War I were responsible for the maximum production of zinc ore in the mining region occurring in 1917, during the time of that war.

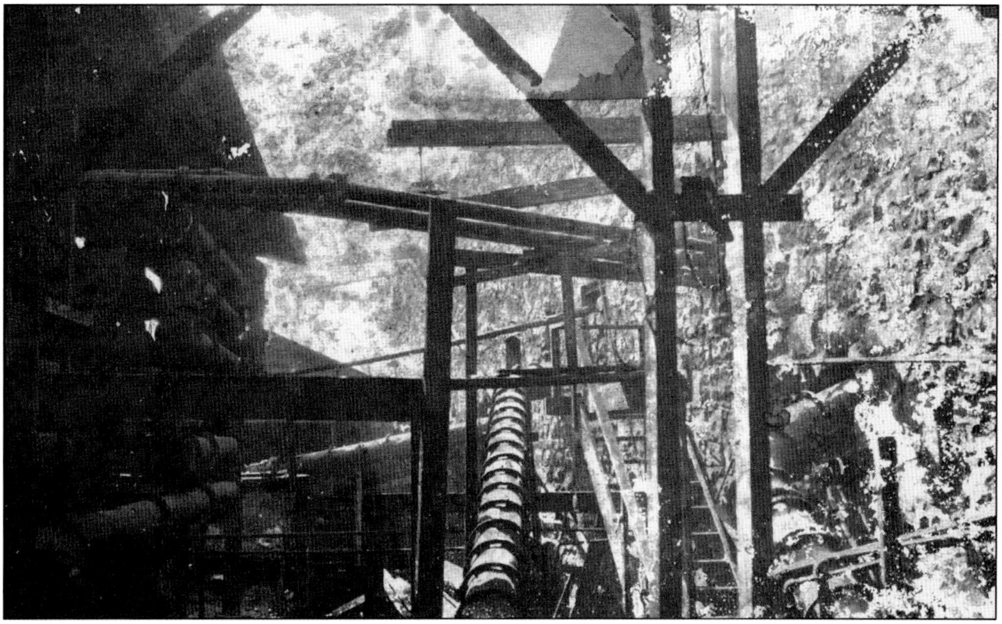

Roasting is a high-temperature process that converts zinc sulfide concentrate to an impure zinc oxide called calcine. The major advantages of this roaster are greater throughput capacities and greater sulfur-removal capabilities.

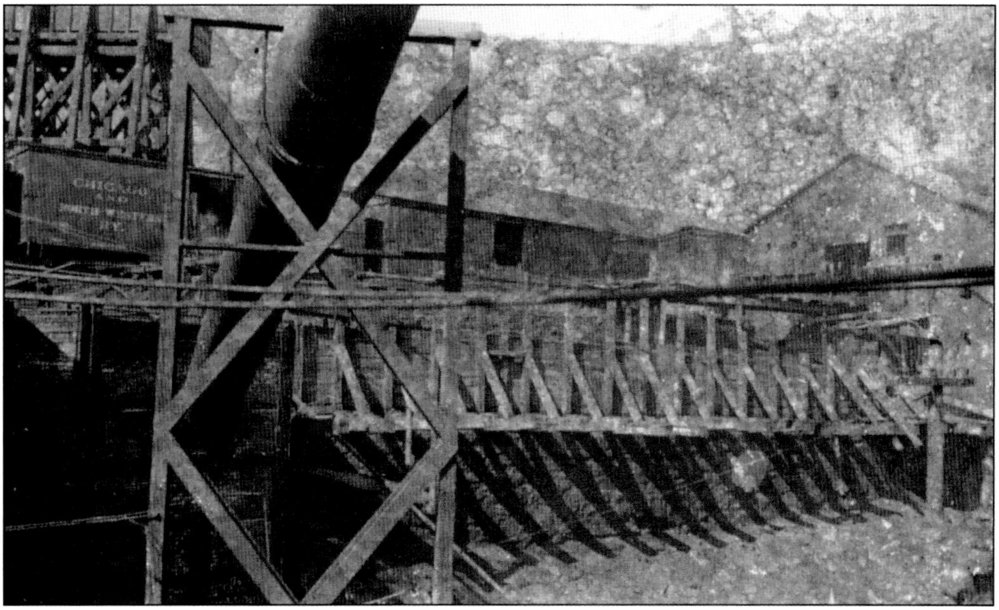

Suspension roasters are also unpressurized and operate at about 1,800 degrees Fahrenheit. This is another step to separate and prepare the zinc oxide from the zinc ore.

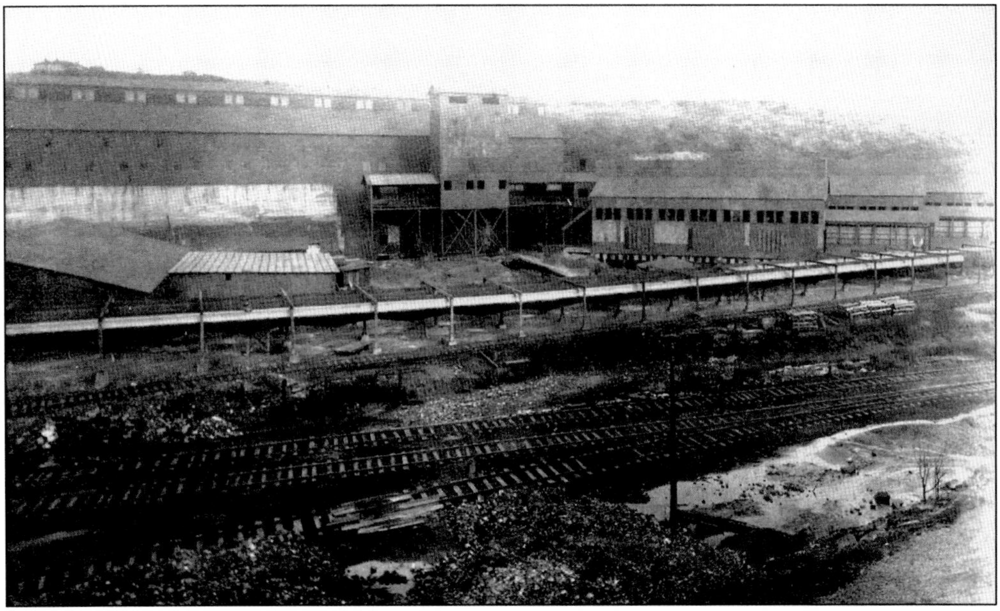

This is the New Jersey and Mineral Point Zinc Works Factory. It was built in part by John Norman, a carpenter from Spizzen, Germany. He worked here for 17 years. His pension was $1 a month for each year, so he got $17 a month. It took two men to lift his tool chest.

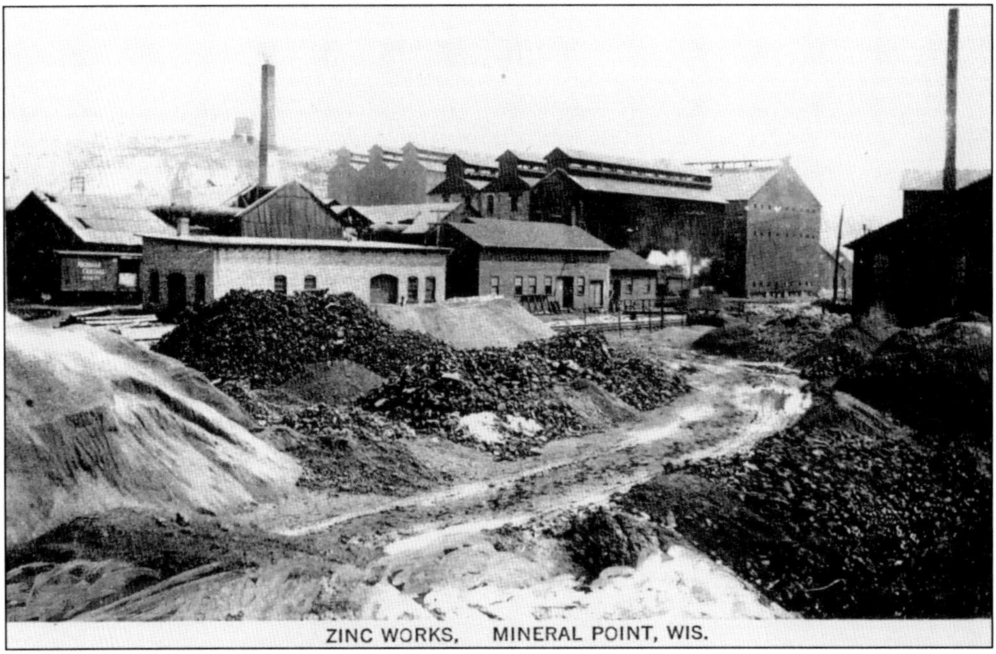

The plant continued to thrive and grow, adding an electrical power plant. After 1920, the output of the plant suffered because of decreased usage, but new uses for zinc oxide and sulfuric acid permitted the plant to continue production until the Depression in 1929.

Two

Mineral Point Trains

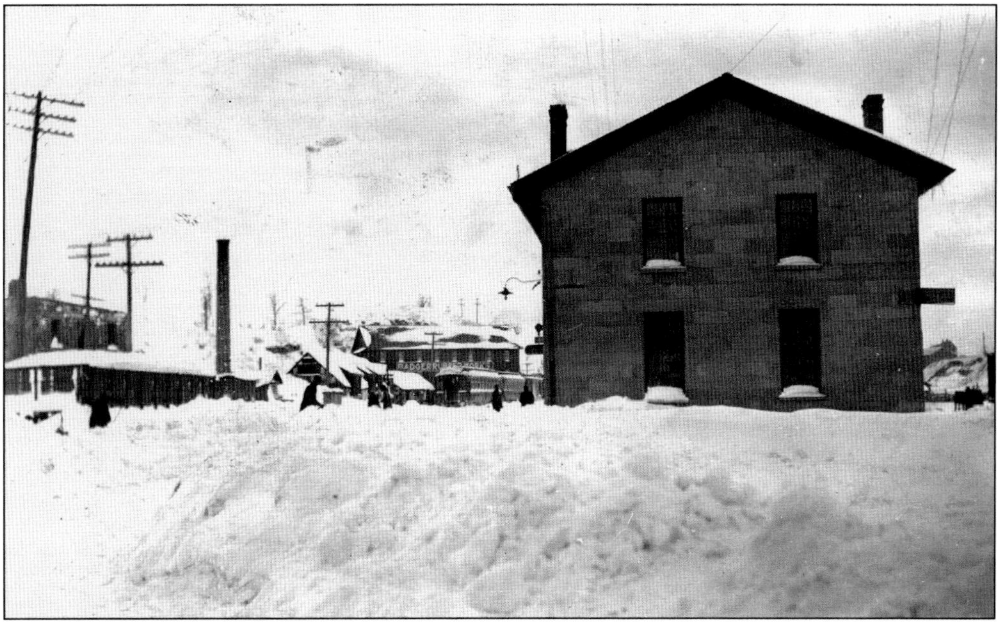

A handful of visionaries from Mineral Point found a way to fund the railroad from Mineral Point that connected to the Illinois Central Railroad. Despite tremendous challenges, the railroad was built and opened in 1857. It survived through good and bad years and eventually was purchased by the Chicago, Milwaukee and St. Paul Railway in 1880. This Mineral Point depot is the oldest depot in Wisconsin, and it is one of the few surviving pre–Civil War depots in the United States.

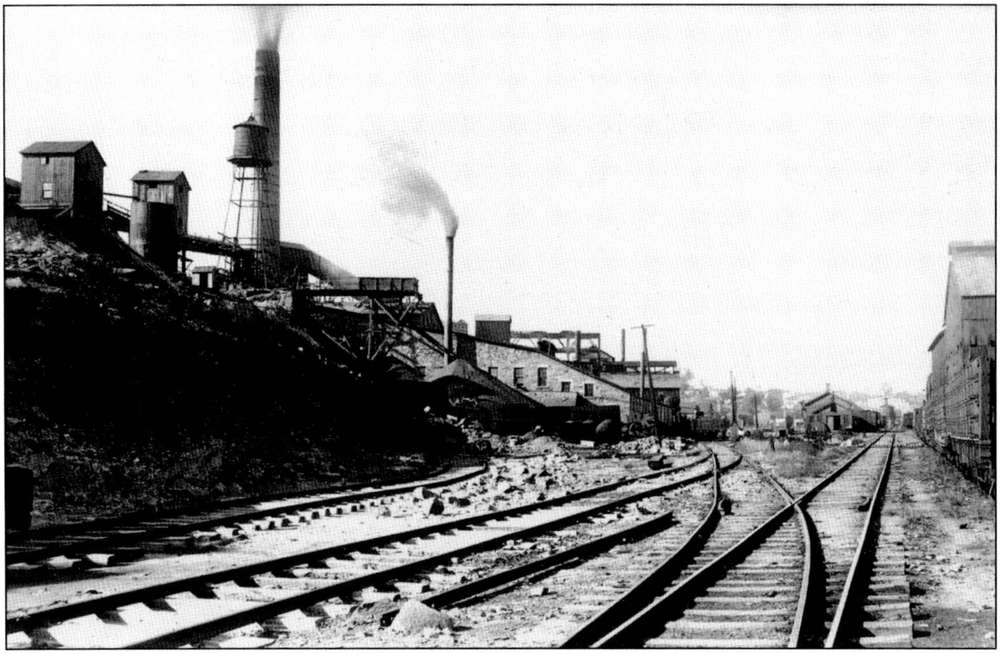

By 1930, the zinc plant in Mineral Point had closed and the town quickly fell into a prolonged recession. By the 1950s, it was not clear how much longer Mineral Point would have rail service. Essentially all of the traffic going out of Mineral Point via rail had dried up when the industry faded away. Much of the goods coming into Mineral Point were coming via truck rather than train.

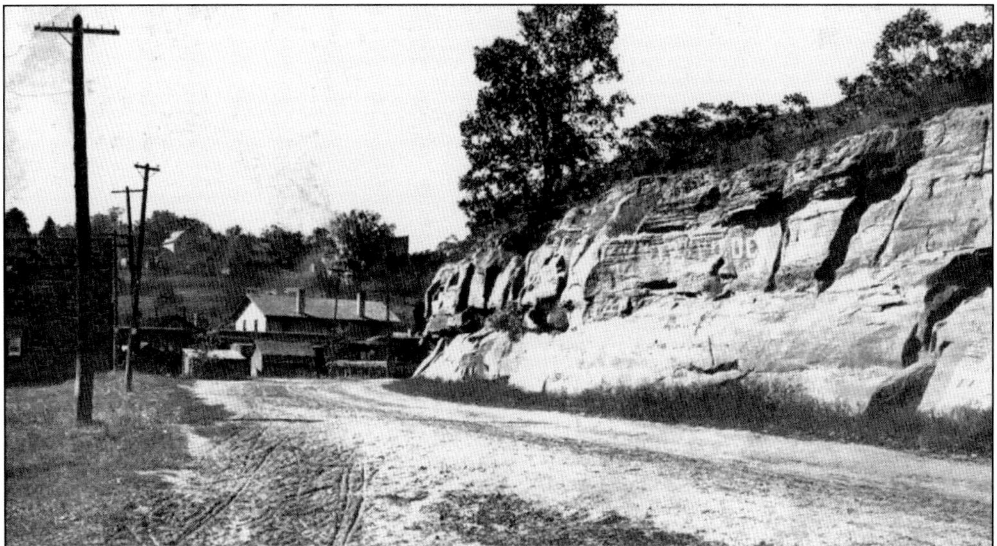

Rock Cliff near St. Paul Depot, Mineral Point, Wis.

This is the Darlington Road leading up to the depot and train tracks. There were grand ideas of connecting Mineral Point to Chicago or at least as far as the state line, but they never materialized. Several railroad lines built stretches of the track, but a variety of financial problems kept the train from becoming a major success.

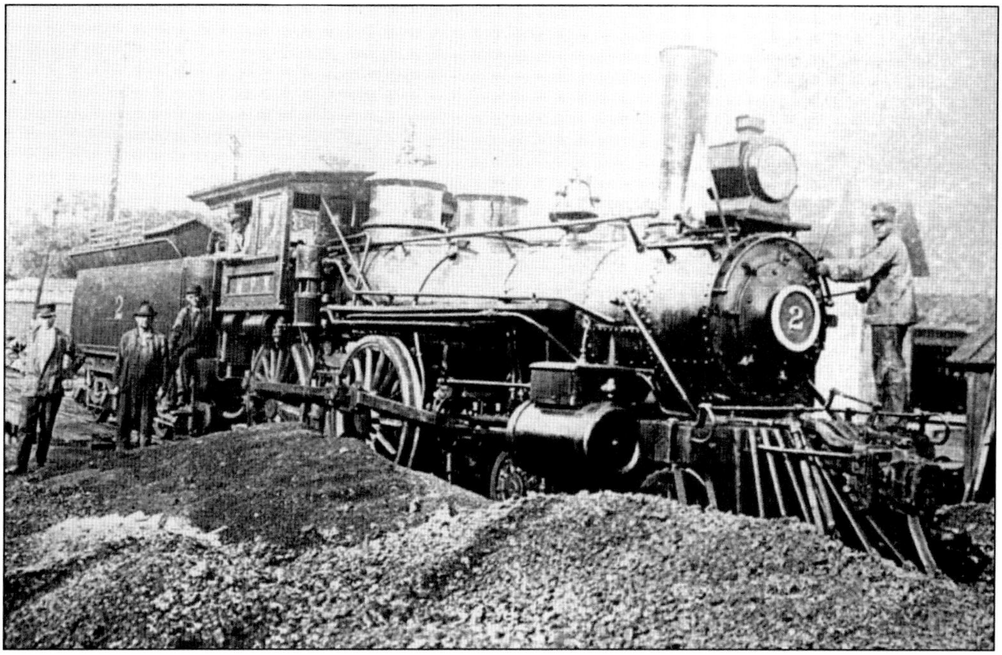

The Mineral Point and Northern Railway (MP&N) Engine No. 2, around 1905, looks powerful and impressive. The MP&N helped the entire region it served to prosper. The people enjoyed greater convenience, as well as regular passenger and freight trains to move people and products from one site to another. (Published by the Mineral Point Historical Society.)

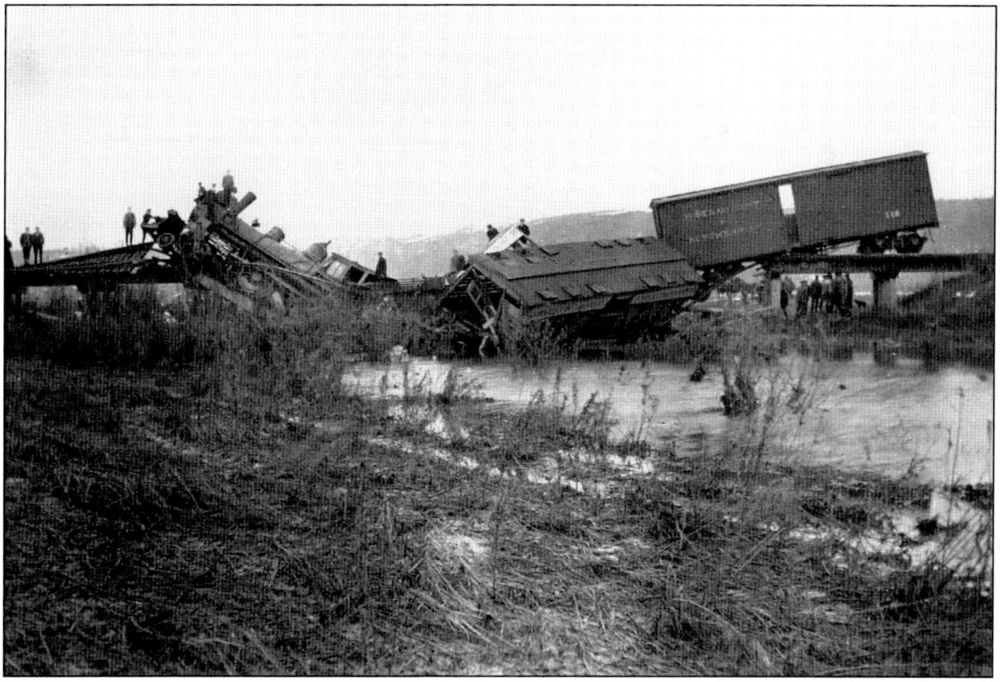

The MP&N train wreck was south of Mineral Point in Lawinger Meadow on February 11, 1911. Local man Henry Waldt was killed in the wreck. Wrecks did happen, including one when the MP&N train went through a bridge, fatally injuring one man and scalding others.

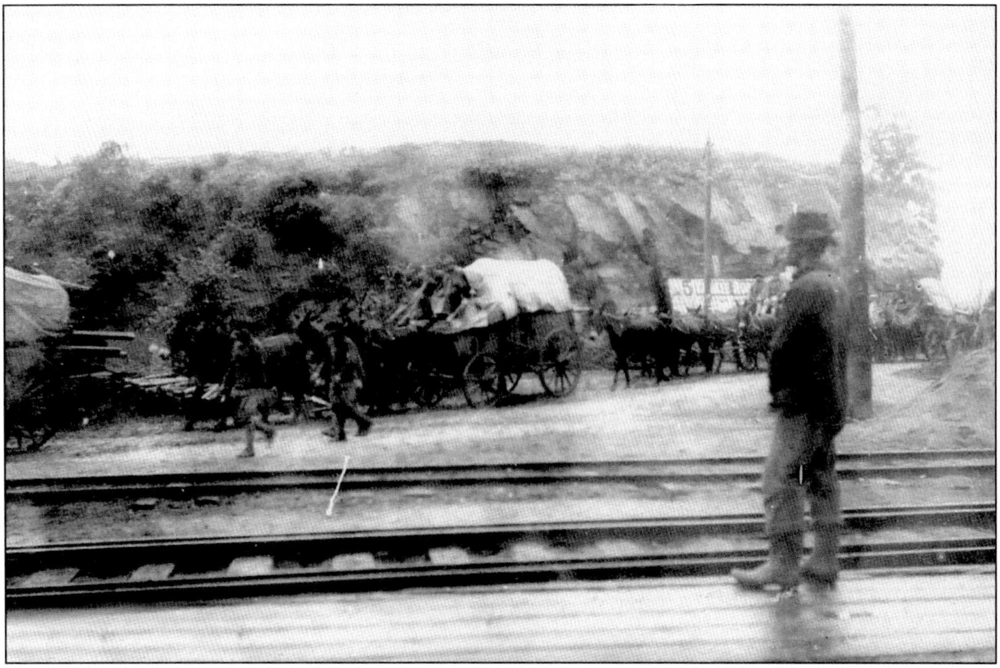

Men with wagonloads of supplies bring their goods to the train station. The trains provided a better and quicker way to transport their products to the big cities. Many times a year excursion trains were made available for special events. Sunday school picnics included a ride on the train. One train ran on August 3, 1905, and carried more than 1,000 people to the Mineral Point fair.

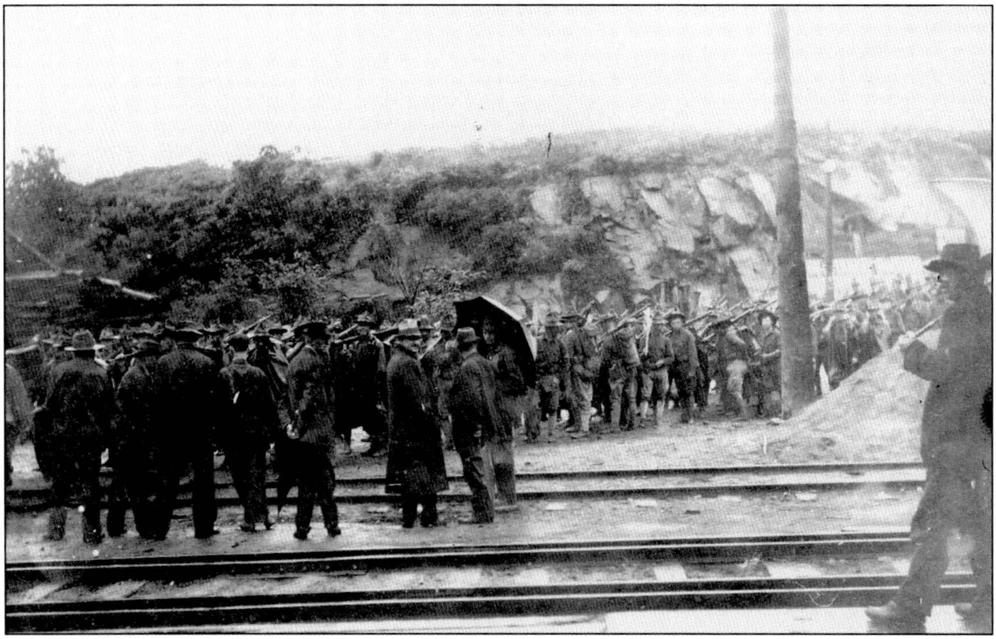

Soldiers going from Camp Grant to Camp Douglas gather at the Mineral Point depot with their guns and supplies, probably during World War I. The depot was a gathering place for happy welcomings and sad farewells.

Three

CHURCHES AND SCHOOLS

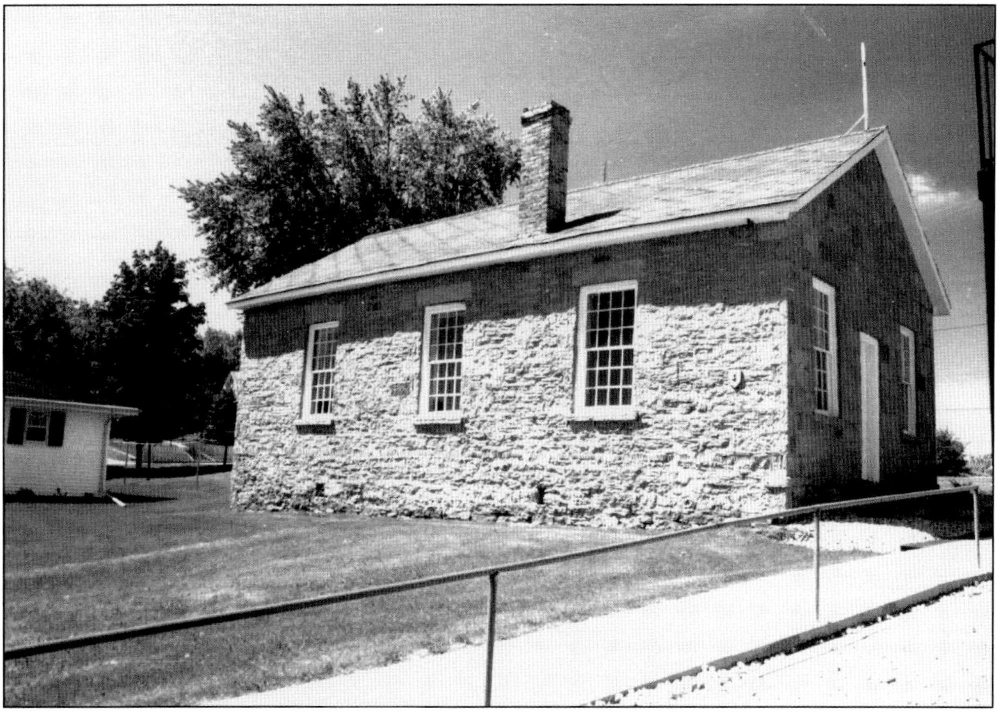

The first Catholic priest to arrive at Mineral Point was Rev. Father Mazzuchelli, an Italian, who celebrated the first mass in 1839. In 1842, ground was secured for a church site. The first church, pictured here, was erected the following year for the Irish Catholics. Father Mazzuchelli is currently up for consideration for sainthood by the Vatican. This is one of the oldest church buildings still standing in all of Wisconsin.

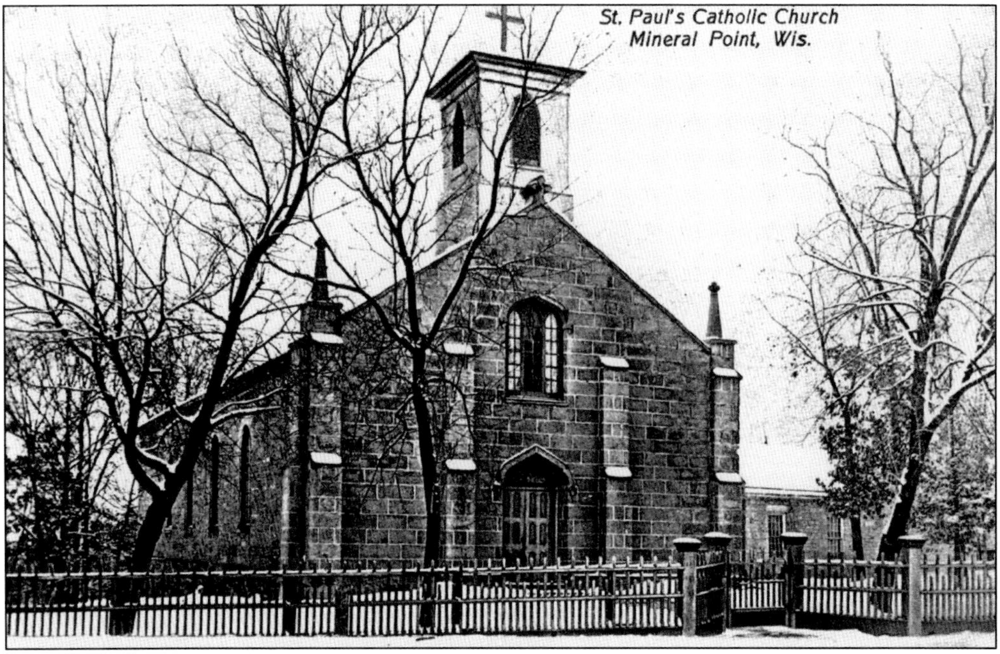

This was the second Catholic church called St. Paul's. It was built in 1860 and was demolished in 1910 to make way for the new church. This church took a long time to build because of lack of funds. This church had a large Irish population.

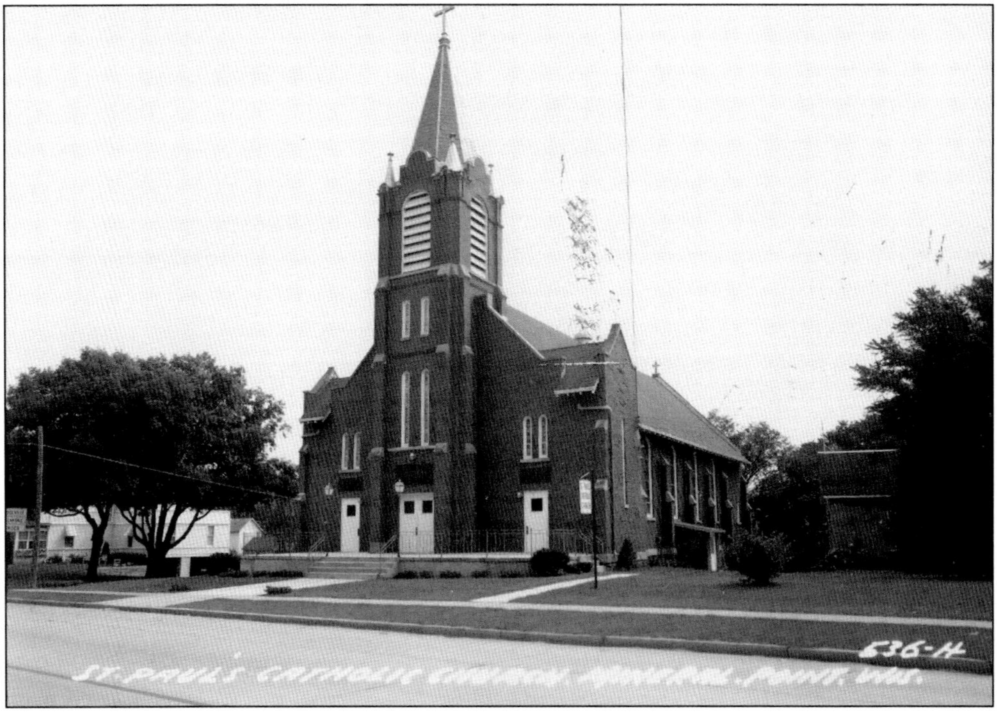

This is the third St. Paul's Catholic Church, built in 1911 at a cost of $20,000. Some of the previous church stone was used as a foundation for this new church. It is vitrified brick with Bedford stone trim. It has a gable roof and seats 450 people.

The United Church of Christ was organized in 1848 as a Primitive Methodist church by Rev. Joseph Hewitt, who came here from England. A year later the stone church was erected covering the area where the chapel of the present church now stands at the corner of Chestnut and Maiden Streets.

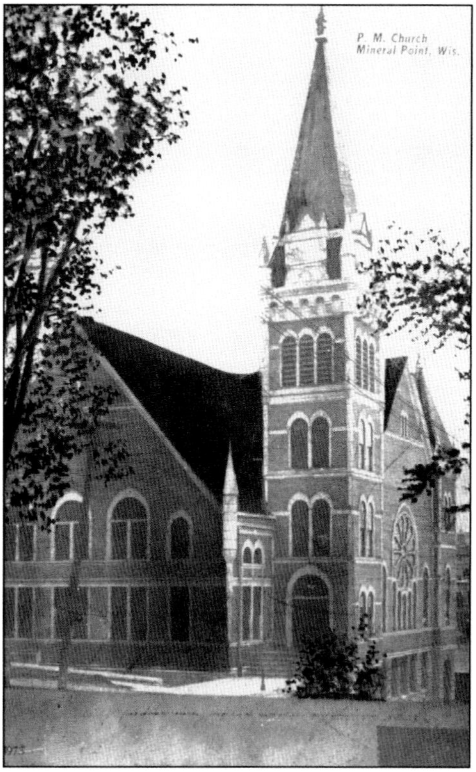

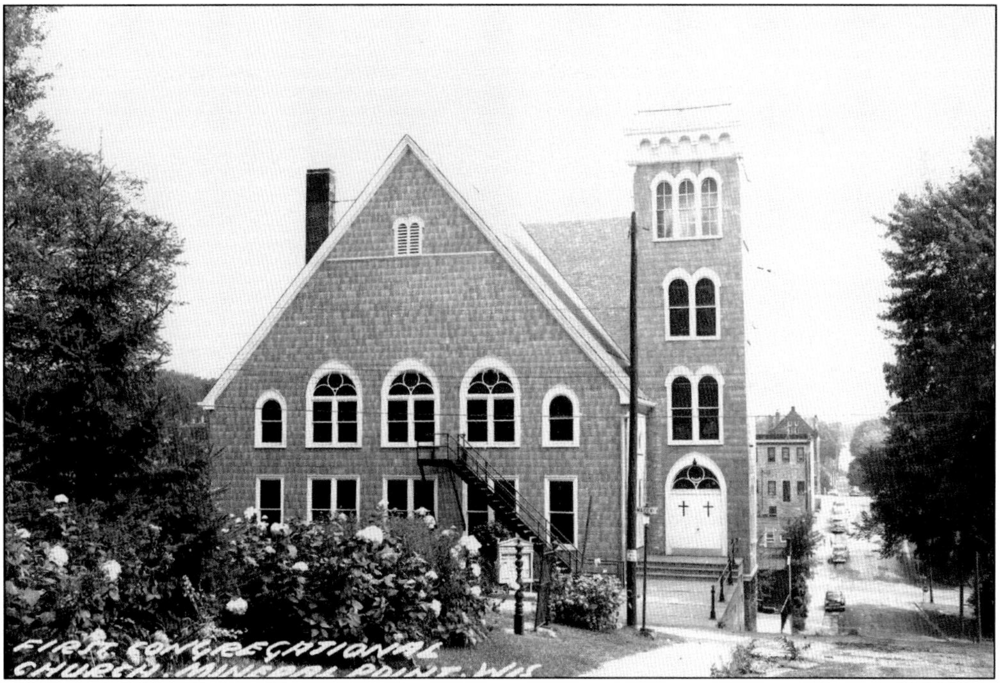

In 1913, the church voted to affiliate with the Congregational Conference of Wisconsin. They later joined in a merger with the United Church of Christ. This church is located on the corner of Chestnut and Maiden Streets.

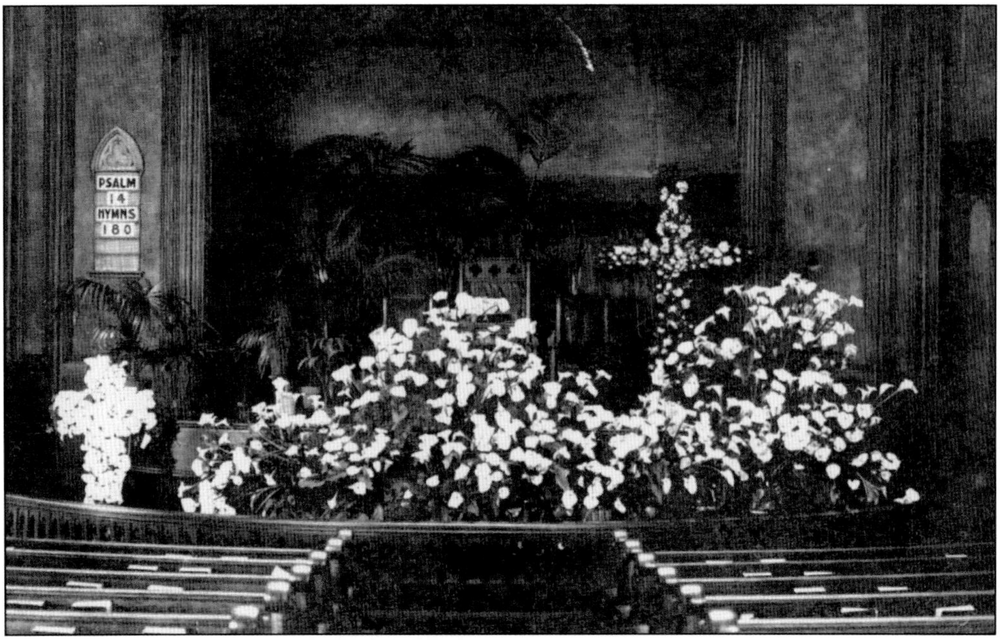

This is the interior of the Primitive Methodist Church, known by locals as the P.M. church. Originally part of the Methodist Episcopal Church, they had a dispute and 70 members withdrew to start the Primitive Methodist Church. The church's altar and crosses are covered with roses, probably for a funeral. The sign says Psalm 14, which is, "The Lord looks down from heaven on the sons of men to see if there are any who understand, any who seek God."

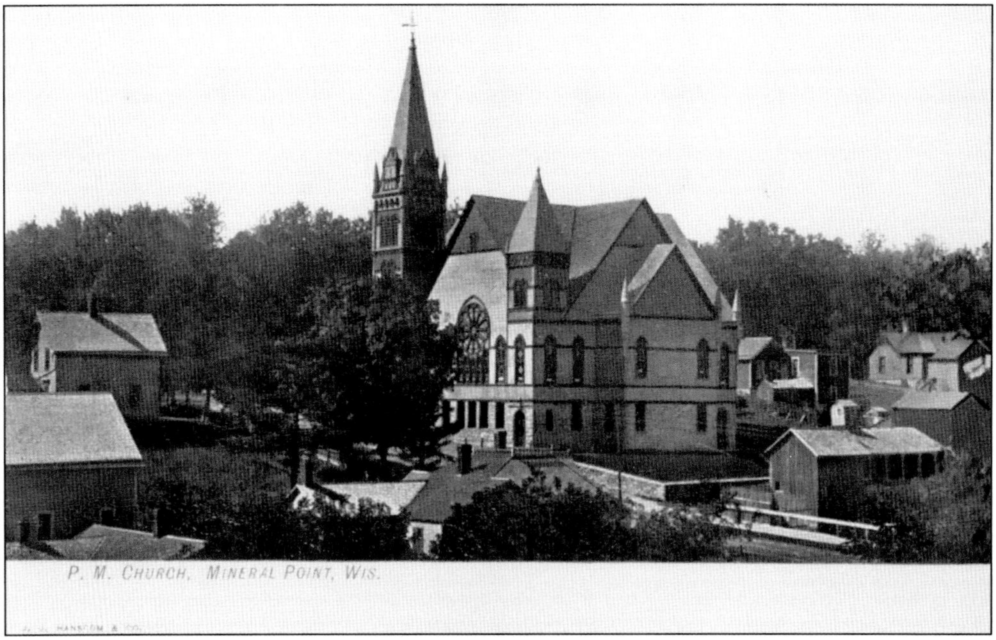

The church started with 70 members and grew until it became necessary in 1890 to raze the building to build a larger and more modern structure. It became the United Church of Christ.

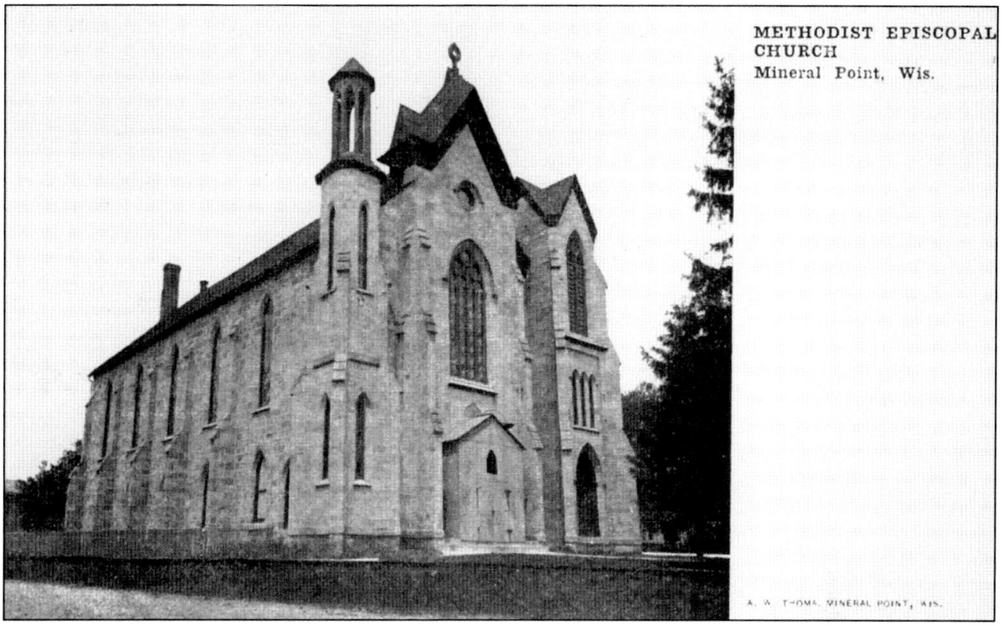

The Methodist Episcopal Church traces its history back to 1834. Its present limestone building is the third one erected by the congregation. The church is the oldest protestant congregation in the state. Over the front door etched in stone it says Methodist Episcopal Church. The sign in the lawn says First Methodist.

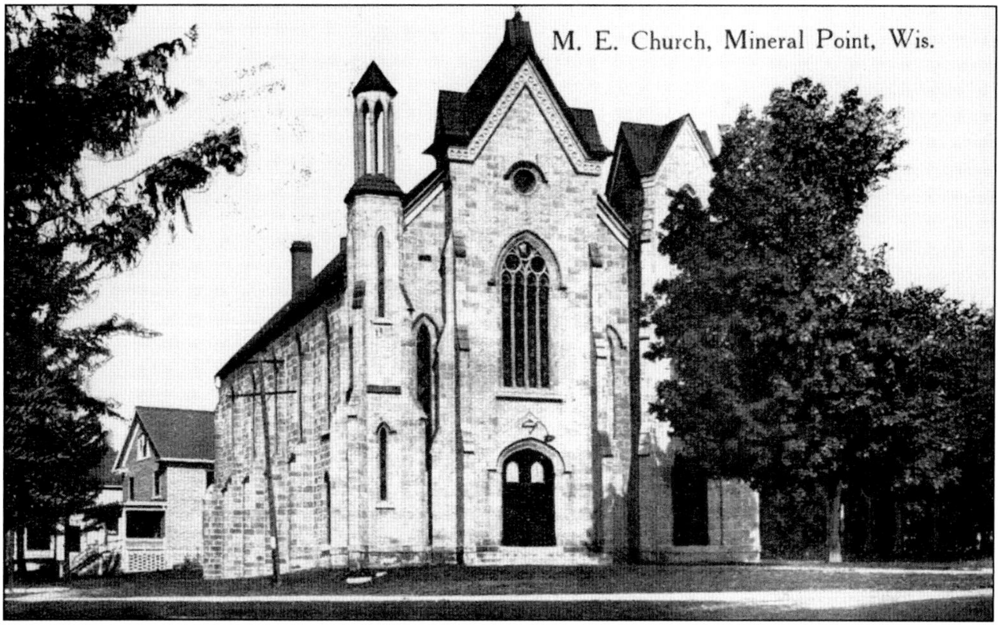

The first building constructed by the Methodists in Mineral Point was a log church near the foot of High Street. The interior of the present church was remodeled and renewed in 1904, at which time a pipe organ was installed. In 1907, an addition was made to provide a rear entrance, a kitchen, and a Sunday school room.

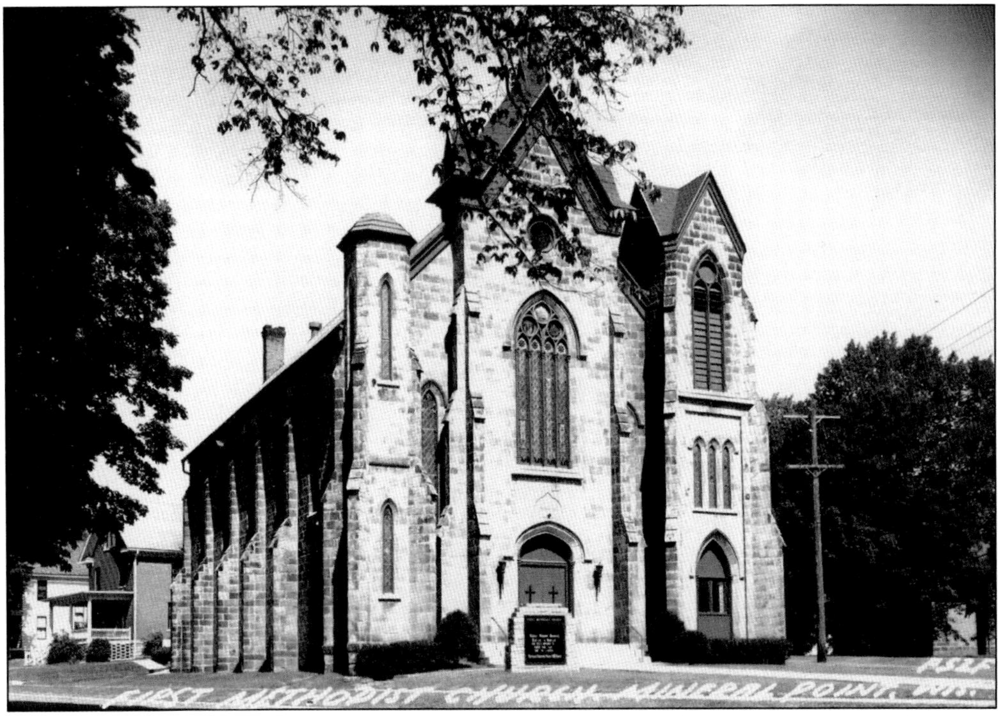

The current church is where author Marian Hendricks played the pipe organ when she was a senior in high school in 1930–1931. It was originally a hand-pumped organ, but it was electrified when she used it.

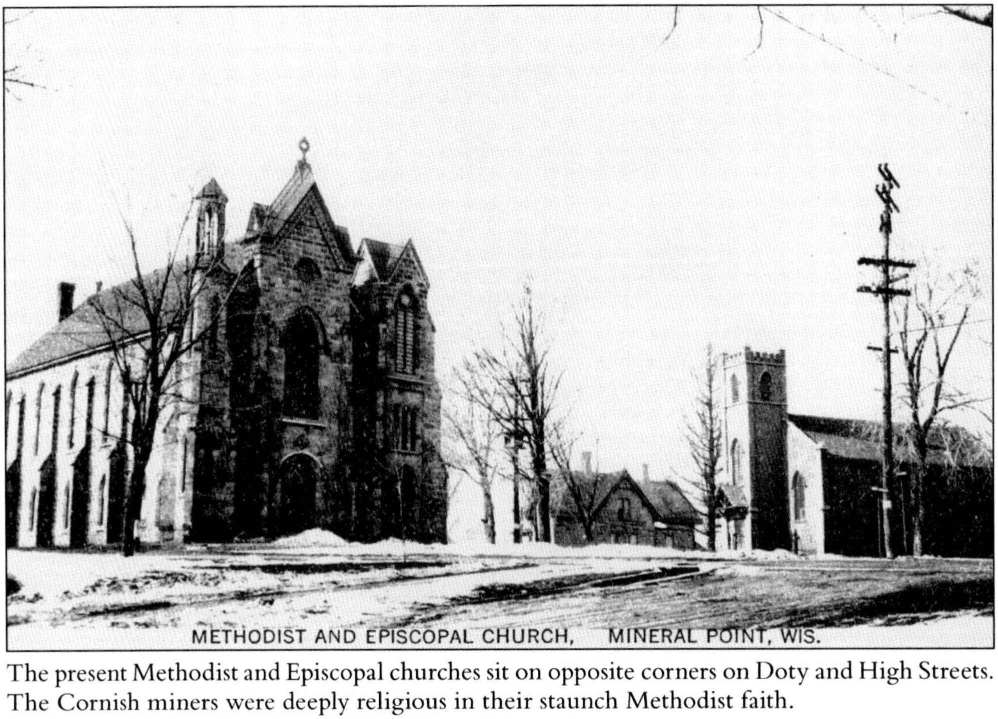

The present Methodist and Episcopal churches sit on opposite corners on Doty and High Streets. The Cornish miners were deeply religious in their staunch Methodist faith.

The Trinity Episcopal Church was built in 1845 at a total cost of $5,000, a sum that was raised by local subscription and by gifts from friends in the East, England, and Wales. It is located at 402 High Street. (Photograph by Mike Mewis.)

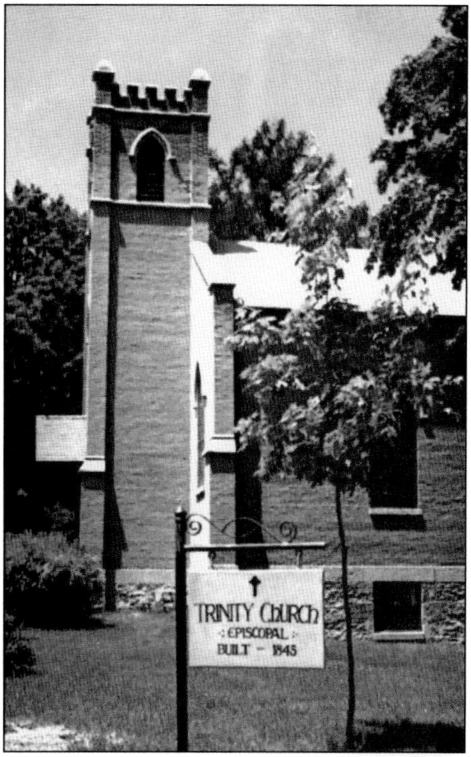

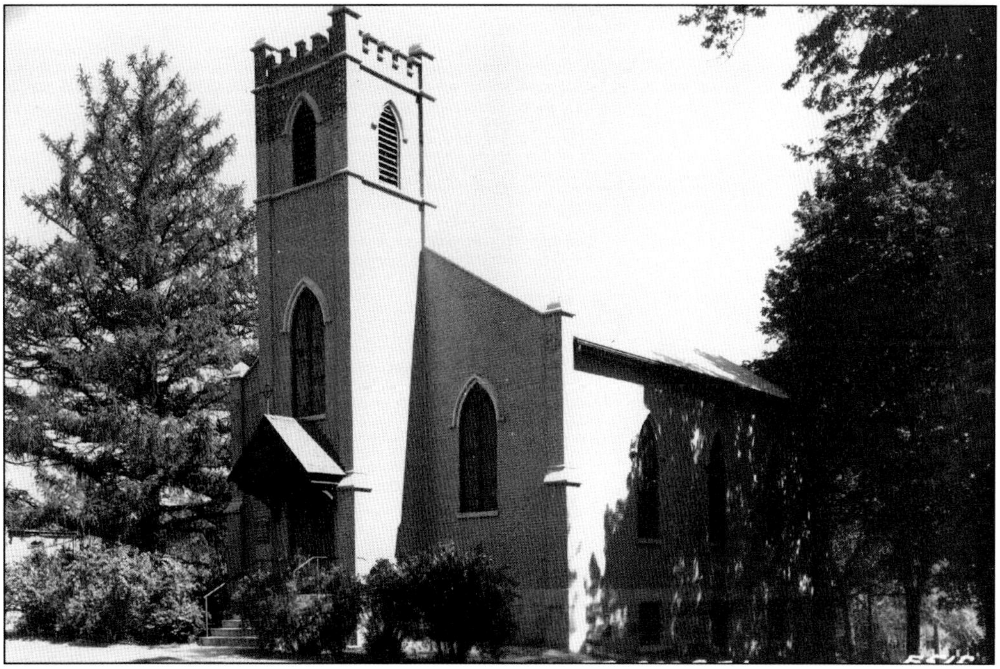

The rectory was erected in 1868 at a cost of $6,720, and the parish house across the street was built at a cost of $2,875. In 1857, crumbling foundations threatened the church building. A program of repair, rehabilitation, and restoration was undertaken, which totaled almost six times as much as the original building cost.

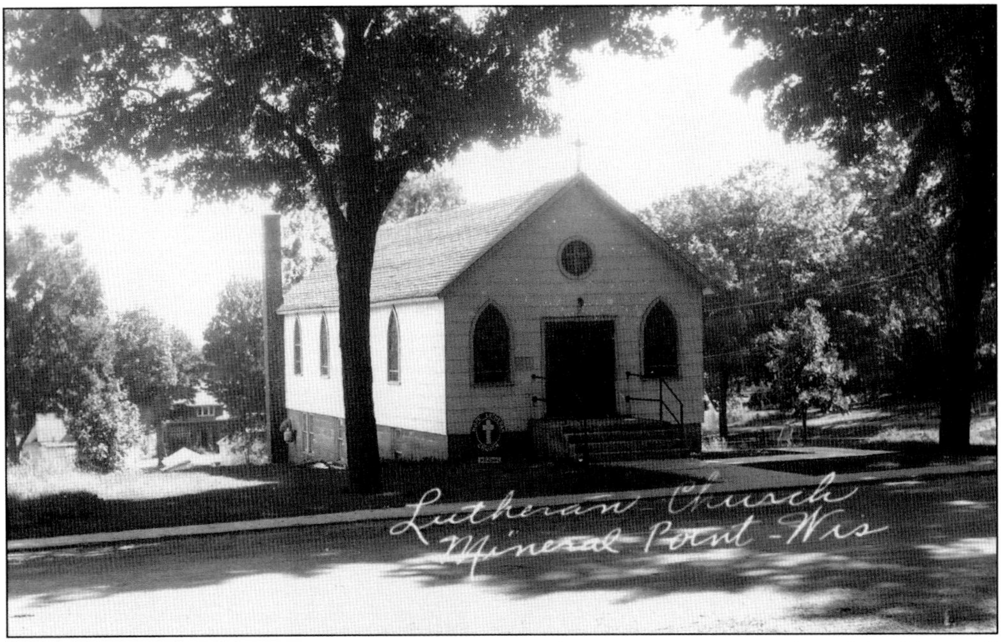

Hope Lutheran Church was organized in 1945. The congregation worshiped in this small remodeled Oak Park Cheese Factory that was bought at an auction for $300. The building was moved from Highway 151 South. Today a house sits on the church foundation.

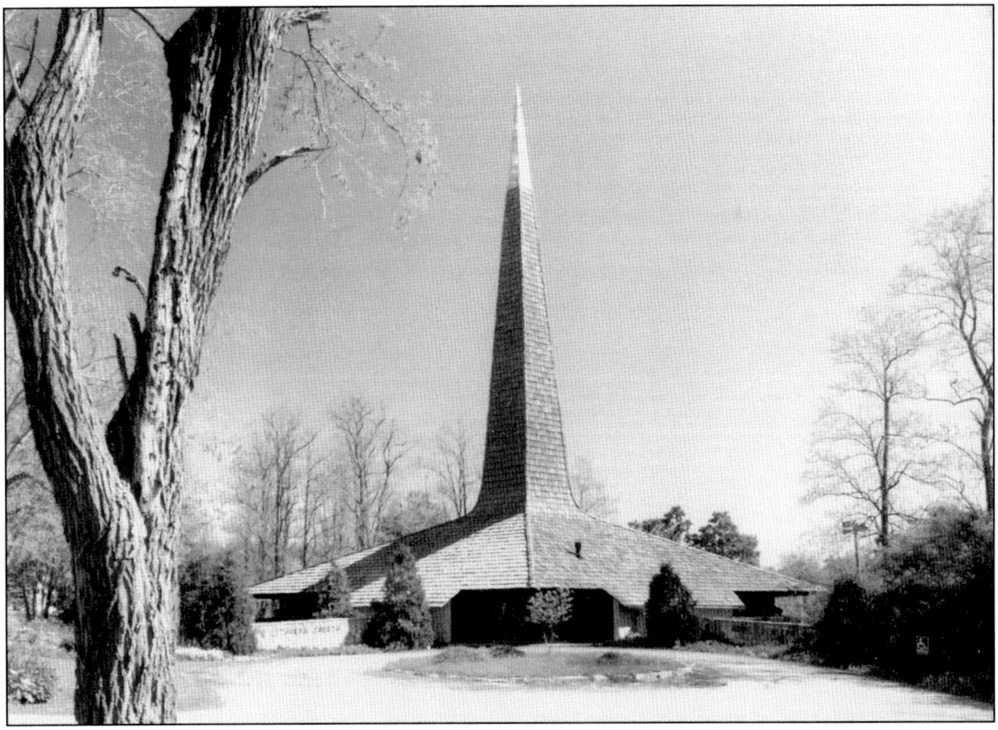

The new Hope Lutheran Church was completed in 1974. This church, located at 555 Commerce Street, near Spruce Street, has an impressive steeple that stands 95 feet above the parking lot. (Photograph by Betty France.)

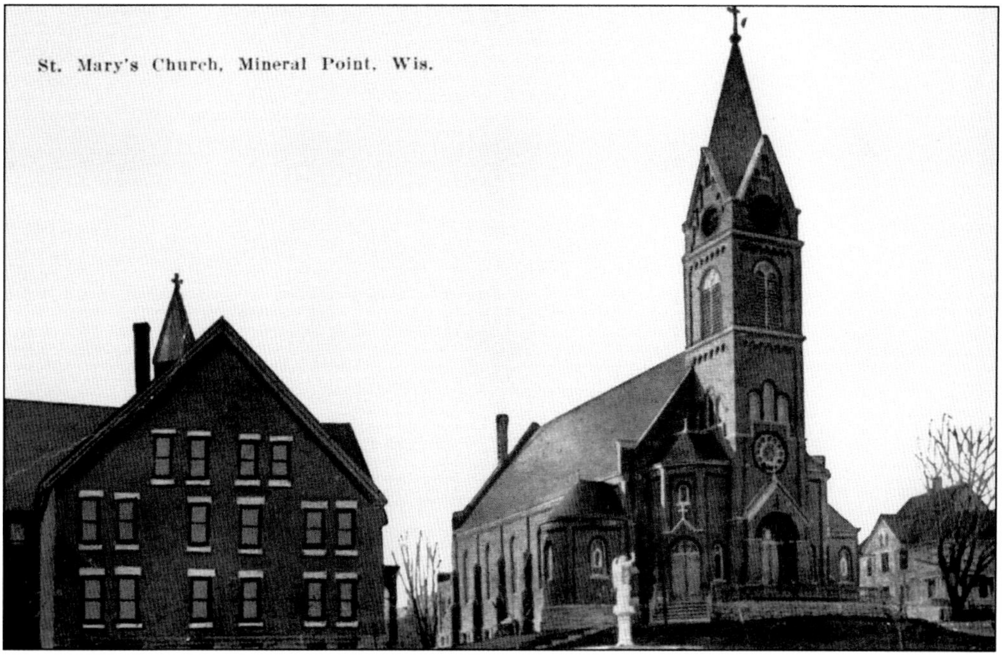

St. Mary's Catholic Church had its beginning in the year 1870. The Germans who came here did not want to go to an Irish church, so they built their own. This solid brick church was erected in 1901 on Davis Street. St. Mary's Catholic school was built next to the church. On the other side was the rectory. Today St. Paul's and St. Mary's Catholic Churches have united to become one church at this site.

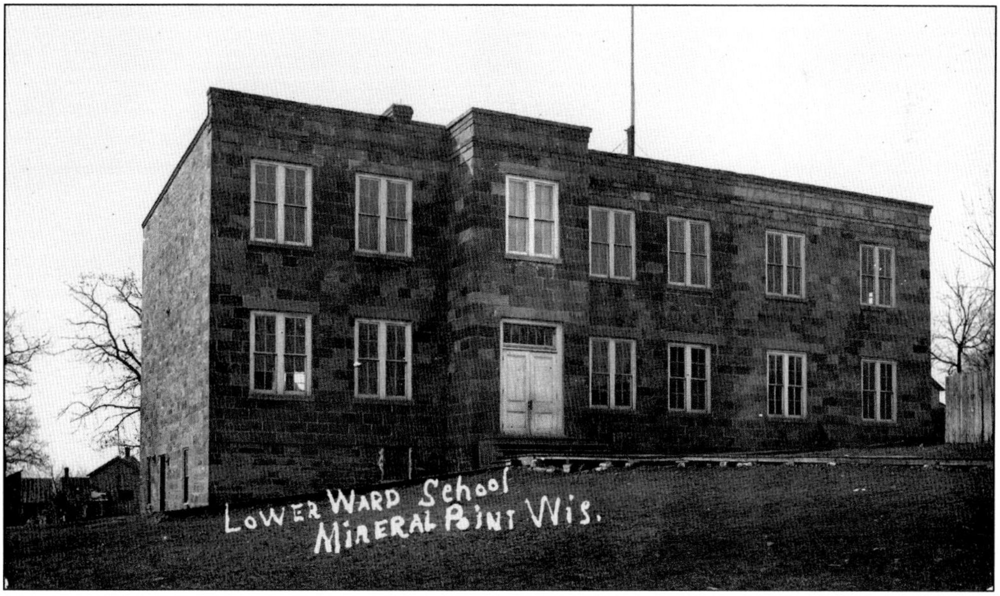

This is the Lower Ward School, also known as the Fourth Ward School, located on Front Street. This was the town elementary school. It has since been demolished. The early Cornish immigrant miners had little or no schooling. Most of them could not read or write. They were hardworking, thrifty, and honest.

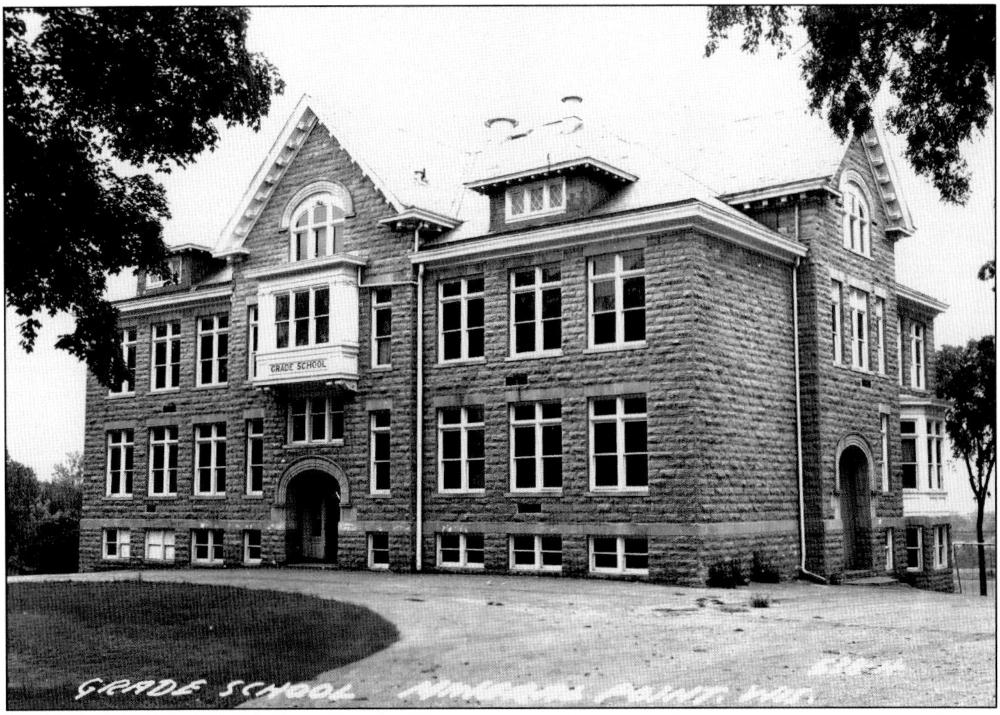

Originally the high school, this became the new grade school after the ward school was demolished. Locals are sentimental about their schools. When they leave town and return to visit they look to find where they went to school.

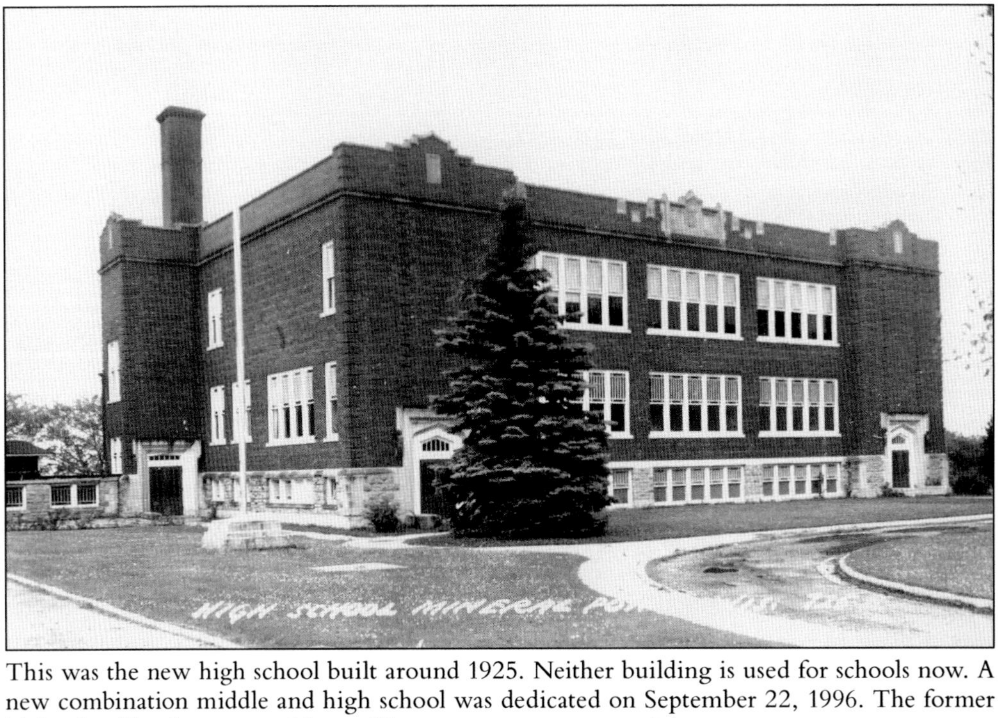

This was the new high school built around 1925. Neither building is used for schools now. A new combination middle and high school was dedicated on September 22, 1996. The former high school has been turned into office space, apartments, and day care.

Four

Pendarvis and Shake Rag Street

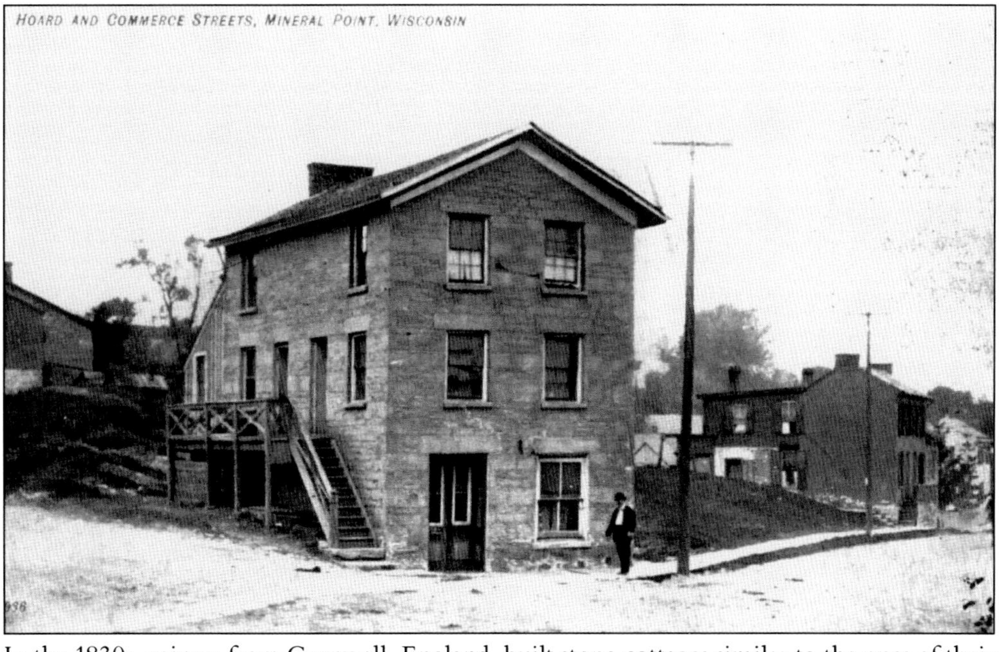

In the 1830s, miners from Cornwall, England, built stone cottages similar to the ones of their homeland. Shake Rag, the greatest concentration of these homes, was so named because at mealtime the shaking of rags by the womenfolk would call the men home from the mines on the opposite hill. This building sat at the bottom of Shake Rag Street. It was the Washington Hotel, constructed around 1860 with additions done in 1895. It no longer stands.

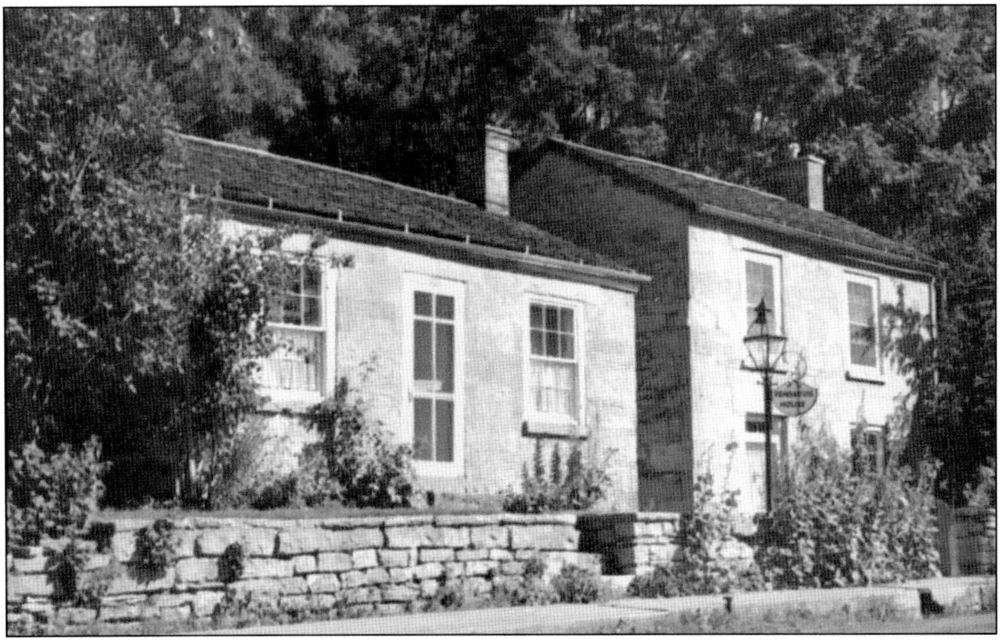

The back of this card says, "Pendarvis and Trelawny Houses of The Cornish Restoration on Shake Rag Street, Mineral Point, Wisconsin. Built in the early 1830s by the miners from Cornwall, England. Nationally recognized for preserving and perpetuating Cornish customs and traditions."

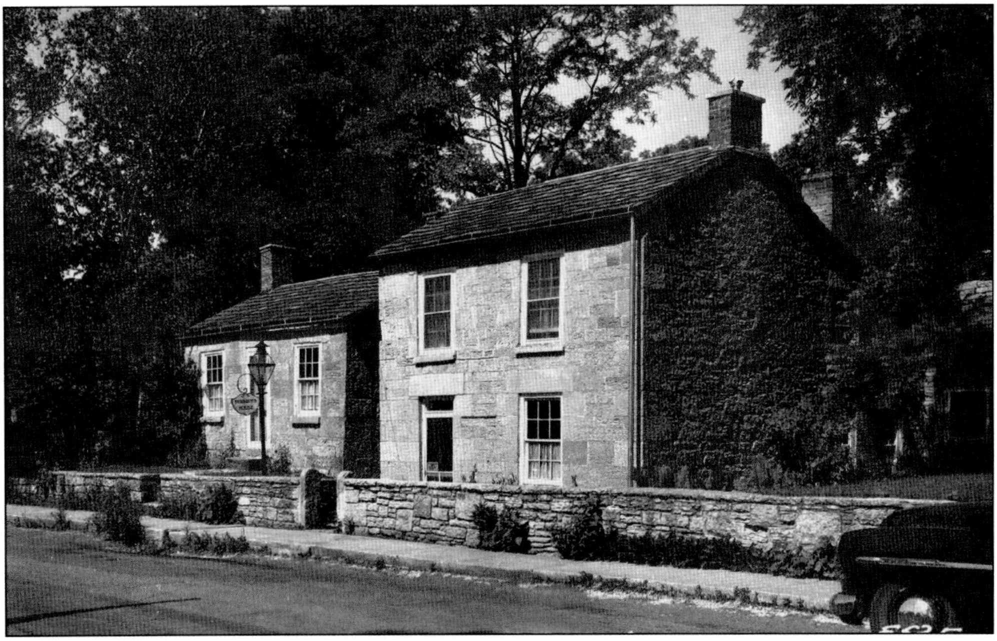

These two limestone houses are restored Cornish miners' homes. There are few examples of this architecture left to be found anywhere in this country. The local people have paid attention to character and detail in their efforts to restore these buildings. Led by Robert Neal and Edgar Hellum, who suggested this restoration idea at a 1936 chamber of commerce meeting, the crumpling ruins of another time came back to life.

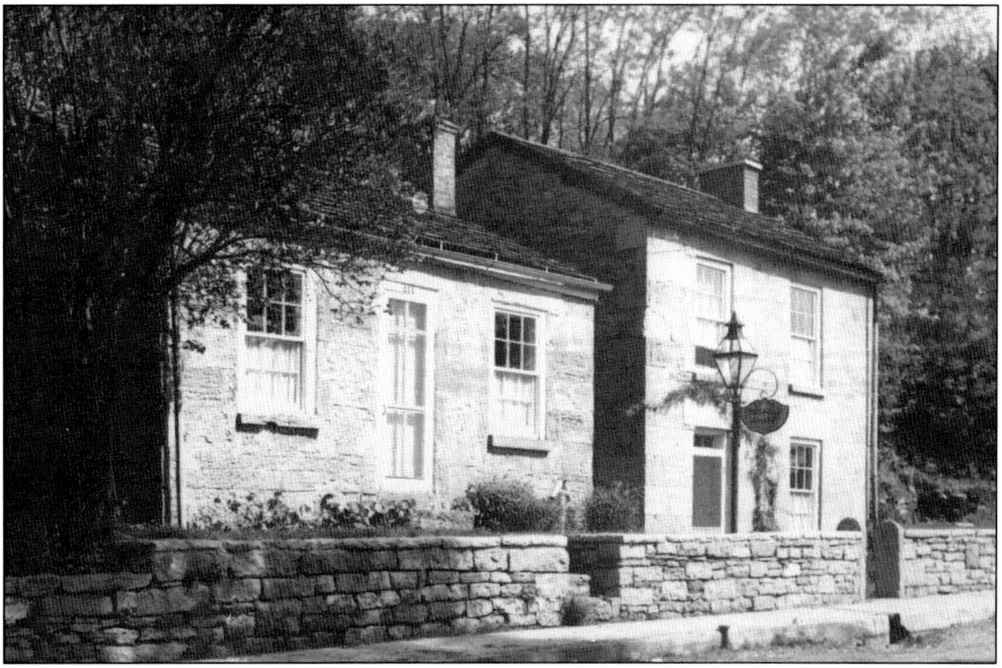

After these two buildings were lovingly restored, Neal and Hellum turned Pendarvis into the finest Cornish restaurant to be found anywhere. Here they served pasties, clotted cream, saffron cakes, and other Cornish dishes. Wisconsin's most prolific author, August Derleth, often ate here along with other noted celebrities.

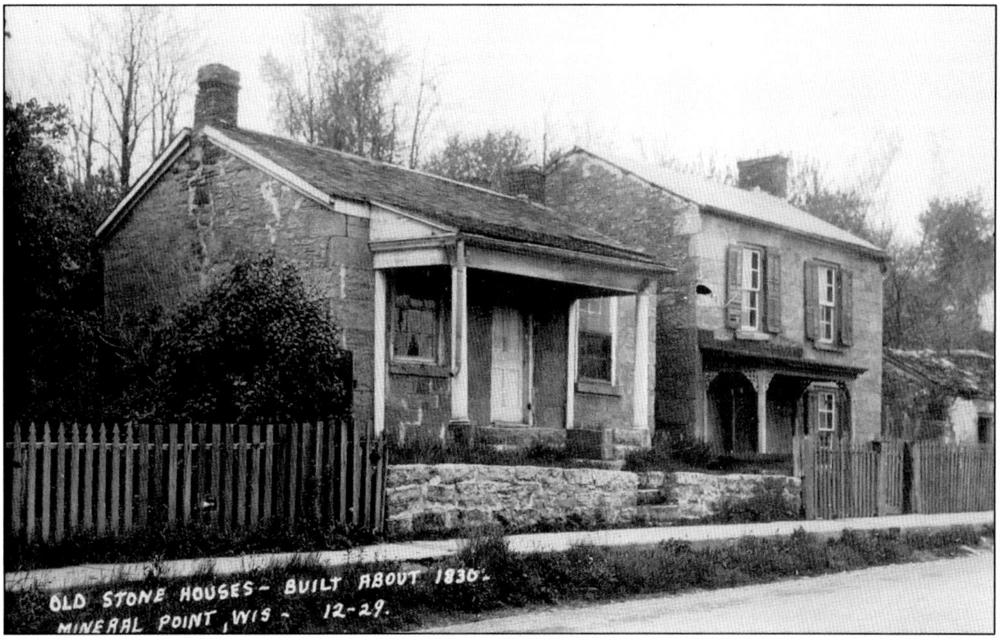

It was here that one tasted treats like the sweet and luxurious Cornish scaled cream, also known as Devonshire cream. While being warned to use saffron sparingly because it was the world's most expensive spice—selling for $150 an ounce—it was used in the saffron breads and cakes served at Pendarvis House.

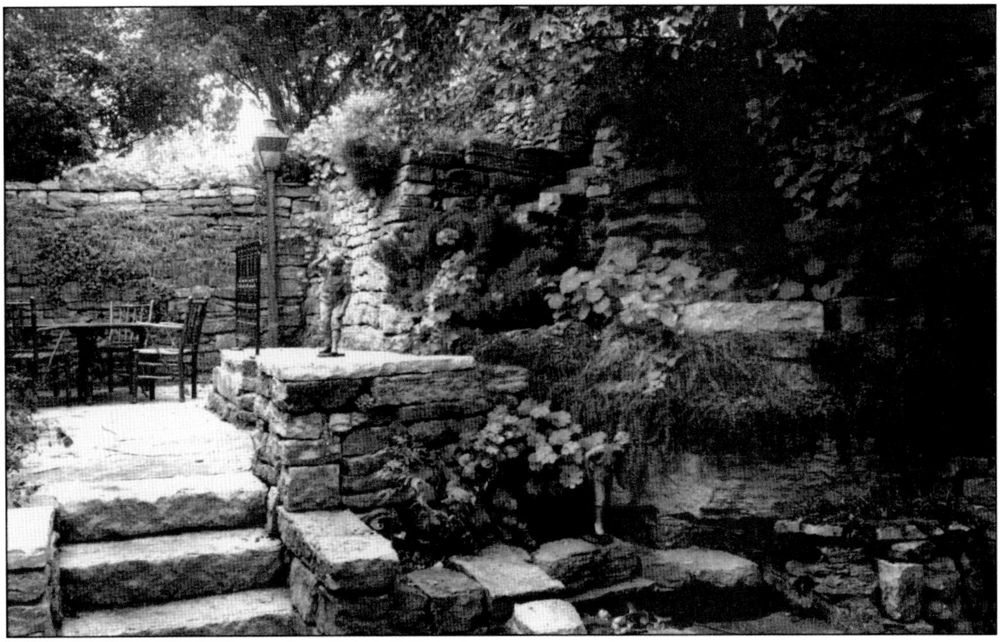

This lovely courtyard is in the back of Pendarvis. Carefully landscaped with stones that create terraced walls, the solitude is comforting. Pendarvis was named after a family estate in Cornwall. (Courtesy of Pendarvis House.)

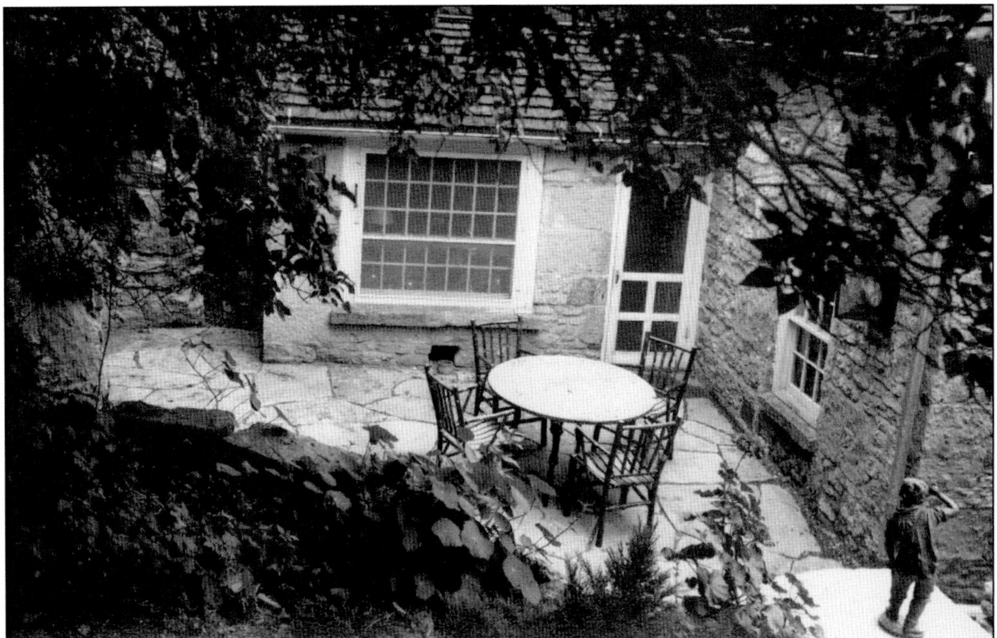

This is the rear courtyard of Trelawny. The building was named for a Methodist bishop. A lot of famous people stopped at this courtyard, including the head of the United Nations, Sinclair Lewis, and Stalin's daughter, Svetlana Peters. (Courtesy of Pendarvis House.)

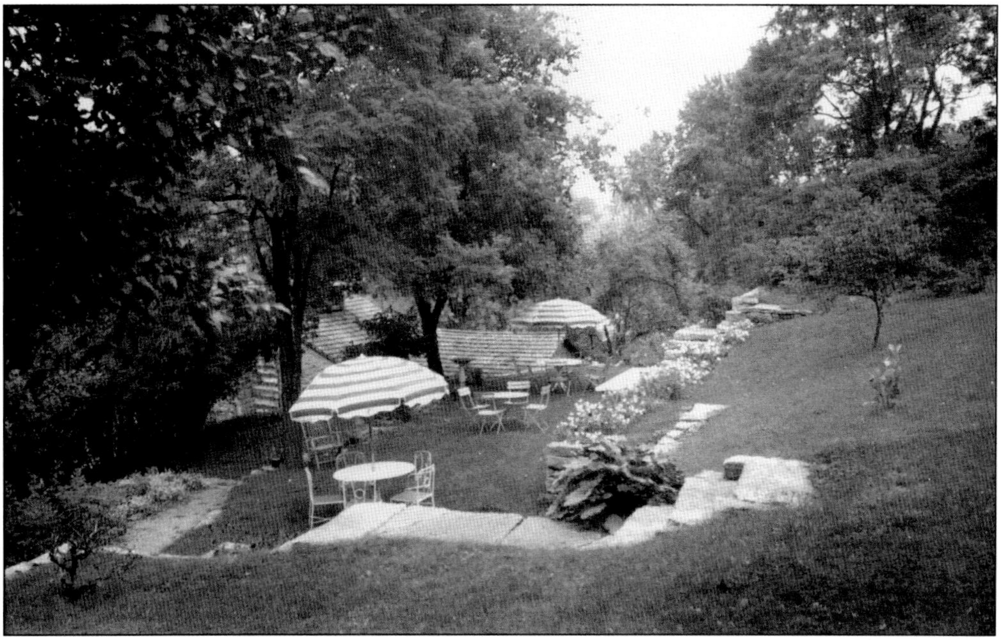

This inviting view is above Pendarvis and Trelawny. Architect Frank Lloyd Wright's head mason, Mr. Curtis, volunteered to help with the restoration work for two weeks. He stayed for two years. He was an expert mason who understood how stone and water and ice interacted. (Courtesy of Pendarvis House.)

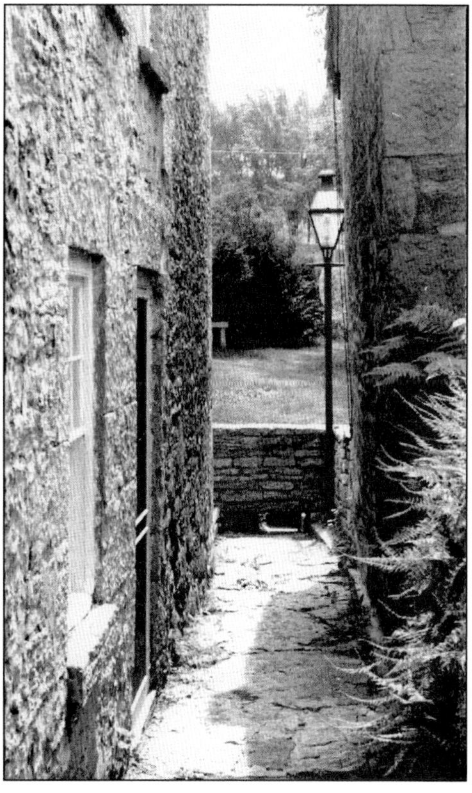

This is the walkway between Pendarvis and Trelawny looking toward Shake Rag Street. Mineral Point was hard hit with the bank's closing, the zinc furnace closing, and the Depression. Nobody had any money. Houses were unpainted. The whole town was pretty decrepit. Robert Neal restored both of these homes during this time. He said, "There was no money, it was really a challenge in how you could do it, and what you could do. We had a roof over our heads, we always had food, we always had people and we always had encouragement." (Courtesy of Pendarvis House.)

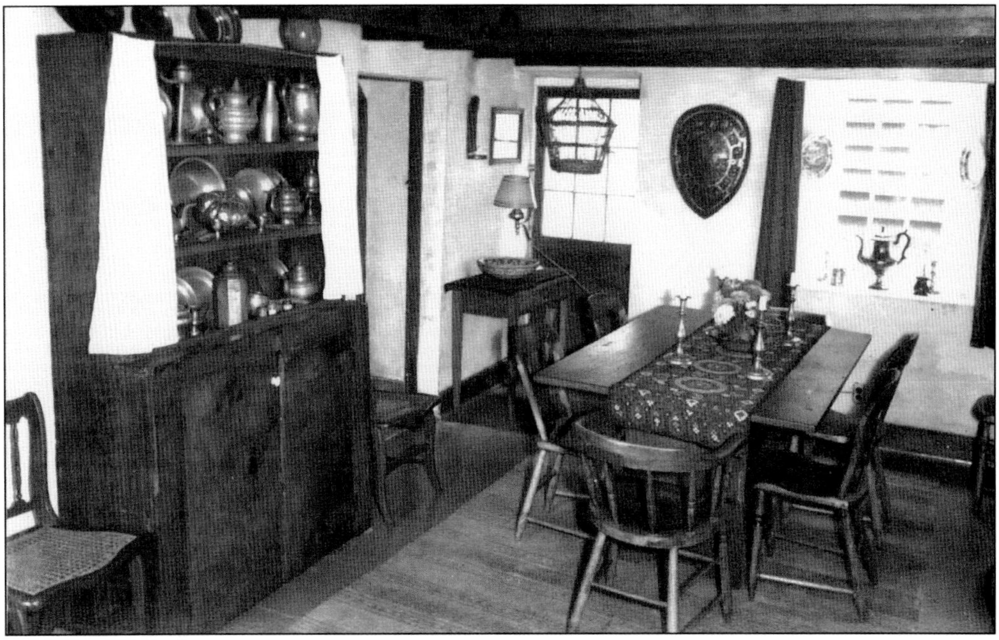

This is the interior of Trelawny's dining room. Robert Neal welcomed visitors to Shake Rag Street with a cheerful old Cornish greeting: "Come, let's touch pipes a bit, and have a dish of tay." With period furnishings, "a dish of tay" seems appropriate for this room. (Courtesy of Pendarvis House.)

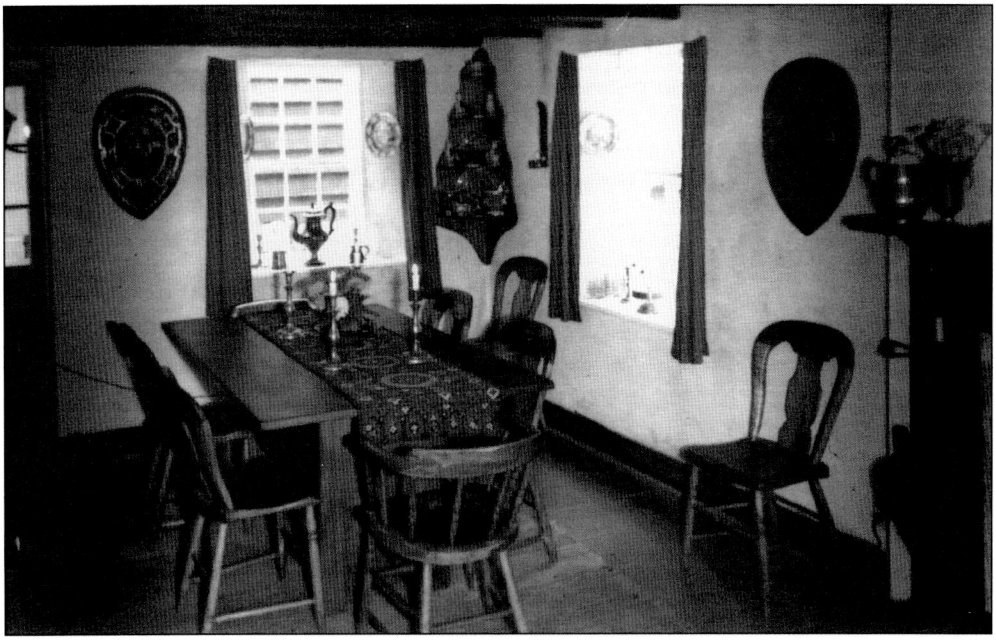

The Trelawny dining room is set up as it would have been in the 1830s. Miners worked long hours in the mines. They were such good workers that their employers would ask if there were anymore like them back in Cornwall. The miner would answer, "my cousin Jack." So the Cornish miners were nicknamed "Cousin Jacks." At the end of their long day they would have welcomed a meal in this room, in this house. (Courtesy of Pendarvis House.)

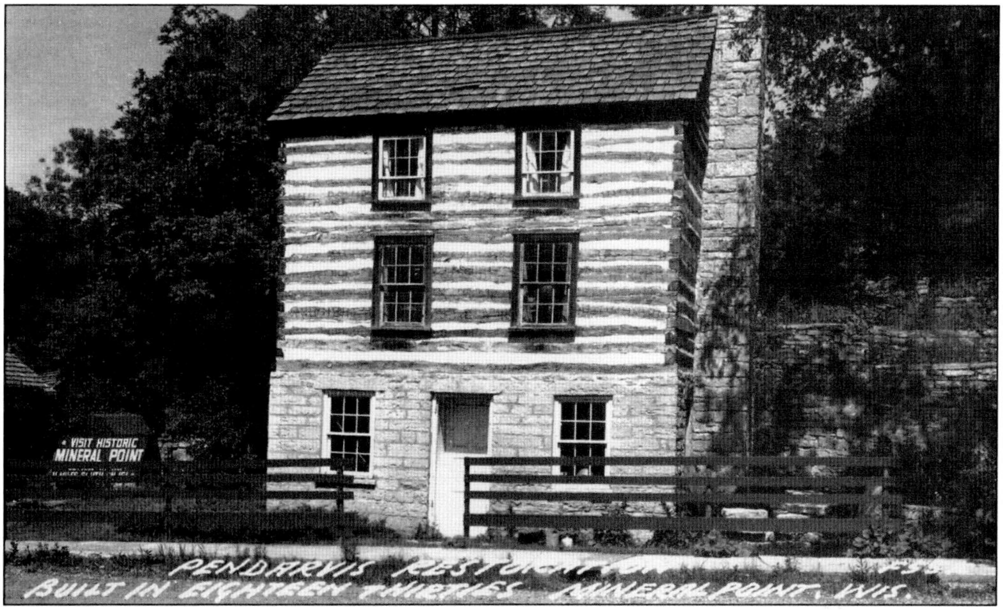

This is the Polperro House. It was named after a fishing village in Cornwall, England. It was built in the 1820s. The log section was built first and probably raised at a later date to preserve the wood. The stone section once may have been a cooper's shop. The root cellar was later joined to the second-floor level. According to tradition, the building was once occupied by three families, one on each floor. The second restoration, by Robert Neal and Edgar Hellum in the 1930s, led to the present operation of it by the state historical society. It is open to the public.

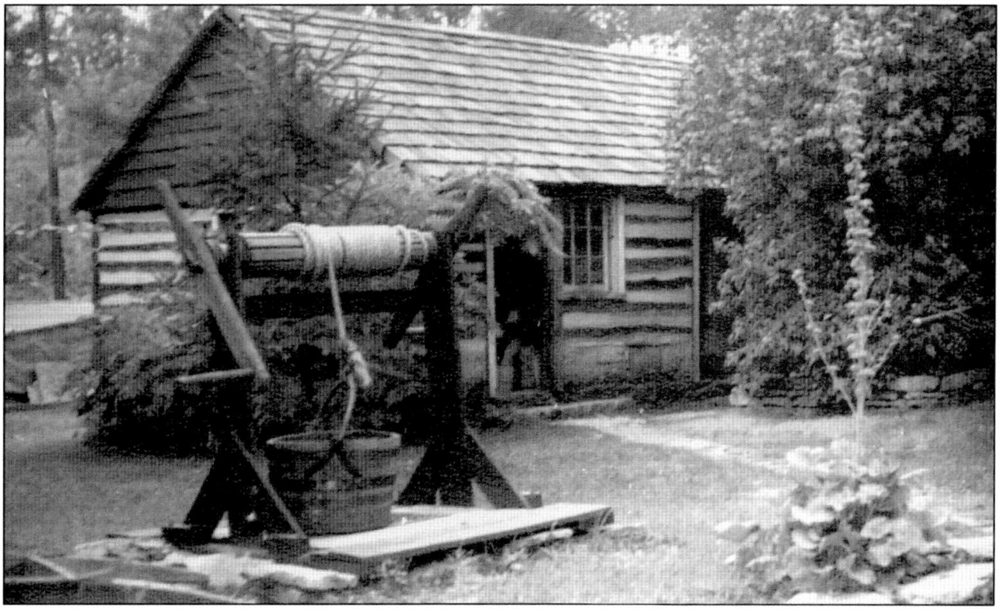

The significance of the mining boom in southwest Wisconsin may never be truly weighed, but it is without dispute one of the most important eras in Wisconsin's evolution. Before mining became a big business, mining was a simple operation. The windlass, as shown here, consisted of a crank set on two posts at the top of the shaft that lifted the ore out in a wood bucket. Tools required were a pick, blasting powder, fuses, a shovel, and candles. (Courtesy of Pendarvis House.)

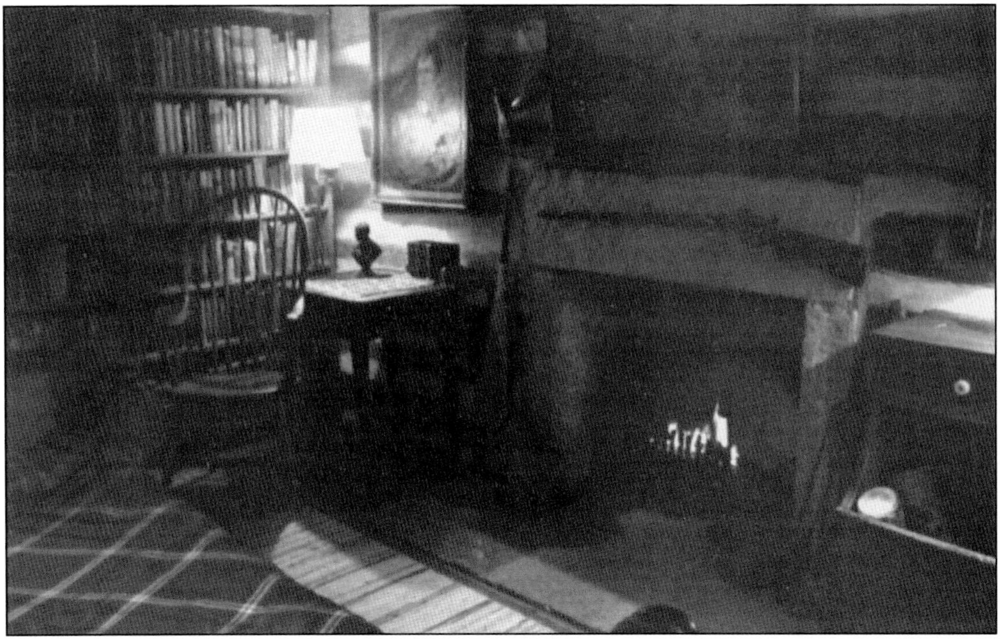

This is an inviting inside view of the Polperro House living room. The wooden walls and ceiling beams, combined with the fireplace and rows of books, offer a cozy environment to spend a winter evening. Period furnishings and artwork add to the Cornish ambiance.

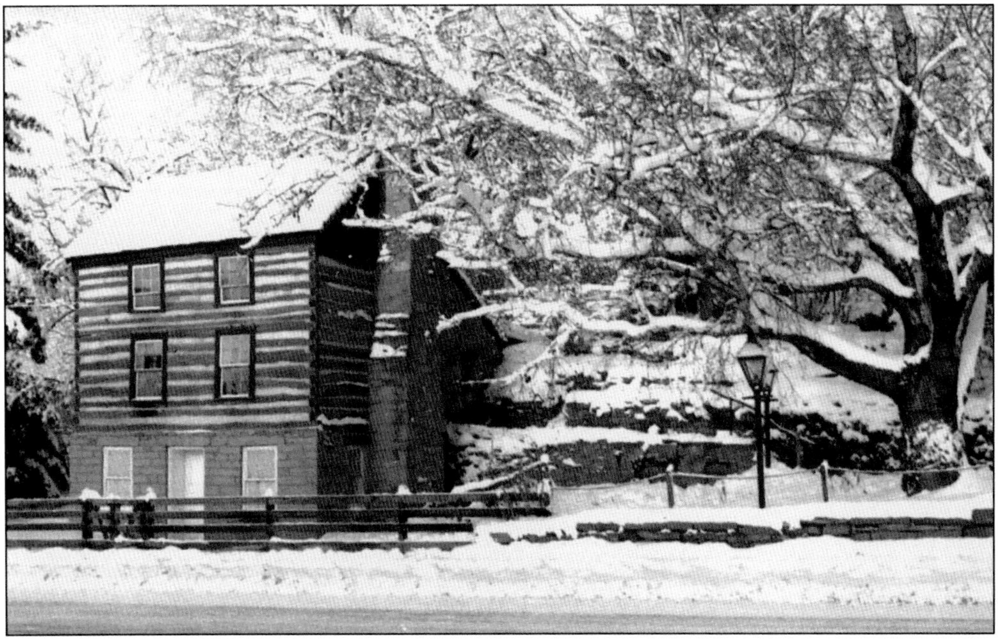

Polperro House shows the beauty of a Wisconsin winter. The snow hugs the house and covers the trees. The house is three stories from the front, but it looks like one story from the rear.

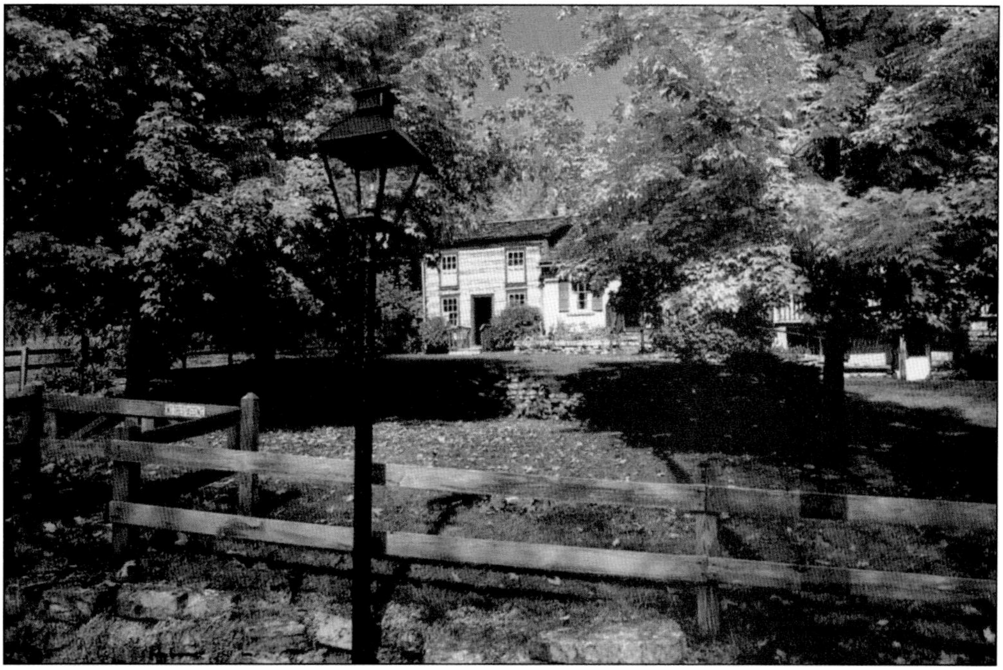

Tamblyn's Row house sits directly behind and above Pendarvis House. By 1834 Mineral Point was a rollicking frontier town of friendly neighbors, frequent duels, and newly discovered copper mines. Many of the 600 people lived in row houses similar to this one. It was built around 1820 as a two-story log cabin. (Photograph by Pat Ripp.)

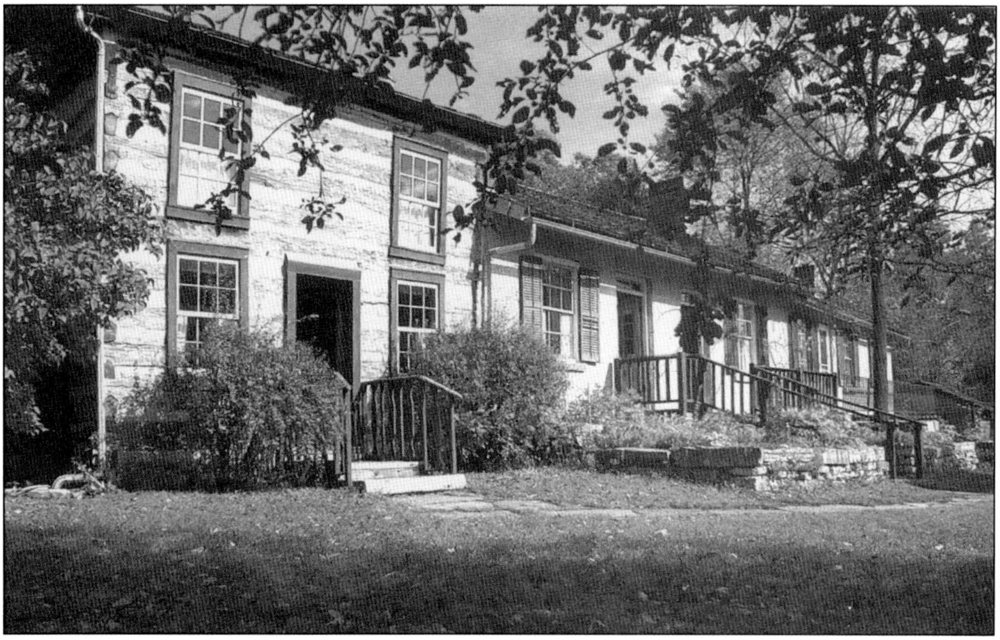

The rock sections were added in the 1830s by Cornishmen. It was in disrepair in 1960, when Robert Neal and Edgar Hellum undertook the challenge to repair it. They discovered a large room that had been completely hidden by dirt and silt. Tamblyn's Row is now part of the Pendarvis Complex and is open to the public.

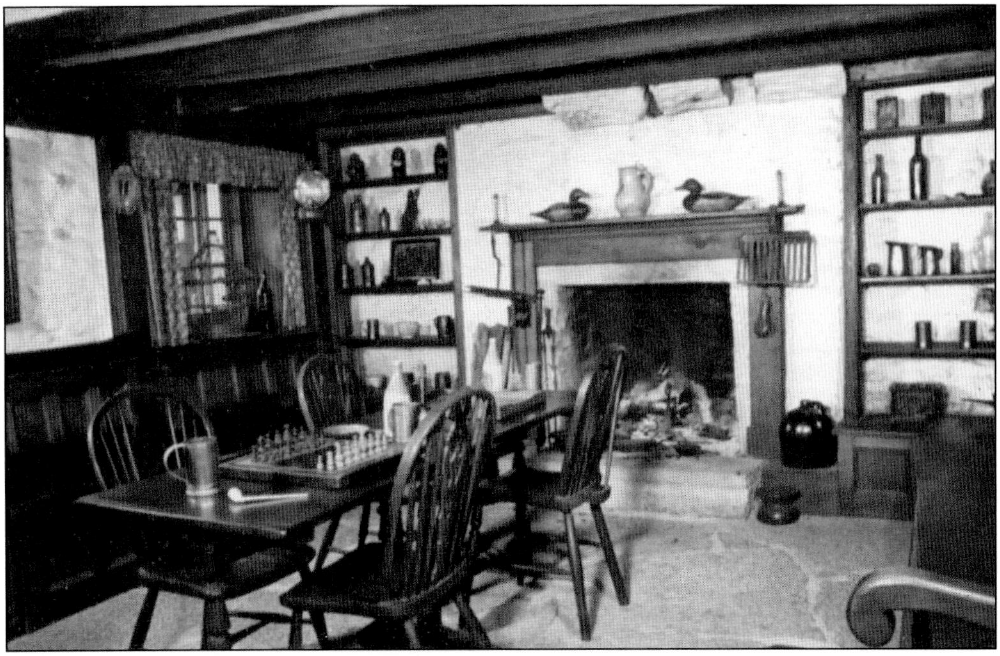

This is an interior shot of the pub at Pendarvis complex, called Kiddlywink. The pub is the "lost" cellar of Tamblyn's Row. During the time when hard liquor could not be served, the pub keeper would keep a secret kettle of brew. When a customer came into the pub and winked at the owner, it was a signal for the hard stuff, thus the name Kiddlywink. The complex is owned by the State of Wisconsin. It is open for daily conducted tours from May through October.

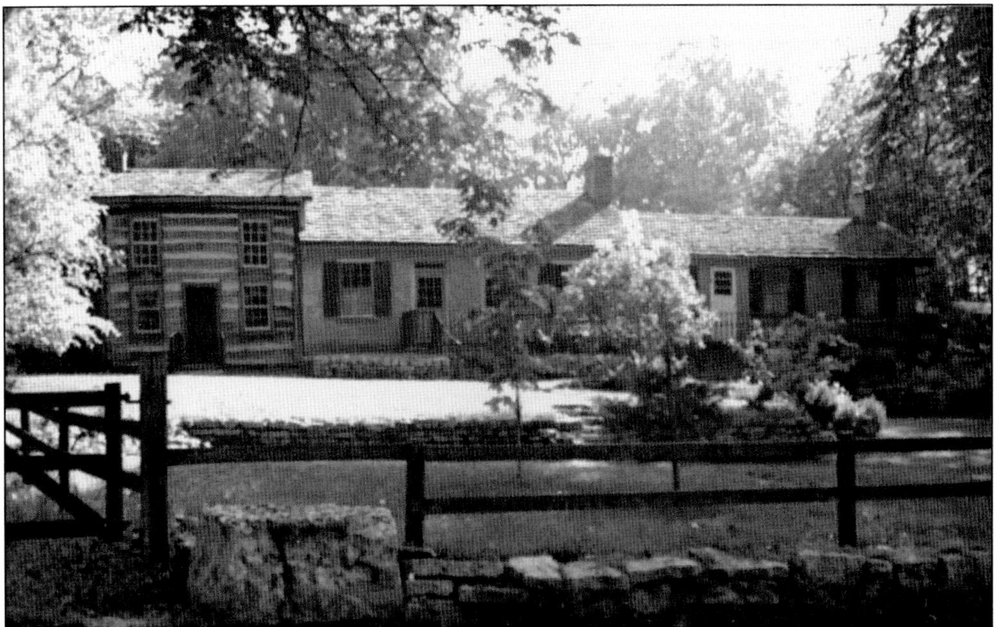

The Tamblyn's Row offered a sense of security because people were close to each other in case of the danger of Native Americans or fires. Fires were always a concern since most houses were made of wood. (Photograph by Mike Mewis.)

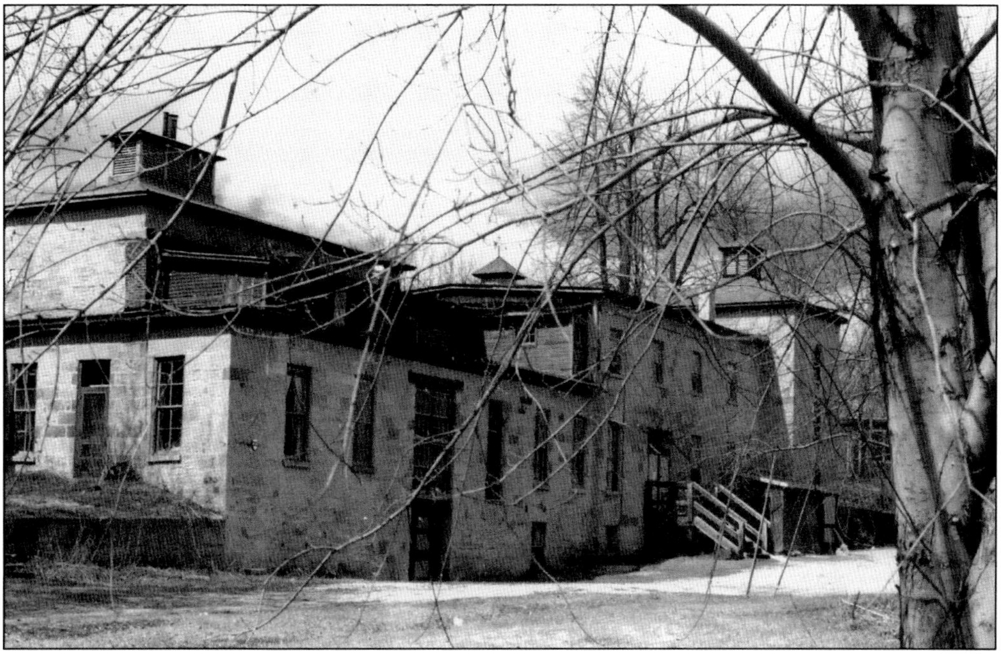

The Mineral Springs Brewery is located at 276 Shake Rag Street. It is currently the home of the Brewery Pottery Studio. Backed up to a hillside mining cave, it was once the source of mineral springs used to create their trademark Mineral Springs Beer. This brewery was a fixture on the Wisconsin scene, serving a local or regional trade. The brewery is significant as one the few resources related to Germans in Mineral Point. The brewery represents one of their contributions to the community. The Germans brought with them their knowledge and passion for beer making and beer drinking. (Photograph by Betty France.)

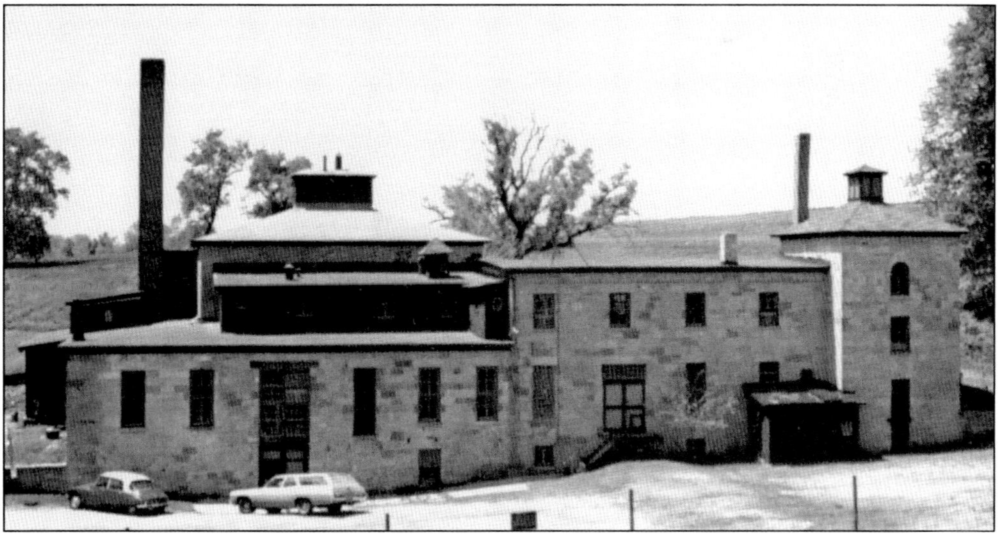

The hill behind the brewery has 5,000 square feet of caves where the beer was stored at a cool temperature. This was a favorite meeting place for the miners to gather and to indulge in the popular Mineral Springs beer. Inside the large room there is a long wall where the brew kettles sat and the ingenious miners hooked up spigots that allowed beer to flow freely into their glasses. (Photograph by Mike Mewis.)

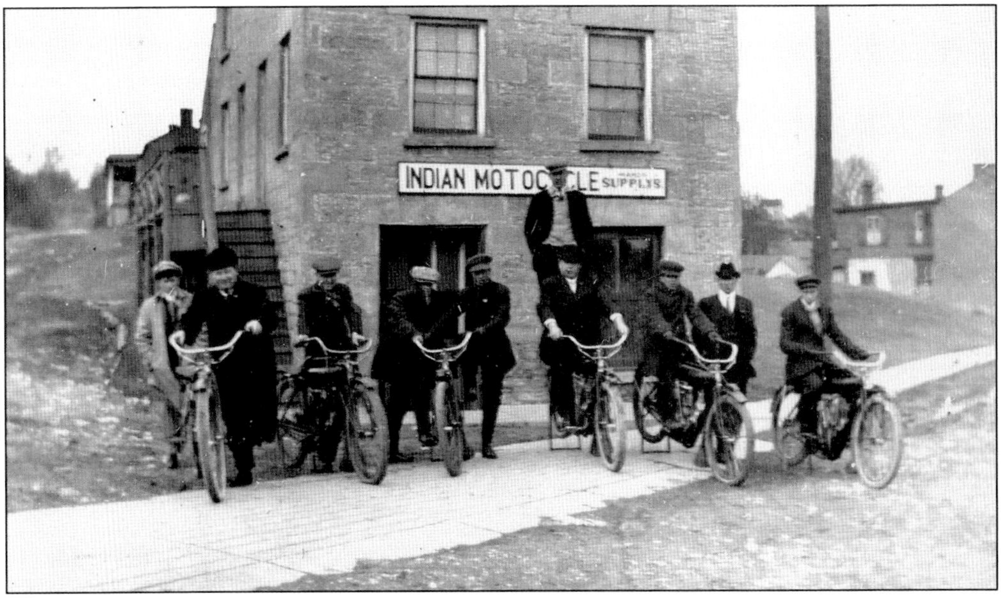

This is the former Washington Hotel on the corner of Commerce and Shake Rag Streets. The buildings behind the hotel were removed when Highway 23 was rerouted. At the time of this photograph, the building was called Indian Motocycle Supplies. Not to be confused with motorcycles, these bikers were the closest thing to motorcyclists of that day.

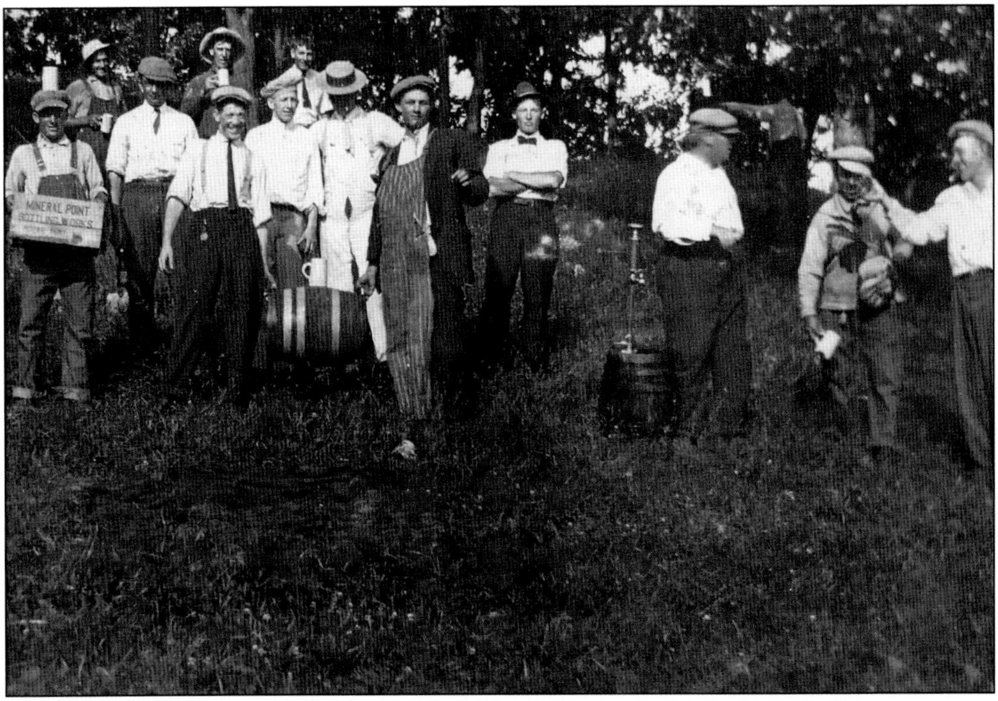

This is the only postcard found that refers to the Mineral Point Bottling Works. The employees are having their picture taken. One man is holding a crate of the soda that they bottled at their plant. Mineral Point Bottling Works made various flavors of soda. It also distributed Potosi beer, which was a big seller because it was cheap.

The restored craft community in historic Mineral Point is where Bernard Klase pottery started about 1850. Today resident potters demonstrate and sell pottery as part of the tour of this restoration on Shake Rag Alley.

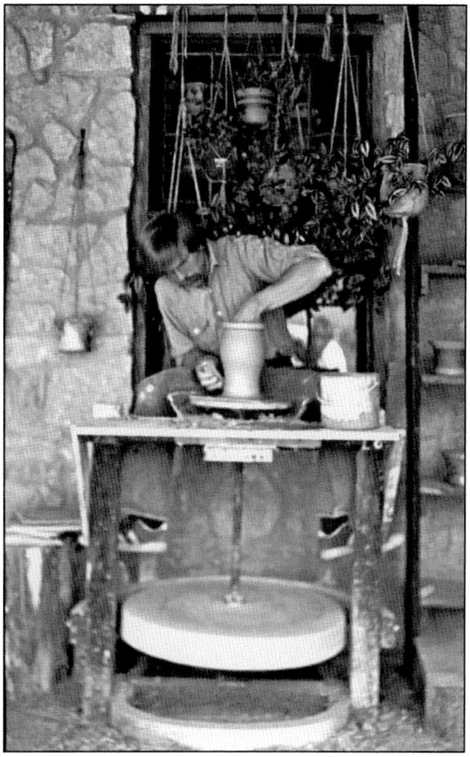

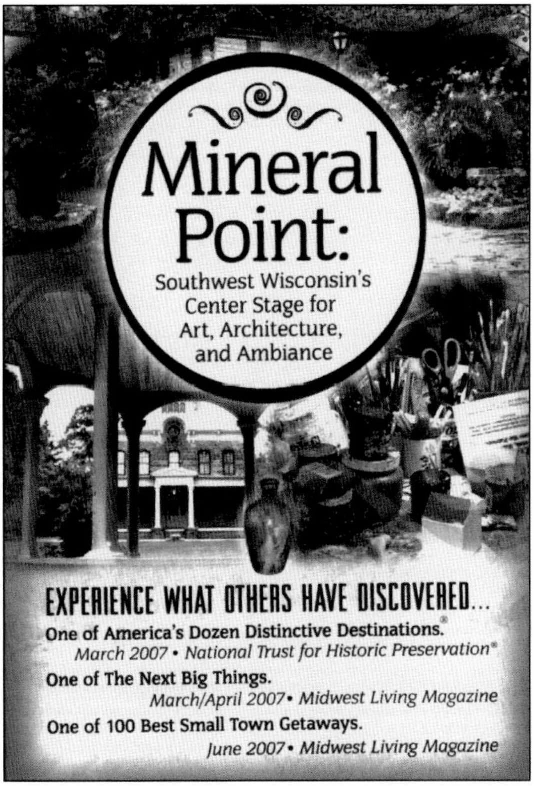

The National Trust for Historic Preservation deemed Mineral Point as "one of America's dozen distinctive destinations" in March 2007. The April issue of *Midwest Living Magazine* says Mineral Point is "one of the next big things." In the June issue it called Mineral Point "one of the 100 best small town getaways." (Courtesy of Mineral Point Chamber of Commerce.)

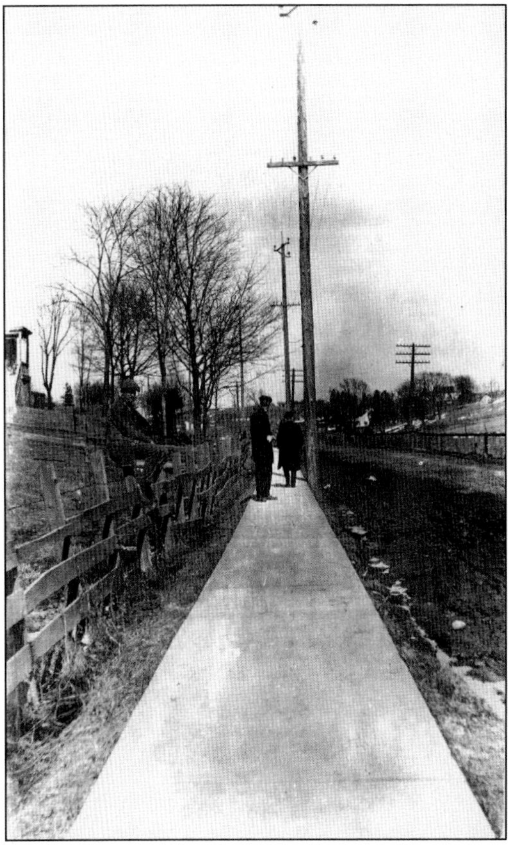

This 1920s view on Shake Rag Street shows the entire street has a fence between the sidewalk and grass lawns. In the beginning Shake Rag was important because it bordered the lead ore mines. It was convenient to build the miners' cottages along this street.

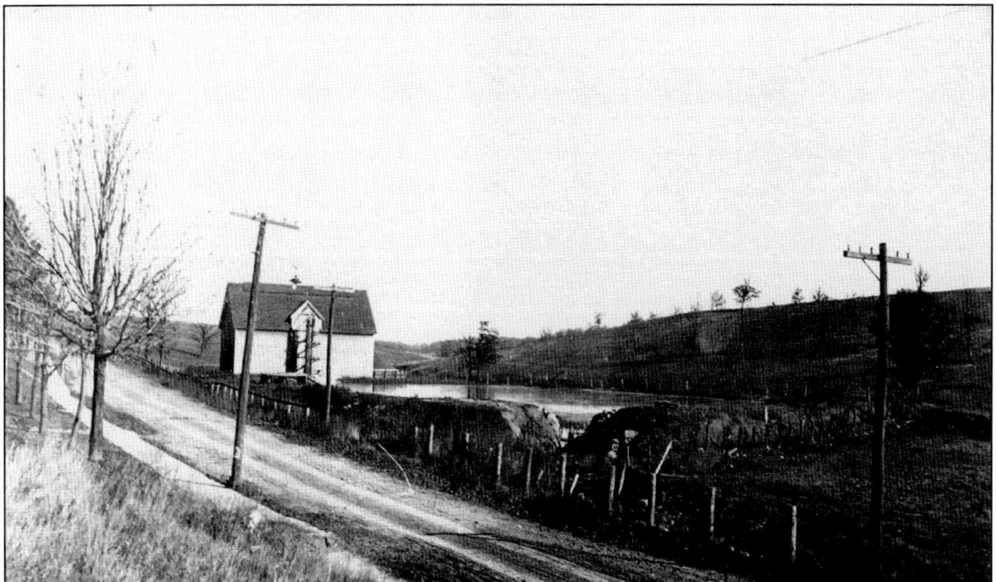

The icehouse used to be located at the Mineral Springs Brewery, at the end of Shake Rag Street. It is no longer standing. The ice was used to keep the beer cool, which was an important step in the brewing process.

Five

Out and About

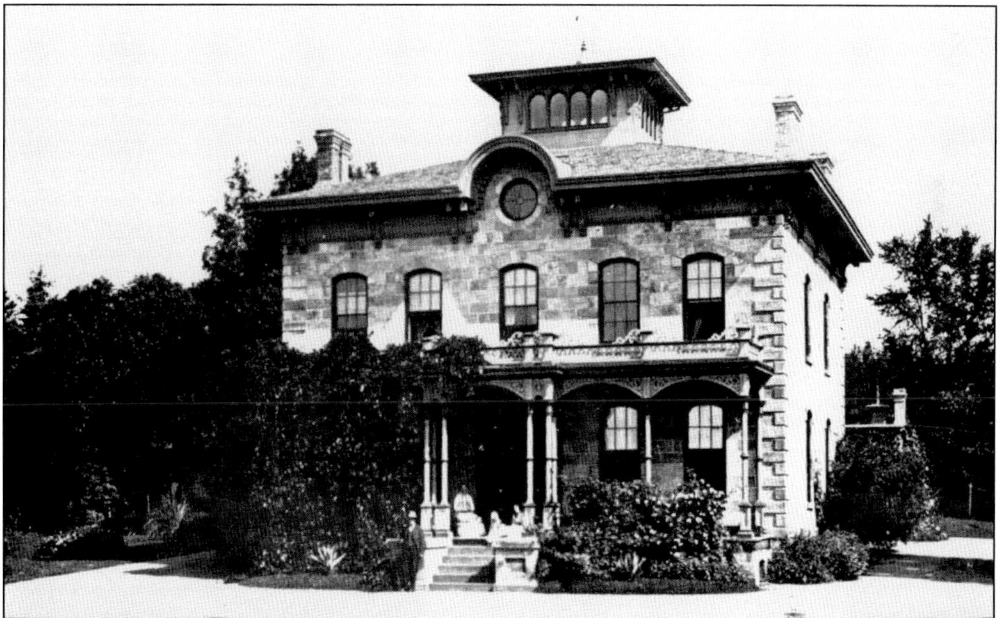

The Gundry House at 234 Madison Street is the current home of the Mineral Point Historical Society Museum, where local history is shown off against the Victorian-era splendor of the home. Joseph Gundry was a native of Cornwall, England. In 1867, he built this impressive mansion on 11 acres and planted native and imported trees and shrubs. The estate was known as Orchard Lawn due to its large apple orchard and gardens. (Courtesy of Mineral Point Historical Society.)

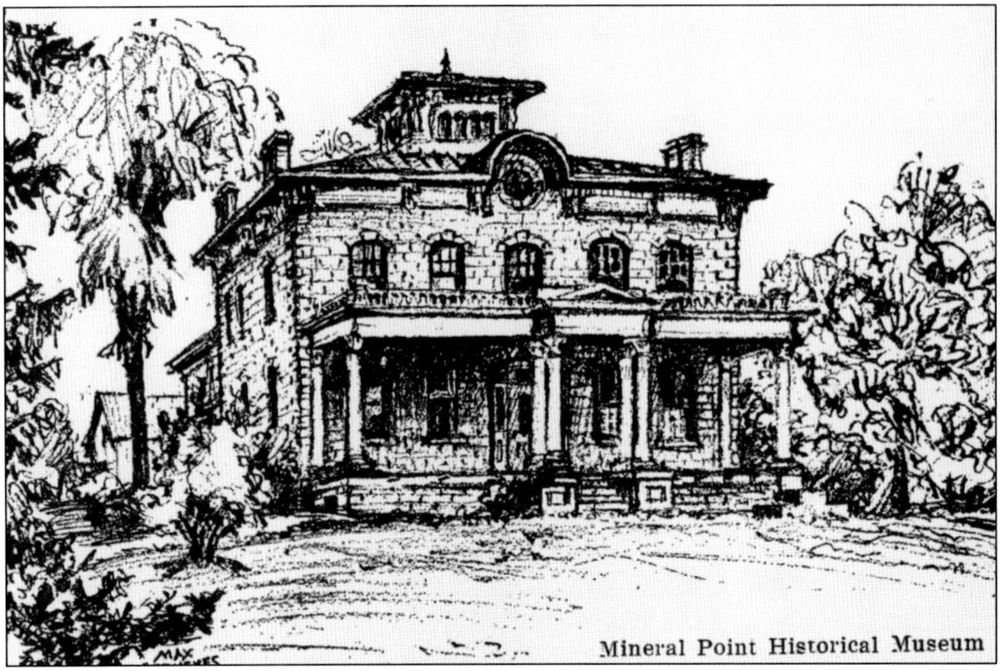

Two of the Gundry children lived in the house until their deaths in the 1930s. Another daughter decided to have the building razed in 1937. She could not stand to have anyone else live in the house. The wrecking crew was met by a group of men from the community who, despite the Depression, scraped together enough money to purchase the building. The group became the local historical society, and the building is now a museum open to the public.

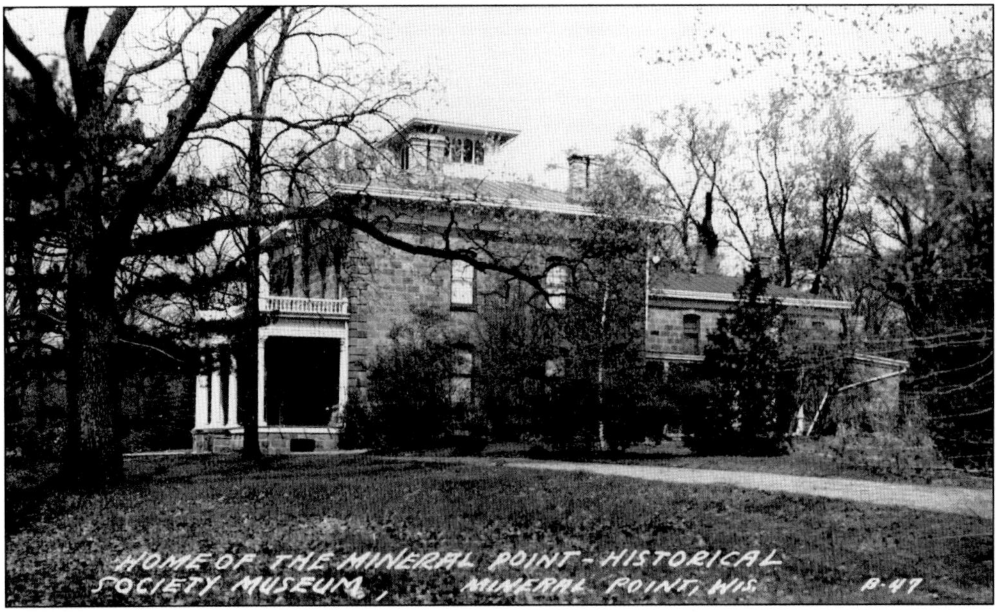

The Mineral Point Historical Society was organized in 1939 to perpetuate the history of this early Wisconsin community. The museum was established in 1940 and contains hundreds of articles of historic interest. Many of the articles dating more than 100 years claim original attachments to the founders of the community, state, and nation.

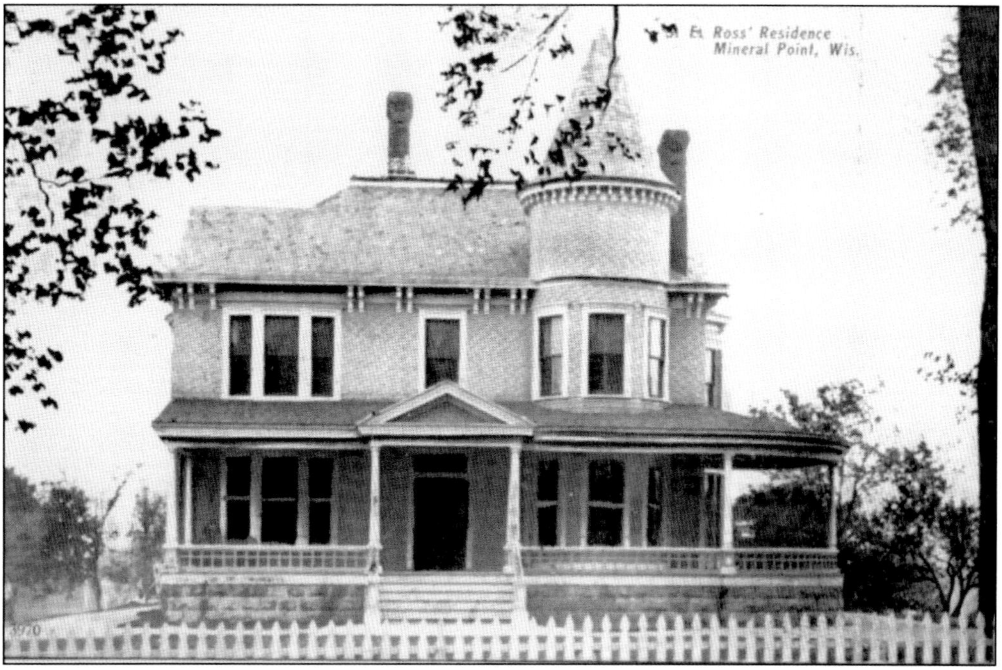

This is the Sam Ross home at 535 Ridge Street around 1910. This Victorian house with its grand porch burned down and was replaced with the Dairyland Motel and Cabins.

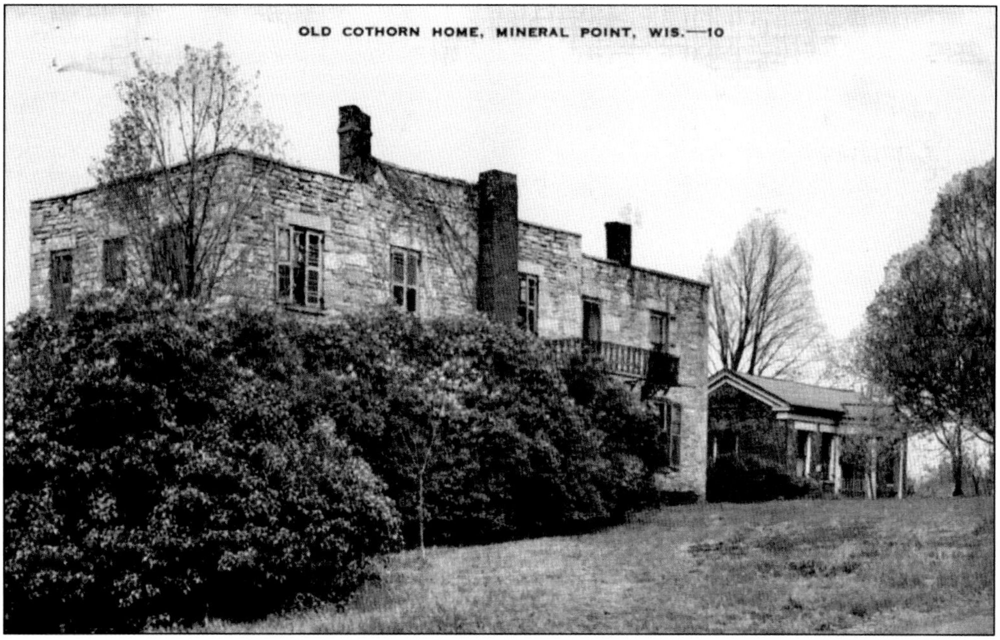

Here stands the Old Cothren Home in 1947. This lordly limestone mansion was built by Judge M. M. Cothren of the 5th Judicial Circuit in 1853 following the Federal style. The kitchen was in the basement following the English fashion. In the original bubble glass windows can be found the etched names of the Cothren family.

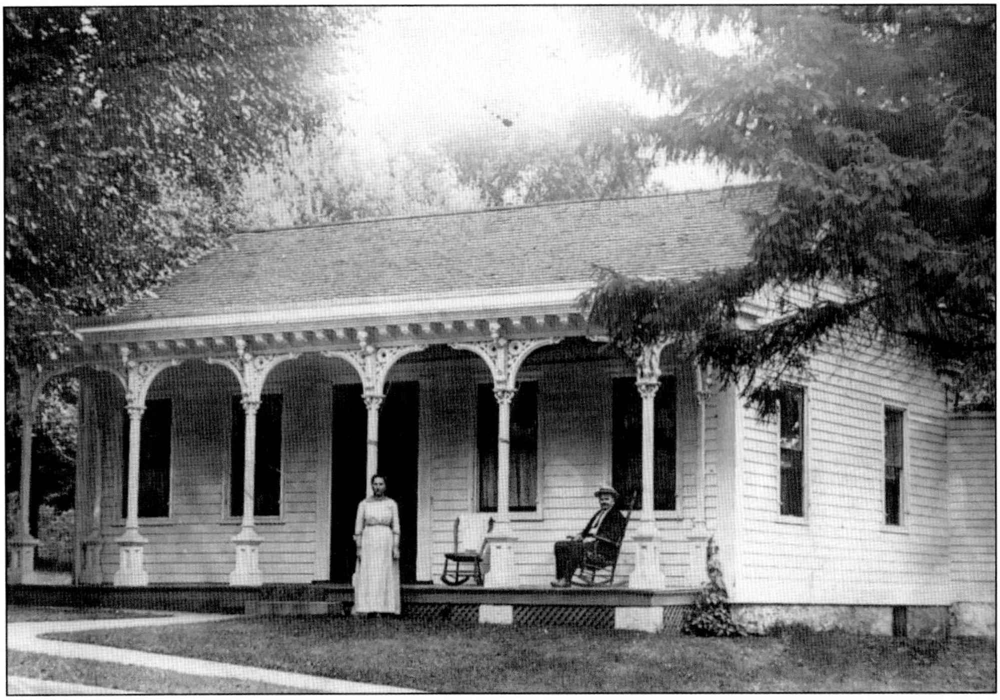

This unidentified local couple, with their matching rocking chairs, enjoys the afternoon together outside their modest home with many pillars.

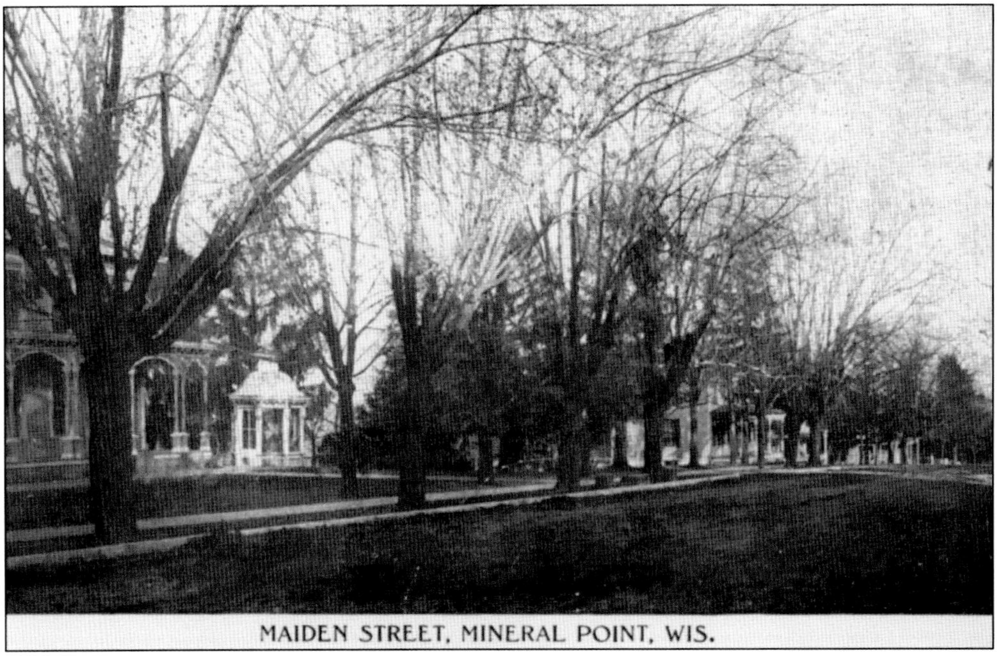

Maiden Street is rumored to once have been the red-light district for the miners and traveling salesmen. Women were scarce and in demand.

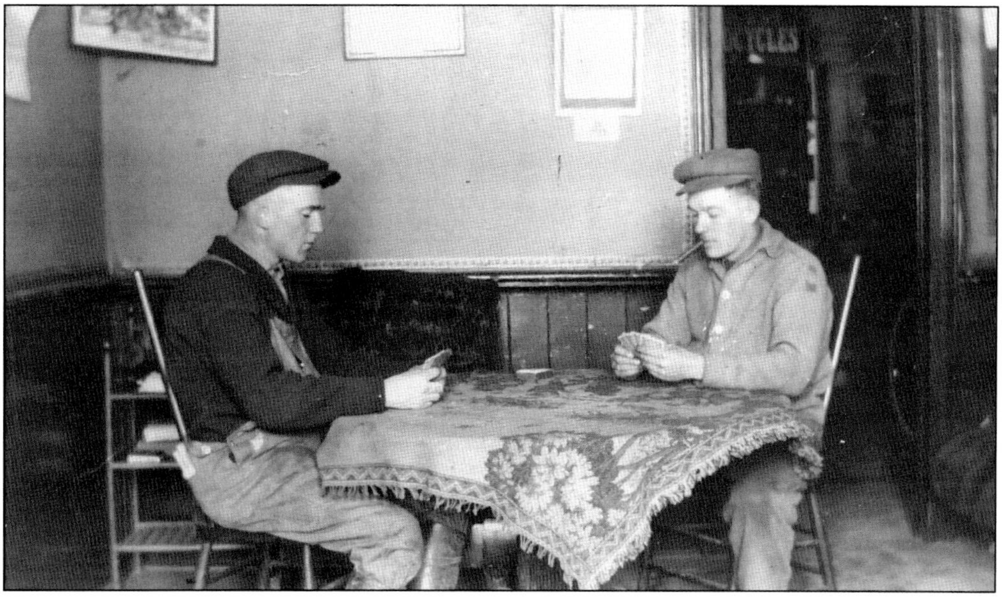

The miners loved to play cards. They often went to church on Sunday and went straight to the horse tracks to gamble, the brewery to drink beer, or somewhere to play cards.

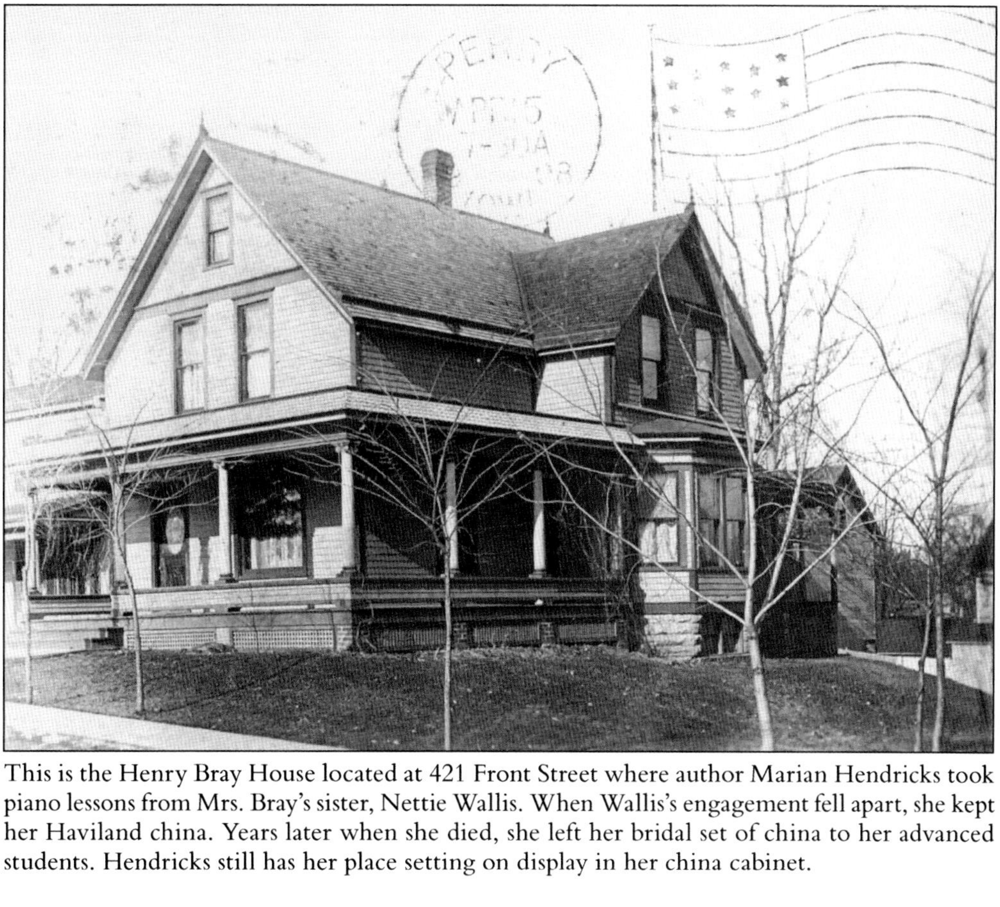

This is the Henry Bray House located at 421 Front Street where author Marian Hendricks took piano lessons from Mrs. Bray's sister, Nettie Wallis. When Wallis's engagement fell apart, she kept her Haviland china. Years later when she died, she left her bridal set of china to her advanced students. Hendricks still has her place setting on display in her china cabinet.

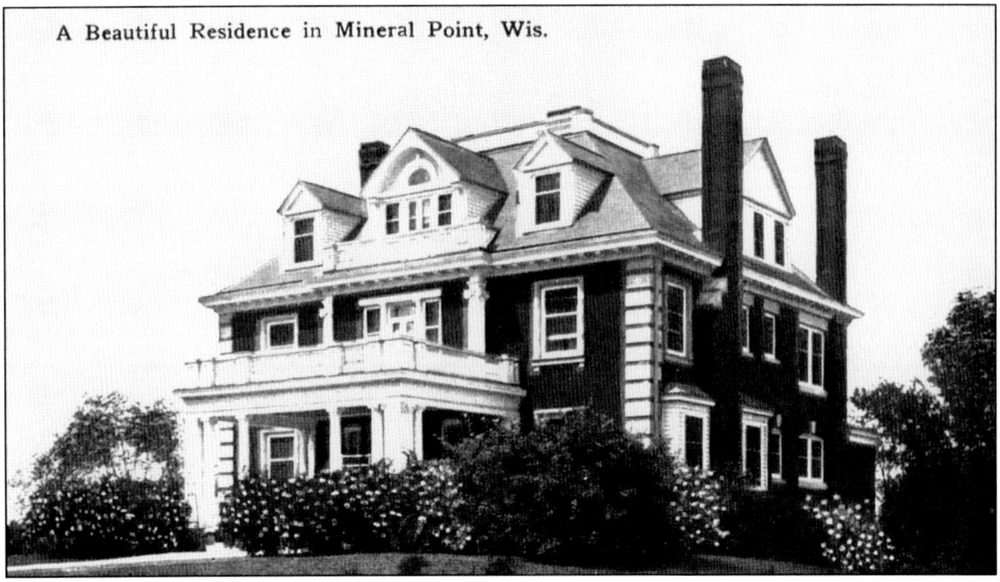

The Jones House was built in 1906 by William Jones from Chicago. The house sits high on the hill on Ridge Street, overlooking the city. It has 16 rooms, eight fireplaces, and four bathrooms. The entrance hall is warmed by a three-story freestanding fireplace surrounded by a balcony and semicircular stairway. Jones imported wood from every state in the union to panel and decorate his home. Each room had a different wood.

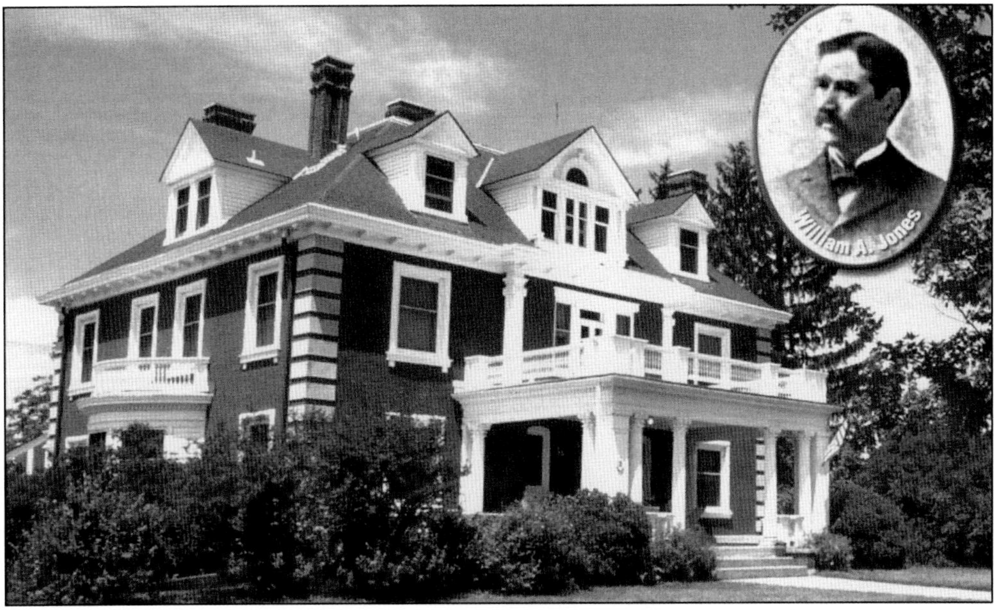

Jones was an icon in Mineral Point history. He was a teacher, banker, legislator and politician, and the first Wisconsin commissioner of the Bureau of Indian Affairs. He was one of the partners of the Mineral Point Zinc Works, and he was the manager of the Mineral Point Railroad. As an old man he lived alone in his big mansion, while his family remained in Chicago. After his death, the family kept the place immaculately maintained until his last daughter died. The house was then used as a bed-and-breakfast for a few years. It currently sits empty most of the time, although it is used for meetings and receptions. (Photograph by Betty France.)

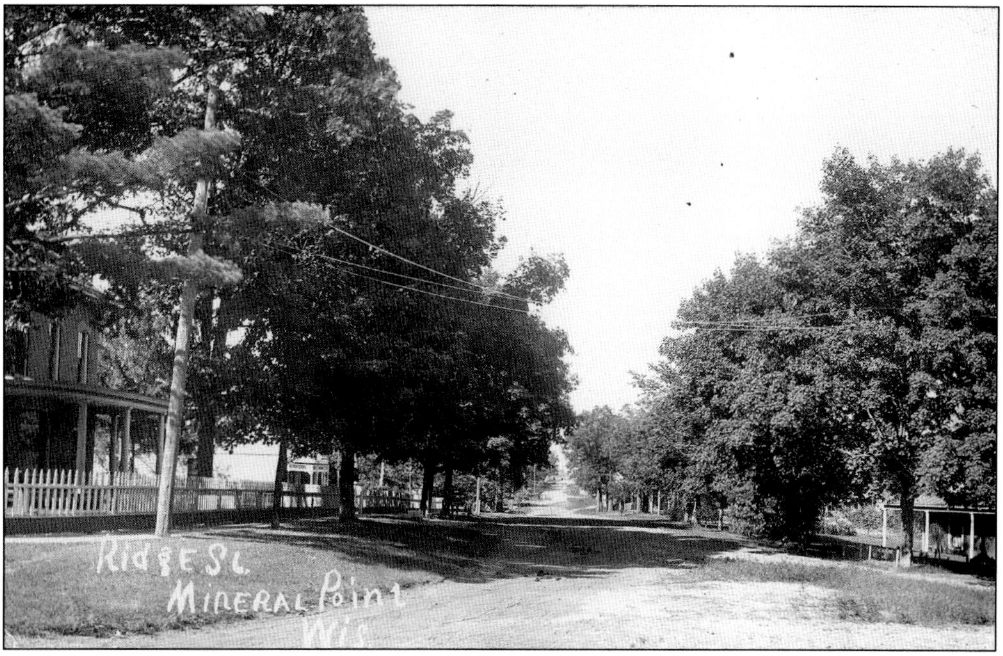

Ridge Street sat high above the town. It eventually became Highway 151, which was a busy thoroughfare. The houses along this street were large, set back from the road with big lawns.

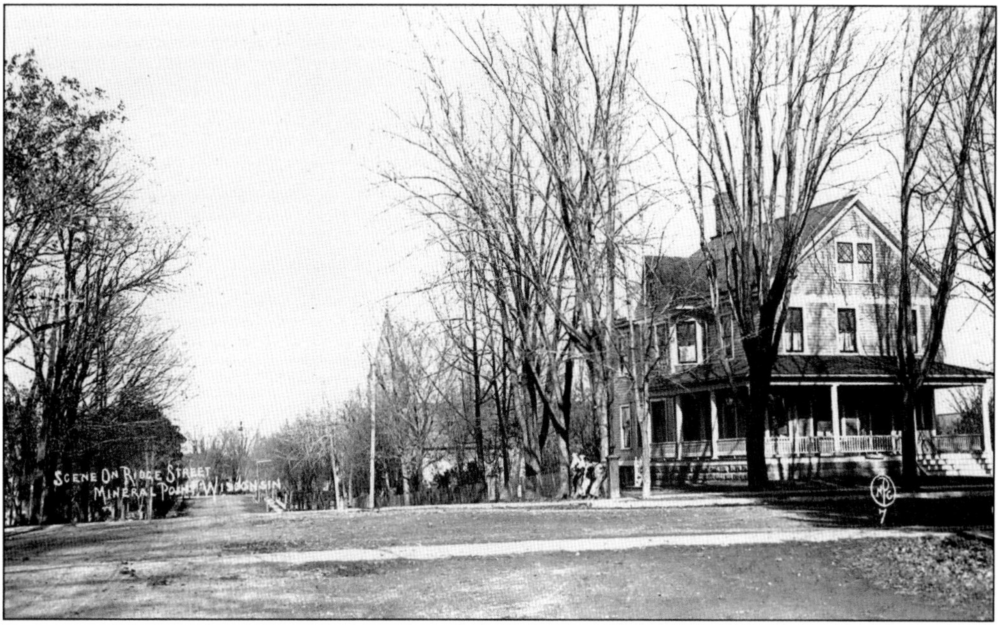

This is a view of Ridge Street looking down Doty Street toward the business district on High Street. The homes of Mineral Point are interesting even to the most casual observer. A drive around the town reveals both tiny cottages and huge mansions. The variety adds interest to the community.

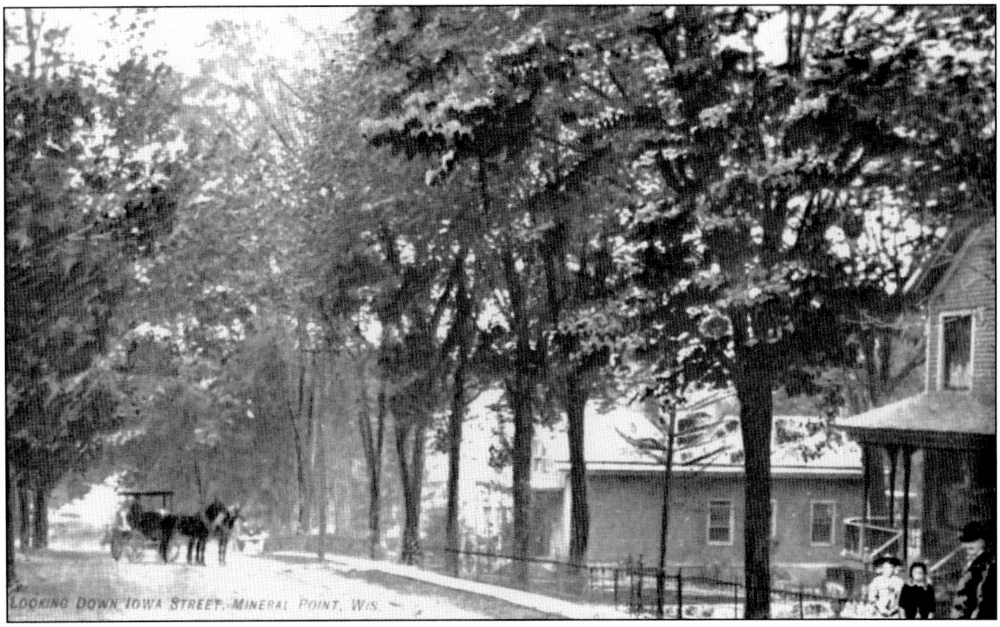

Looking from Maiden Street down South Iowa Street is a winter scene with horse and carriage that was common in the 1800s.

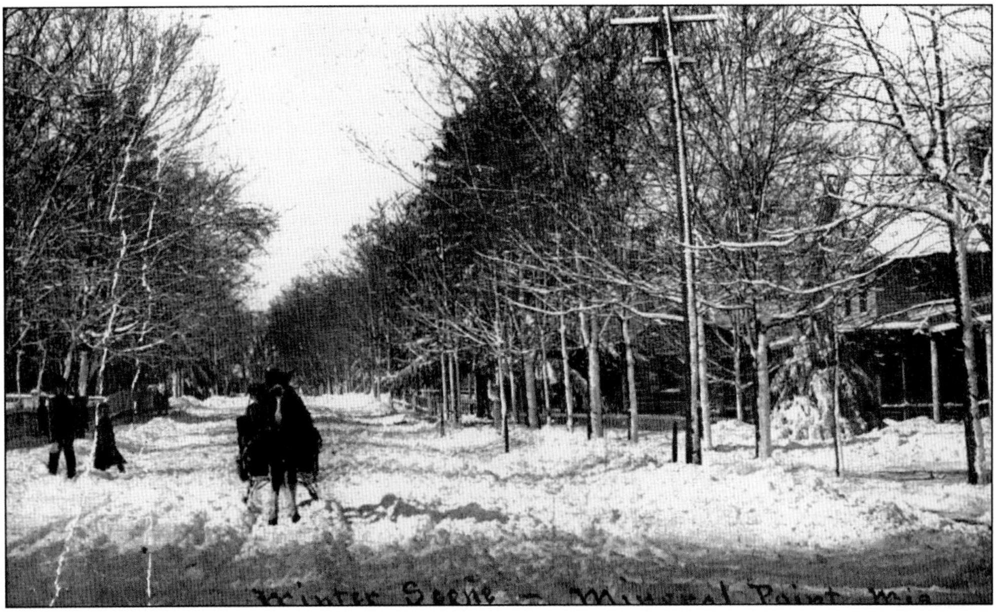

A horse and sleigh enjoy an outing on a Mineral Point street. Mineral Point is in Iowa County. The county derives its name from the powerful and, at one time, invincible tribe of Ioway Indians, whose hunting grounds engrossed the territory that has since proved the foundation of several states.

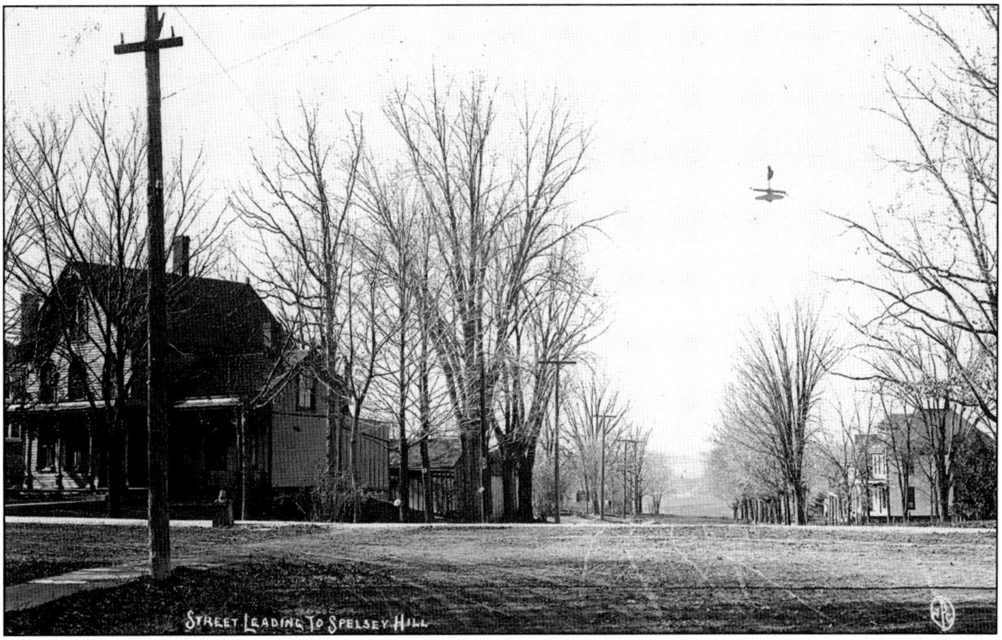

This trip down Dodge Street heads toward Spensley's Hill. The Northern Photo Company of Wausau had this card made, but it spelled Spensley without the *n* and reversed the *l* and *s*.

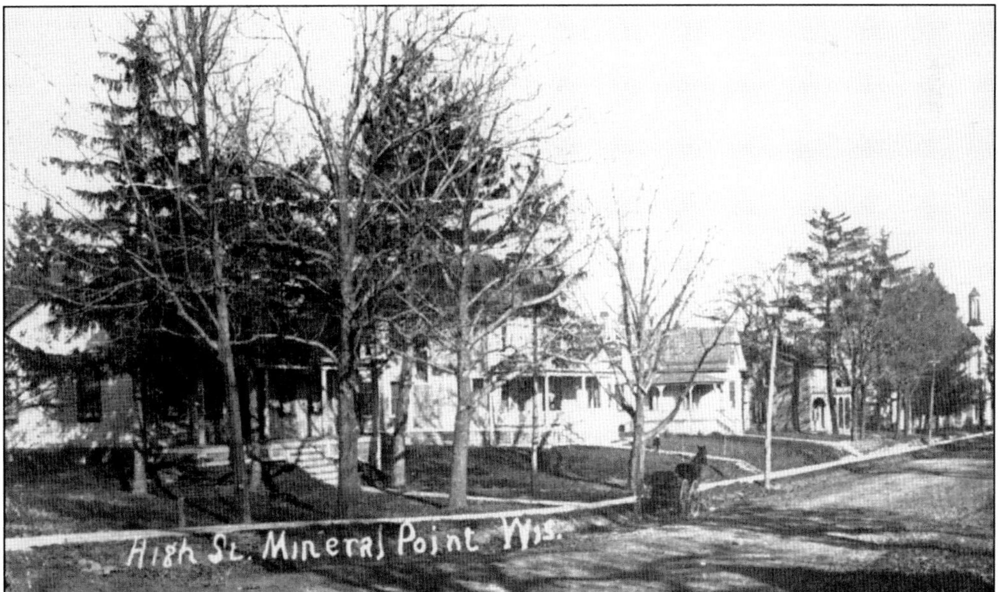

This postcard says it is High Street, but it is really Doty Street. The two streets intersect each other by the Methodist church.

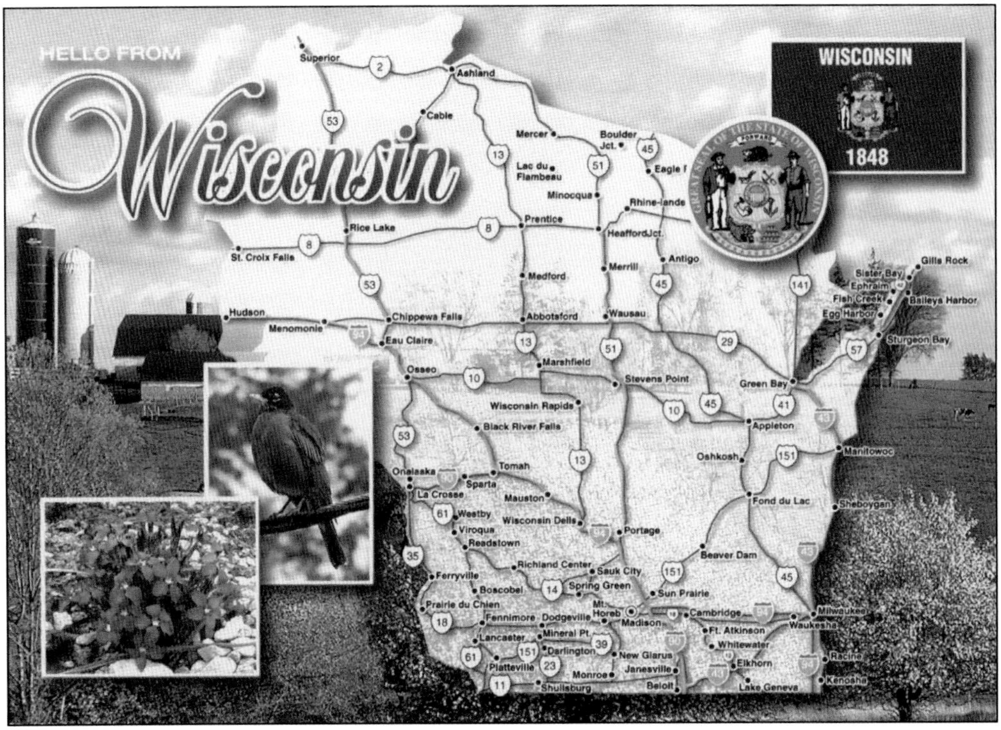

Mineral Point is located near the southwest corner of the state. It is one of the few villages that still can show the architecture of the Cornish miners. Here is where Wisconsin began in the 1820s, when prospectors were swarming over the hills looking for lead to make their fortunes. A lead rush resulted from mineral discoveries, and a mining camp formed around the diggings that eventually were called Mineral Point. (Photograph by Betty France.)

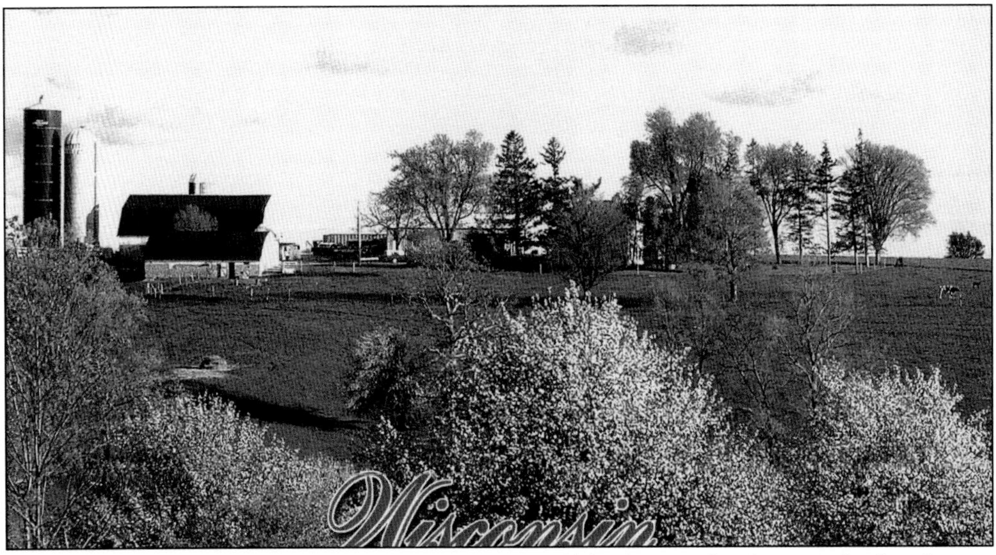

The early miners worked the mines and had to import all food. Later they became the first farmers of the area, often having small mines on their property. Agriculture thrived on the fertile land. Family dairy farms are now important to the rural economy of the state and identify Wisconsin as the "Dairy State." (Photograph by Betty France.)

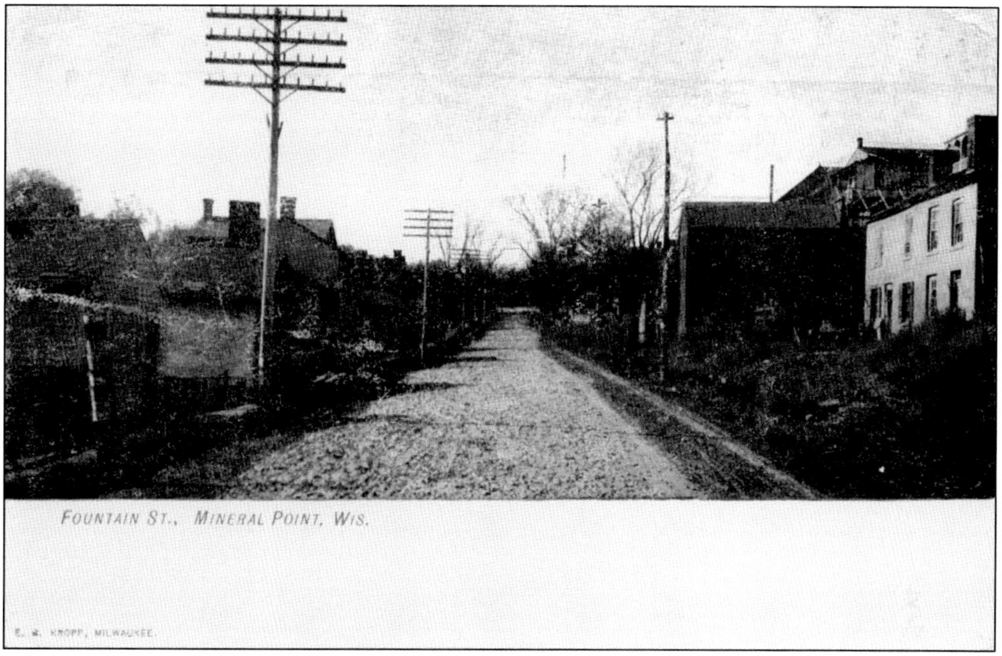

This is an early view of Fountain Street, which is located below the main street called High Street. There used to be a spring on the left with a water fountain and a small area called Jerusalem Park, after a particular spring in the park.

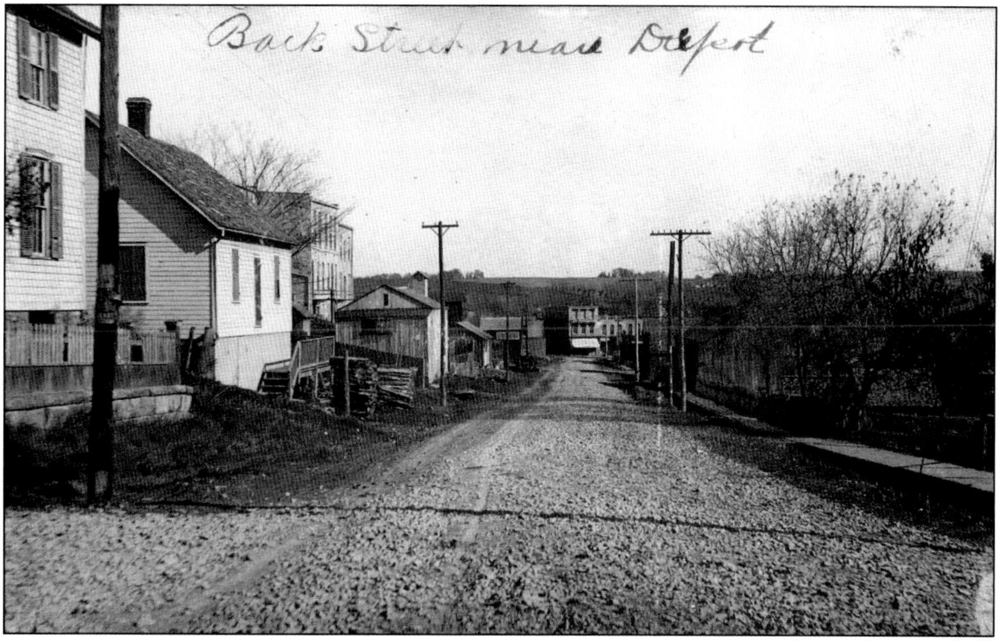

This view is looking the other direction on Fountain Street, from the corner of Chestnut Street. Moses Strong, a pillar from the past, lived on this street. He was suave, tactful, and dignified. In 1838, he was appointed United States attorney for the territory of Wisconsin.

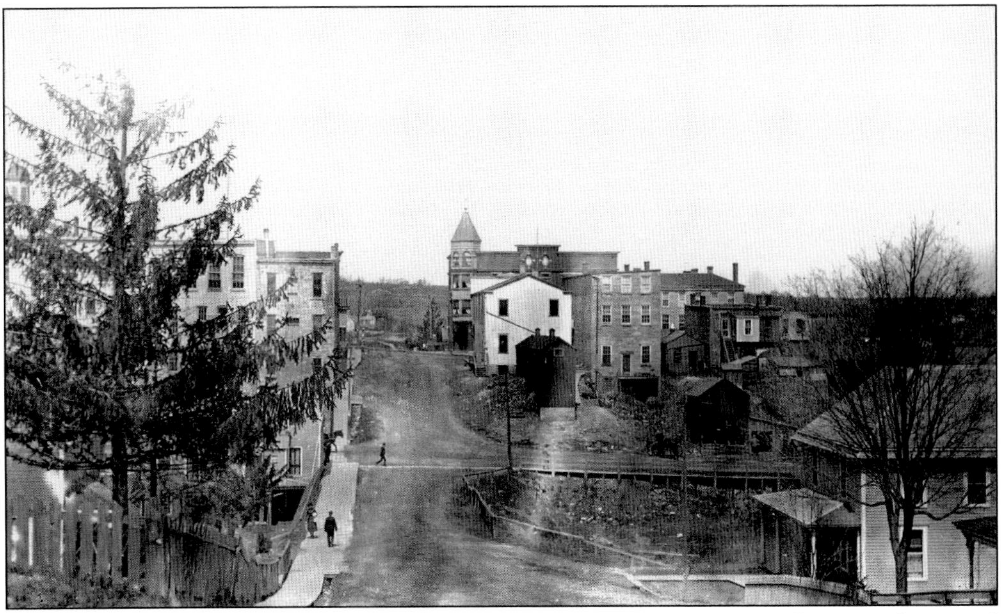

This card is looking north up Vine Street to High Street where one will notice the Royal Hotel cupola. The hilly town was surrounded by limestone caves and hills, making walking a daily chore.

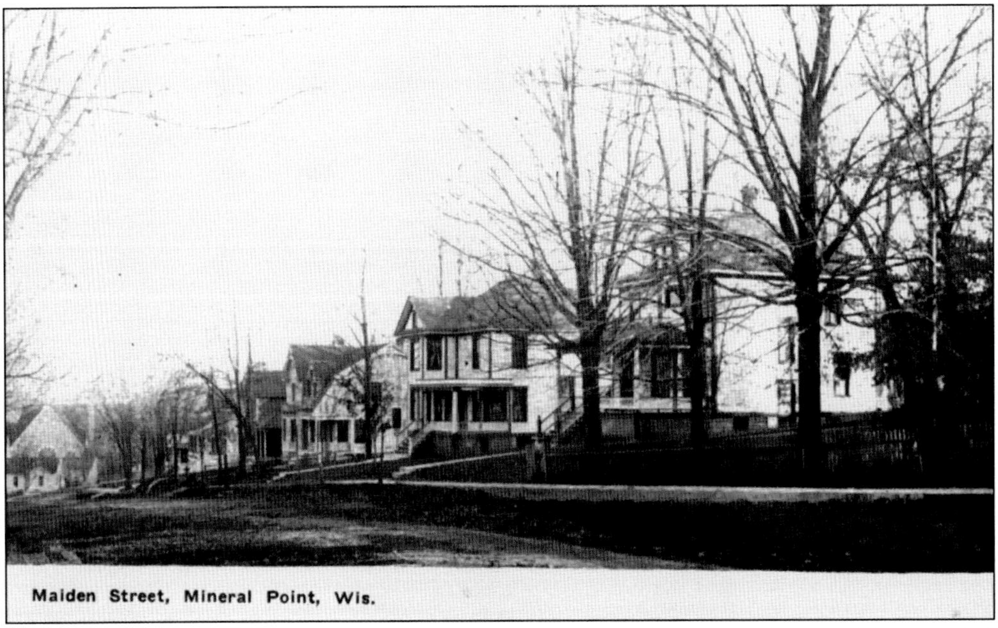

Prosperous times arrived, and six big new houses lined Maiden Street. This card is dated 1910.

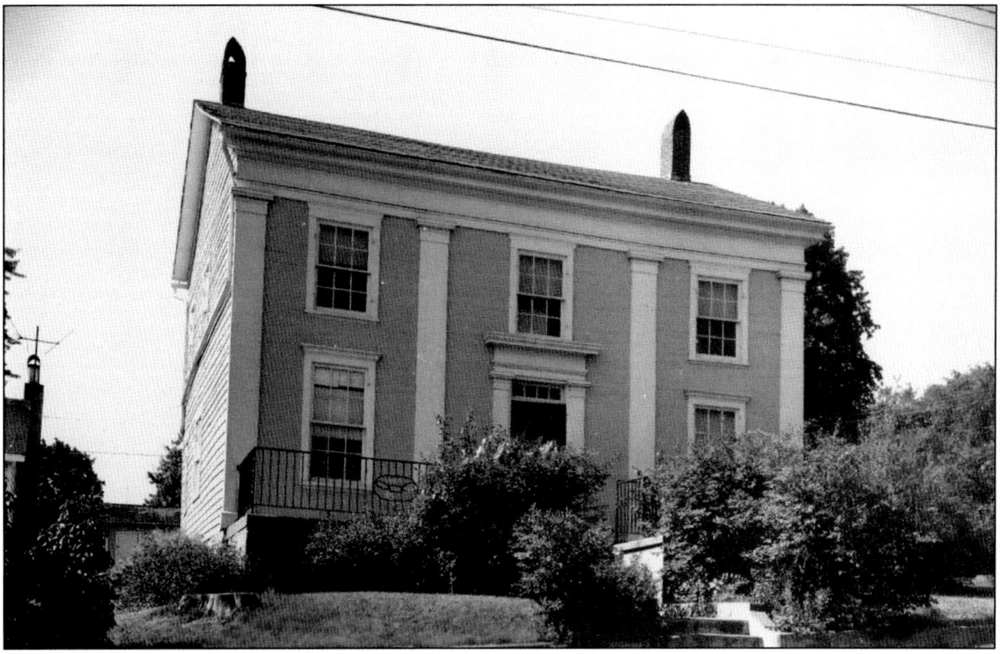

The Odd Fellows hall was built in 1835. This very historic building was the first such lodge building west of the Alleghenies. It is a charming Federal style building on Front Street that also contains the Rebekah Museum. The Odd Fellows was organized to protect and care for members at times when there was no welfare state, trade unions, or National Health Service. The aim was (and still is) to provide help to members when they need it.

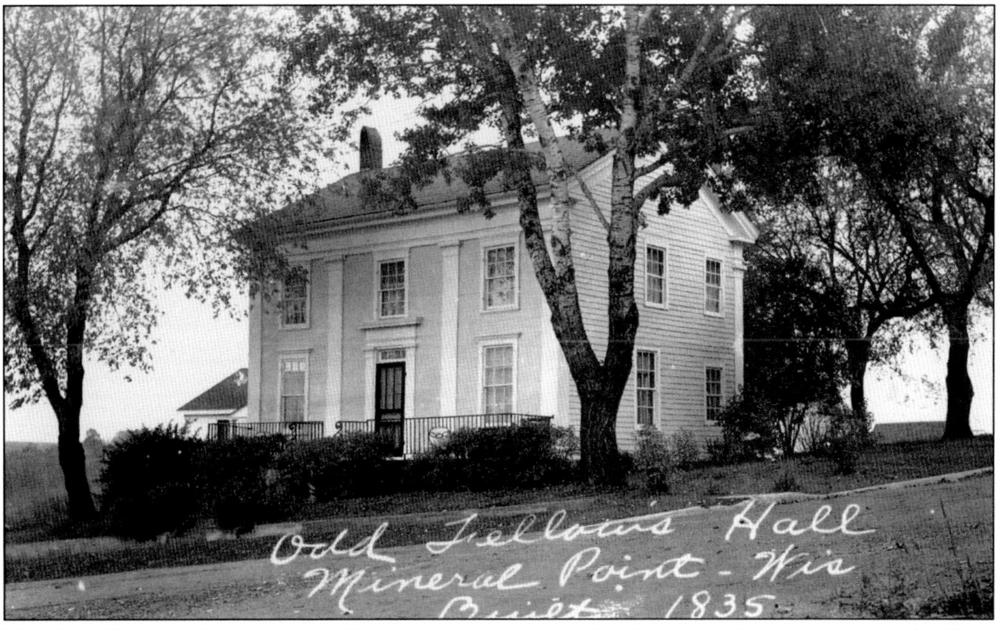

The friendly societies are nonprofit organizations owned by their members, not by shareholders. All income is passed back to the members in the form of services and benefits. The Odd Fellows are fund-raisers for both local and national charities. Branches raise money for local good causes and the societies as a whole raise large amounts for charities.

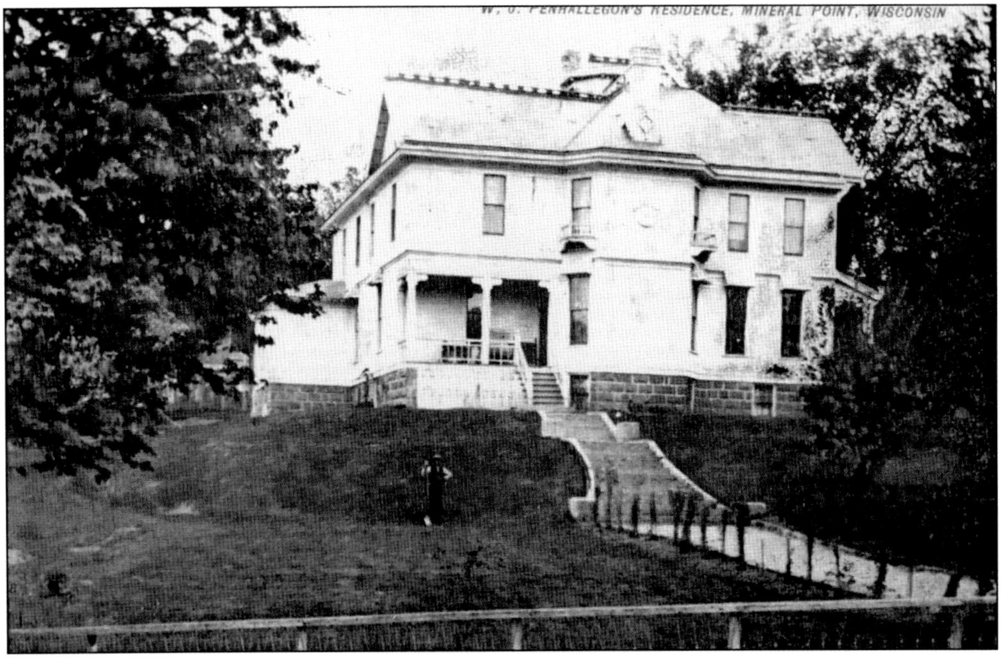

This is a side view of the beautiful Penhallagon residence on 216 South Iowa Street. It was in the upstairs apartment that author Marian Hendricks spent one cold and memorable winter with little heat. The owners left for the winter and shut off the lower furnace. The pipes from the second furnace lost heat, as they were exposed going up 12 feet to the second floor.

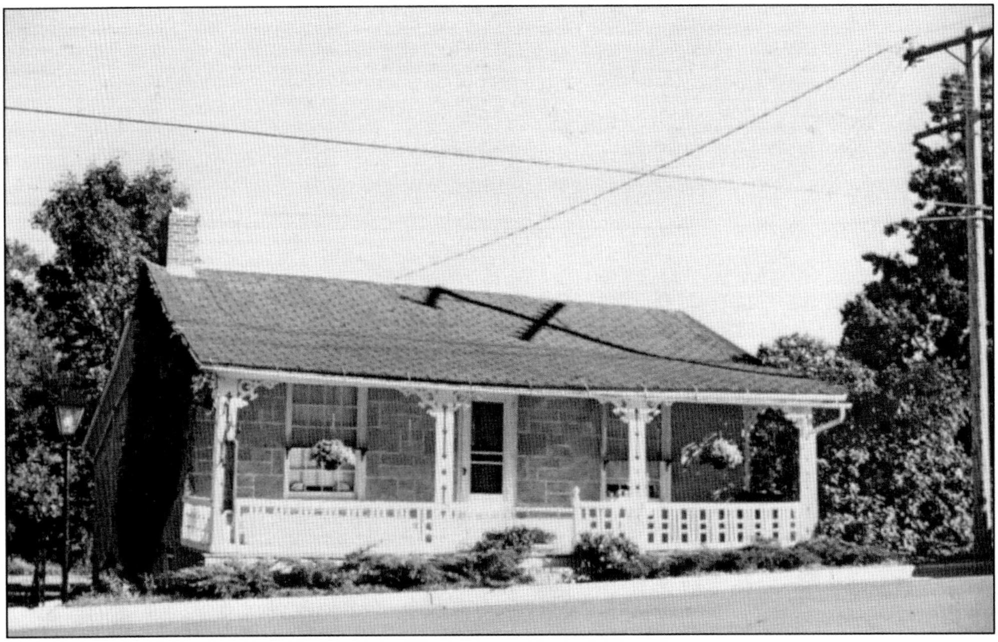

The Welsh House has a lacy porch look. It invitingly sits on Shake Rag Street. It was a cottage restored by Al Felly of Felly's Flowers of Madison, who still occupies it today. (Photograph by Mike Mewis.)

Six

Downtown Business

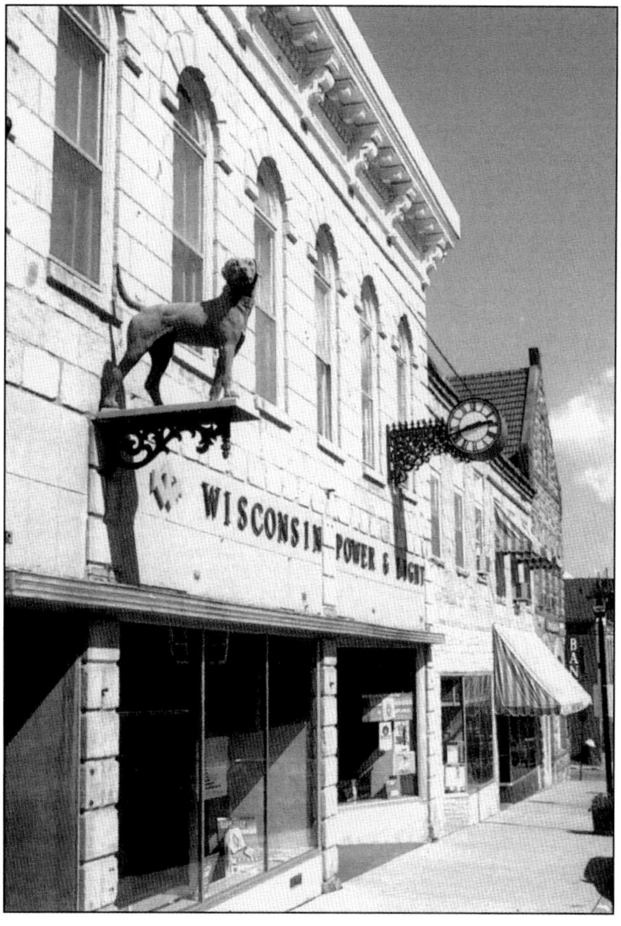

Mineral Point's mascot has overlooked the downtown business district on High Street for 130 years. The zinc cast statue originally promoted the elegant Gundry and Gray department store. Both men were from Cornwall and brought with them the British tradition of identifying stores with animal statues. The pointer has become symbolic to the city that had its origin in 1827, when people came to settle during the lead rush. Locals are quite attached to this dog. (Photograph by Gari Walz.)

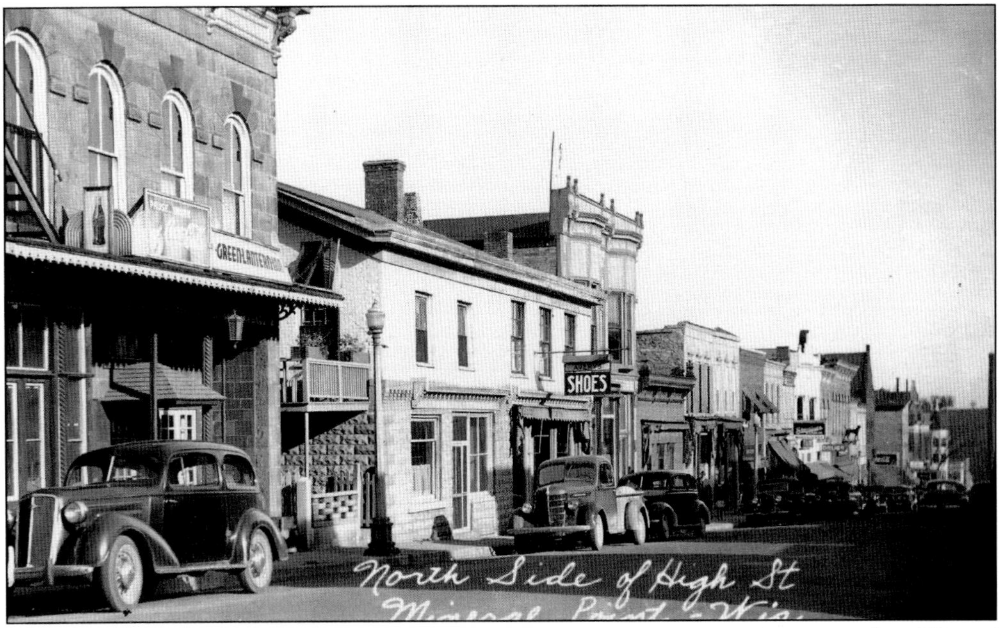

Mid-block is Avery's shoe store sign dating from the 1950s. Prior to that it was the office of Dr. Brown. On the left can be seen the end of the U.S. Hotel, where an arsonist simultaneously set four fires in 1927. The Mineral Point fire department extinguished the fires, and the arsonist was caught.

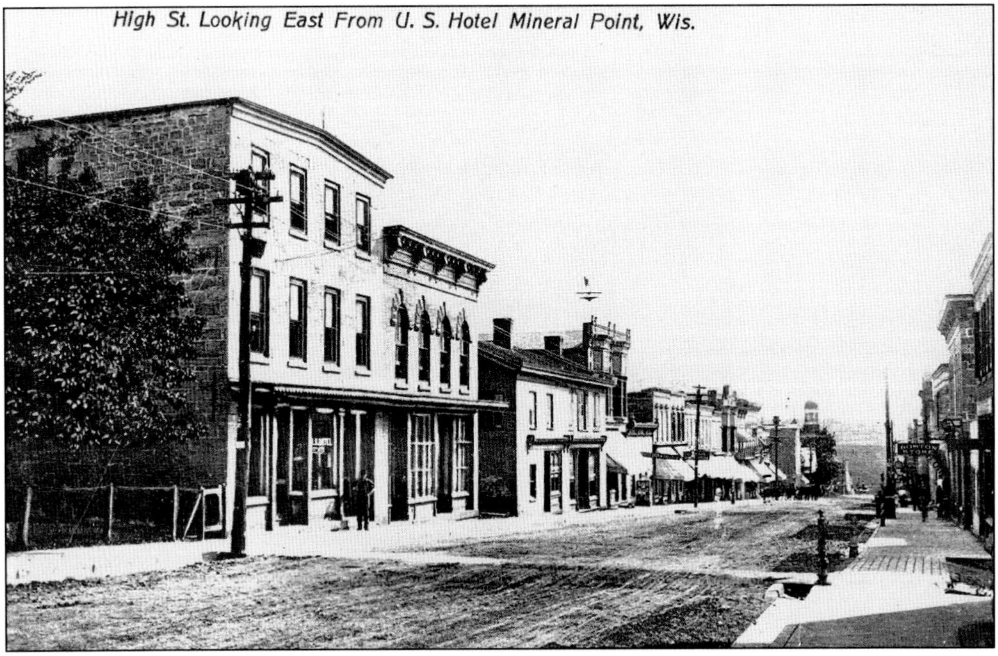

This is the U.S. Hotel at 267 High Street, looking east. Many early dignitaries, including Gen. Ulysses S. Grant, stayed in this hotel. The exterior is plain and simple, but solid. It was built in the 1840s. The hotel was regularly used by traveling salesmen who came in by train with trunks of merchandise and clothing to make sales to local merchants.

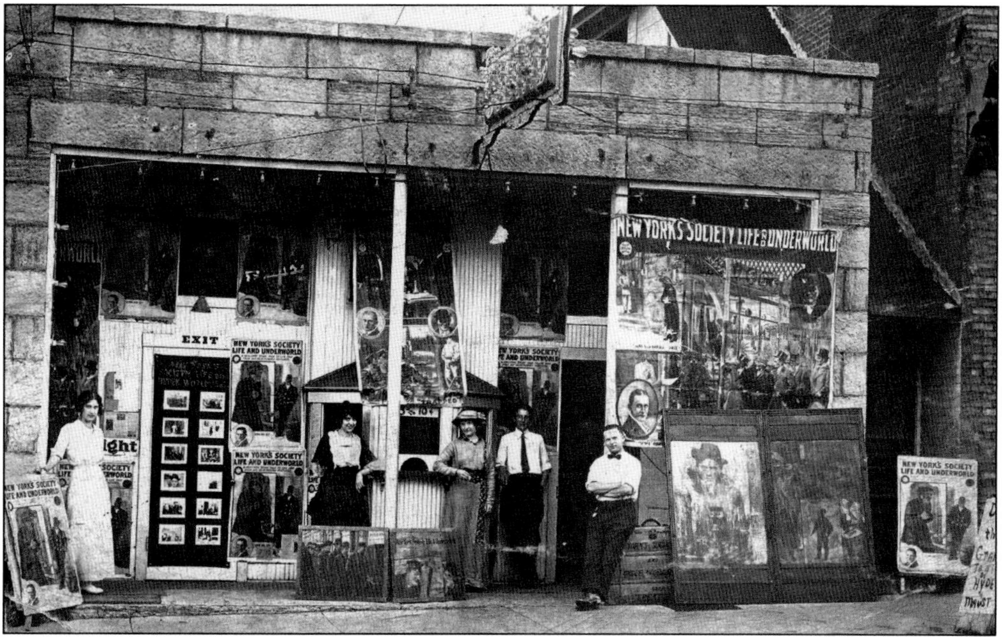

This 1914 photograph is near the Mitchell Hardware store across from the U.S. Hotel. As can be seen, it carried a hodgepodge of merchandise.

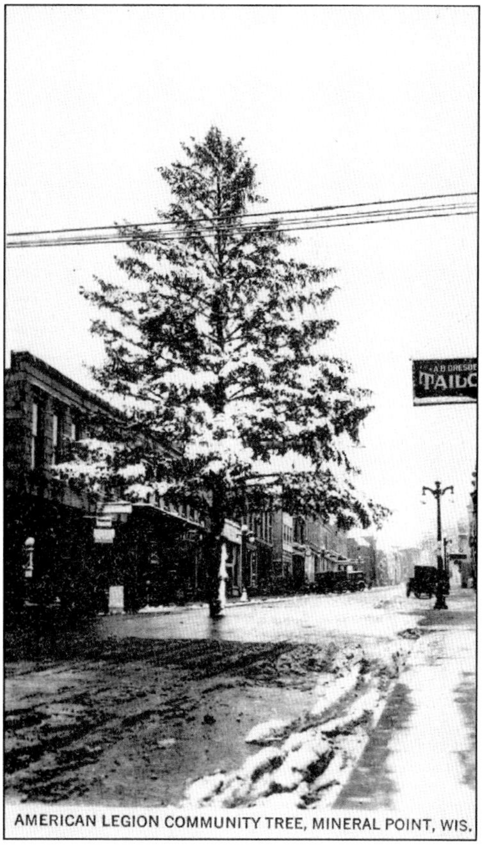

The American Legion's community Christmas tree lights the way to the downtown art community. Potters, weavers, glass artists, photographers, painters, sculptors, and woodworkers work and live here. This artist colony has added charm and color to the town.

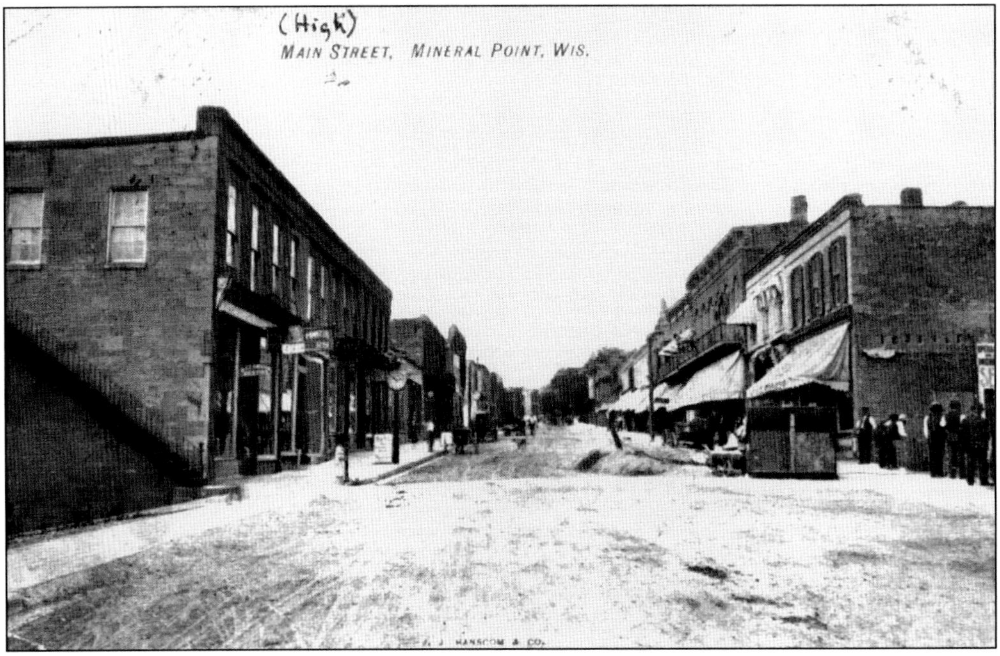

High Street looking west from Chestnut Street shows an unpaved main street being used by horse and buggies and men on horseback.

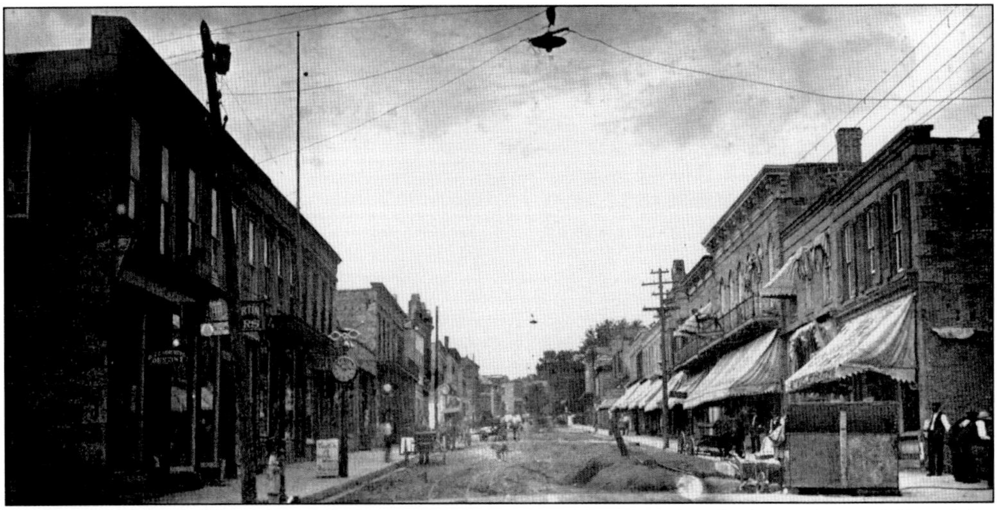

In this similar photograph electric wires are seen overhead with a light in the middle of the street. The same men appear on the right as in the previous photograph but in this one posts and wires have magically appeared.

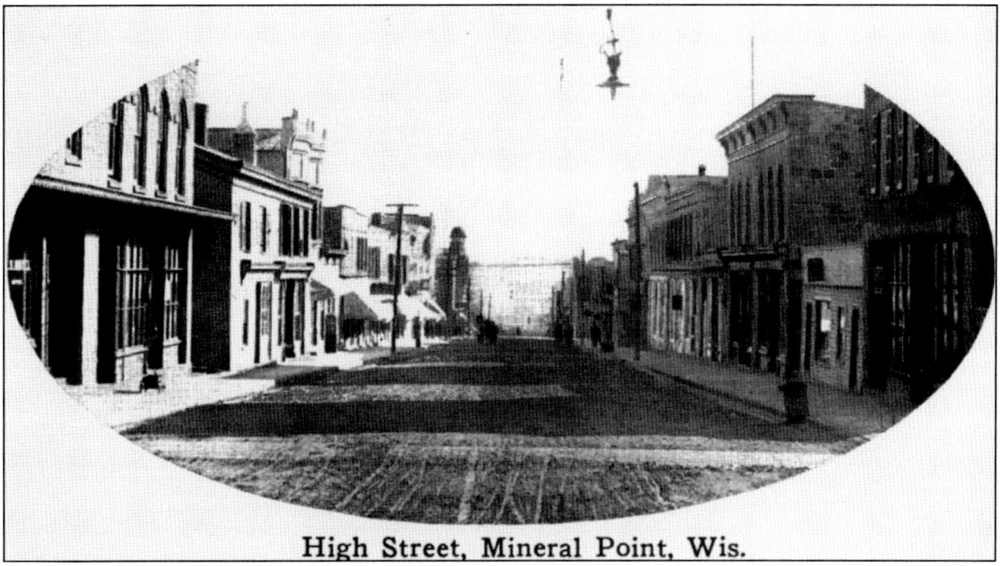

Looking down the High Street business district, students from the School of the Art Institute of Chicago recently visited Mineral Point to study wallpaper scraps, fabric remnants, and hand-written graffiti. They were shocked to find that the humblest house in the city, Pendarvis, has had the largest influence on the city's identity.

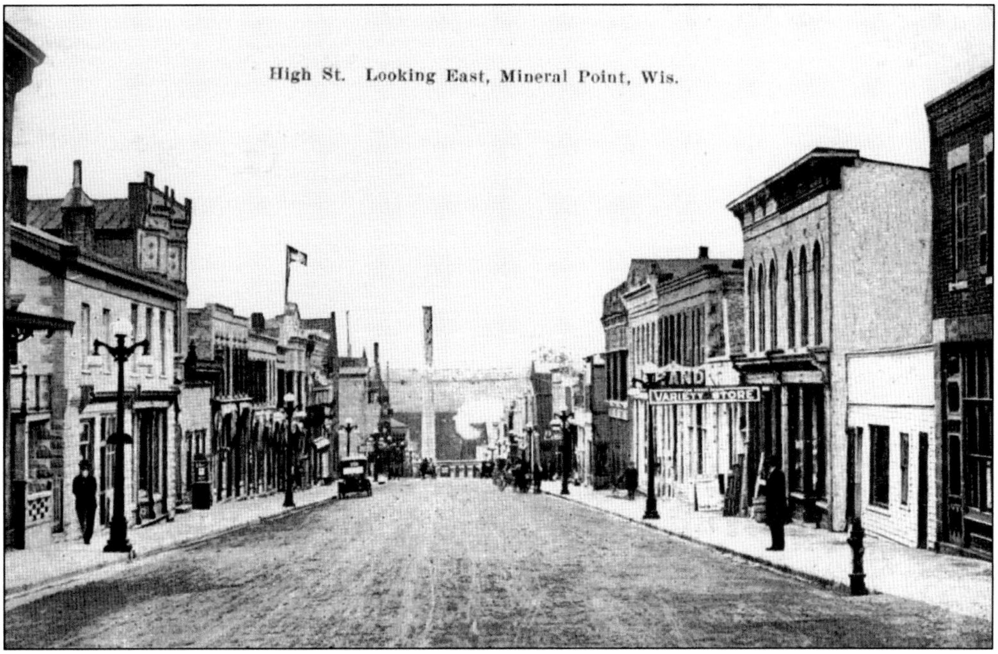

The electric power plant smokestack is visible at the bottom of High Street. The city lights brought a welcomed change to the residents who had voted to get electric lights a couple of years before they arrived.

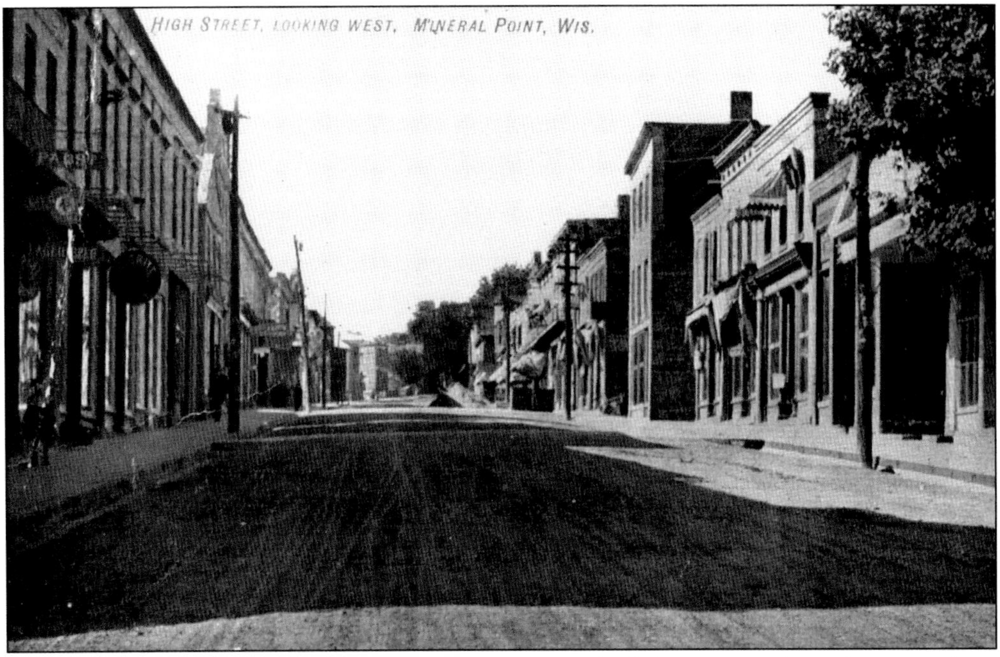

Looking up High Street from Vine Street, a tavern on the left is seen with a Pabst Lager beer sign. Thanks to its welcoming attitude and tremendous community pride, Mineral Point has achieved a standard many communities strive to emulate.

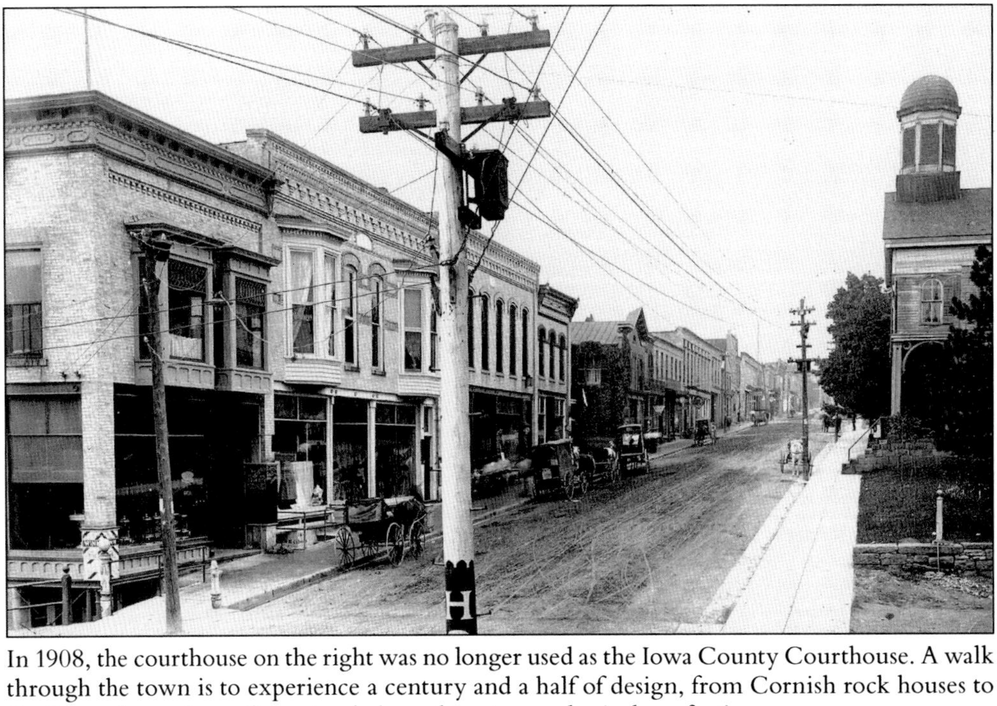

In 1908, the courthouse on the right was no longer used as the Iowa County Courthouse. A walk through the town is to experience a century and a half of design, from Cornish rock houses to Craftsman bungalows, from simple log cabins to neoclassical confections.

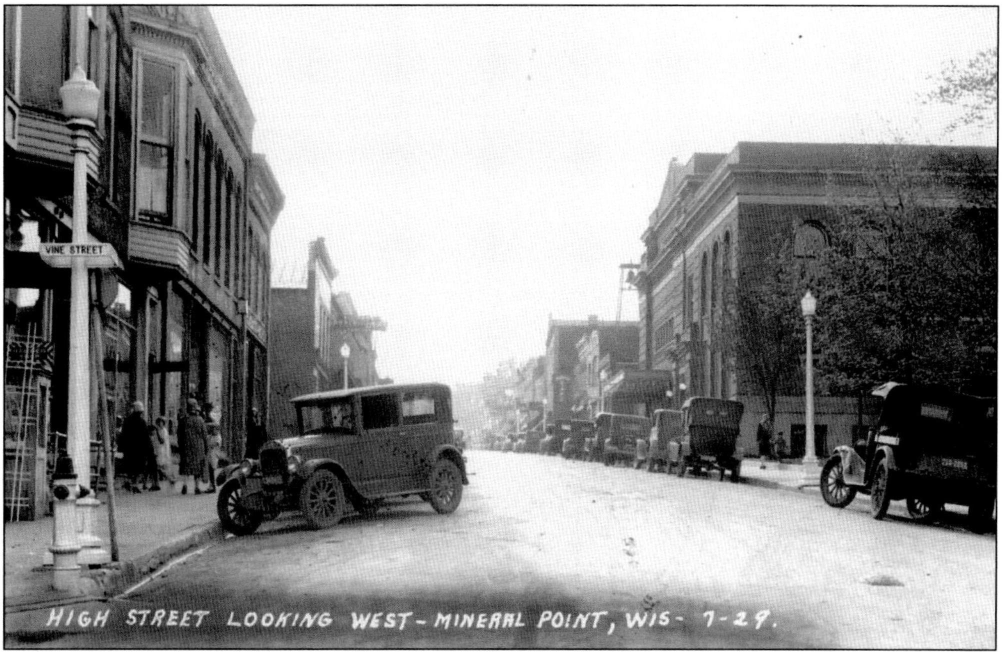

The municipal building is visible on the right in this 1920s postcard view. Residents have taken care to preserve this building with its fine opera house, library, and archival room.

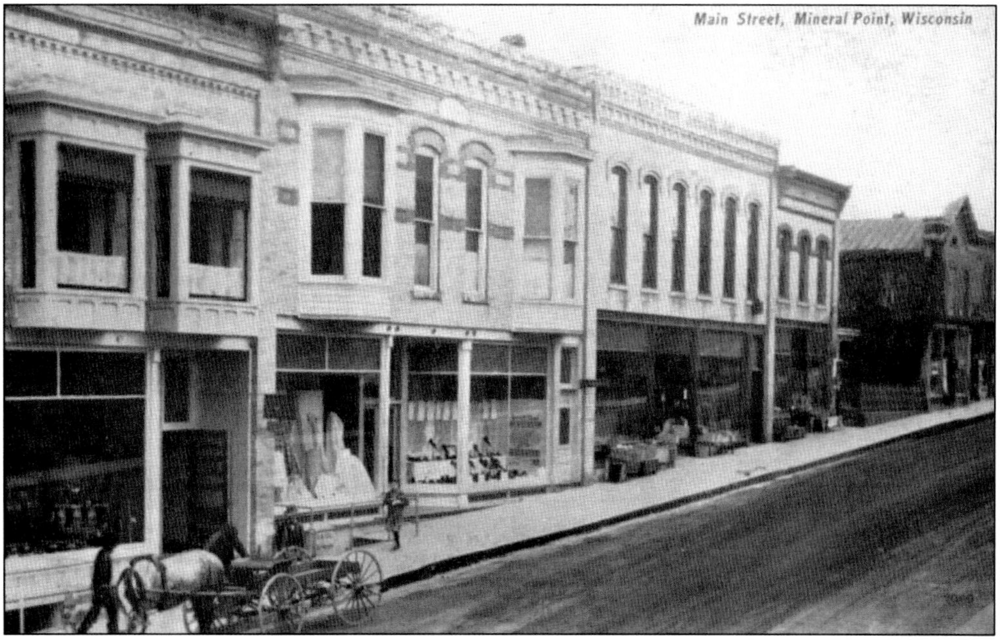

Author Marian Hendricks's father had his doctor's office in this building on the second floor. On the first floor was Martin's Hardware store.

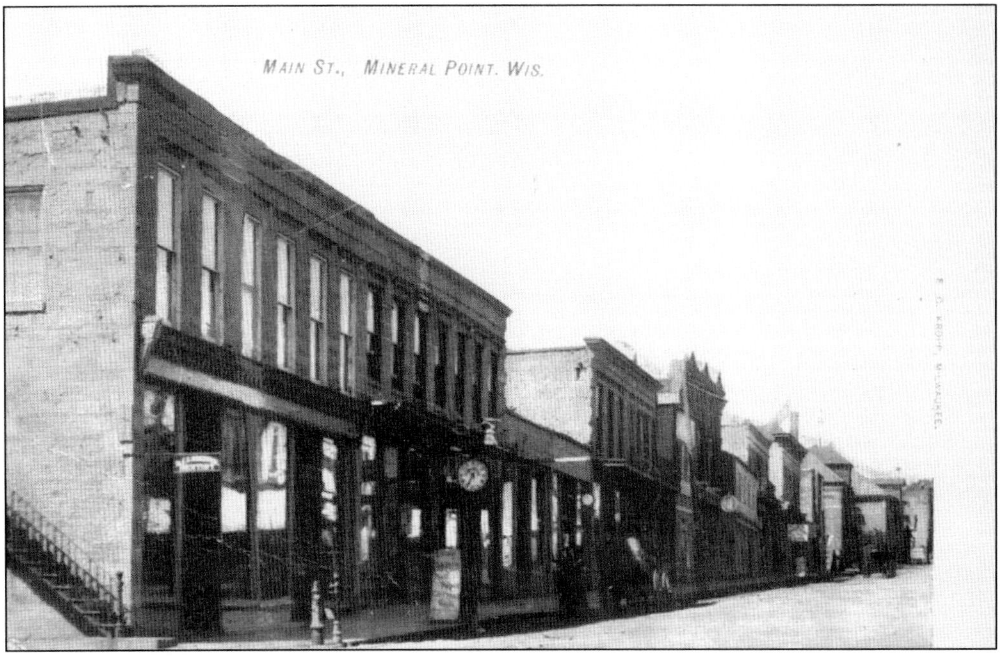

Correll and Martin Clothing was located here. A dental office was upstairs. Ben Franklin now occupies this building. The commercial district at first benefited from the gold rush, selling supplies to people leaving for the west. Then by the 1850s it went into a slump. Eventually the business district stayed stable, serving the city's permanent residents and the area farmers.

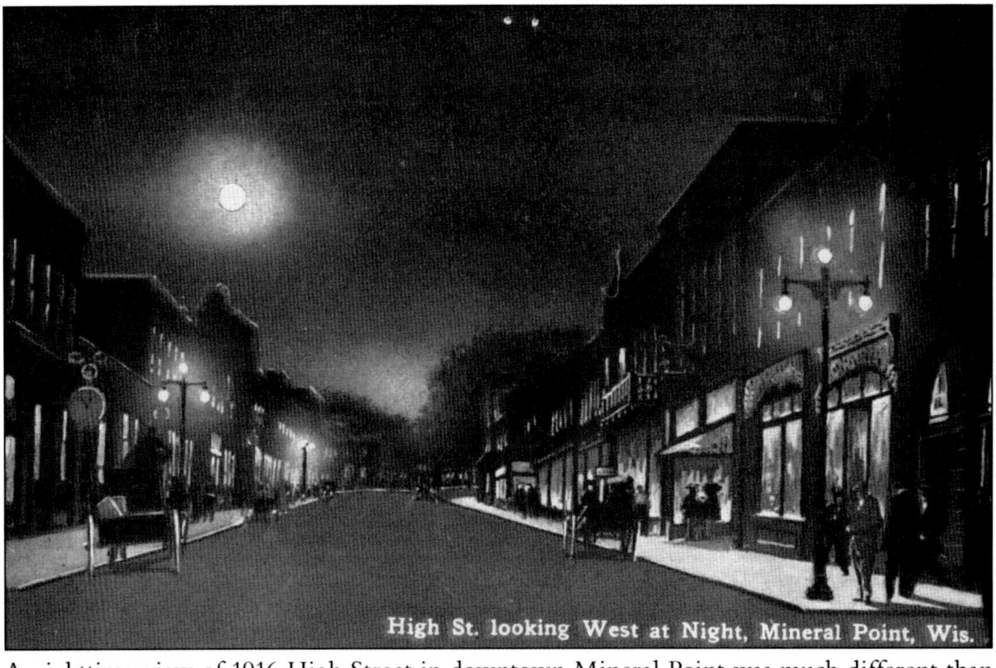

A nighttime view of 1916 High Street in downtown Mineral Point was much different than the previous century when the community retained its frontierlike characteristics and crude, sometimes temporary buildings, due to the transient nature of the miners, the boom and bust lead-mining cycles, and the lack of formal land surveying.

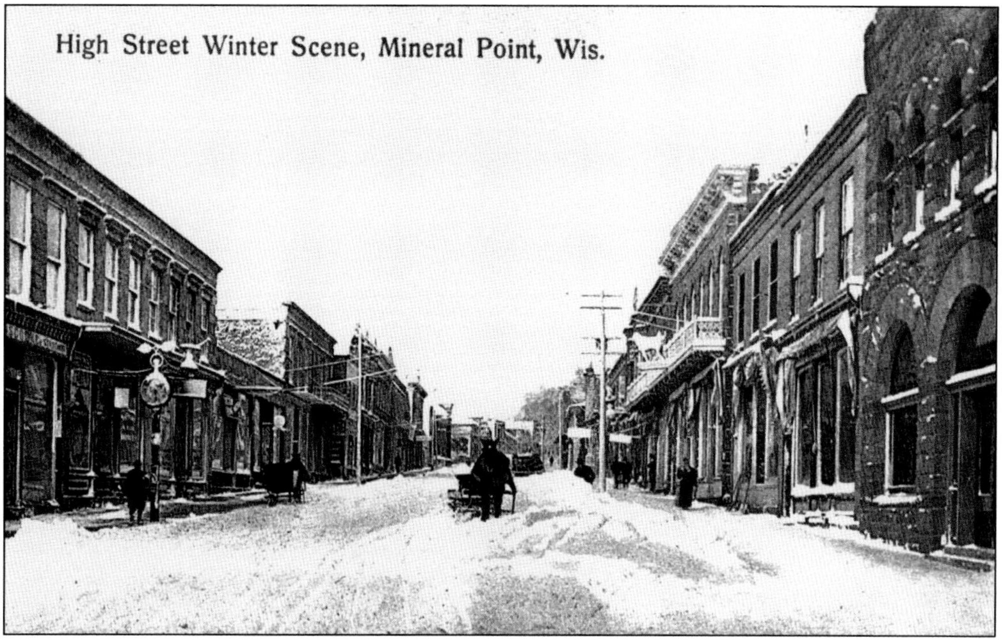

This 1911 High Street winter scene postcard shows why Wisconsin winters then were a big challenge. Without snowplows or snowblowers life was not easy. To harness the horse, hook it up to the sleigh, and ride over the bumpy drifted streets to get to one's destination took a lot of effort.

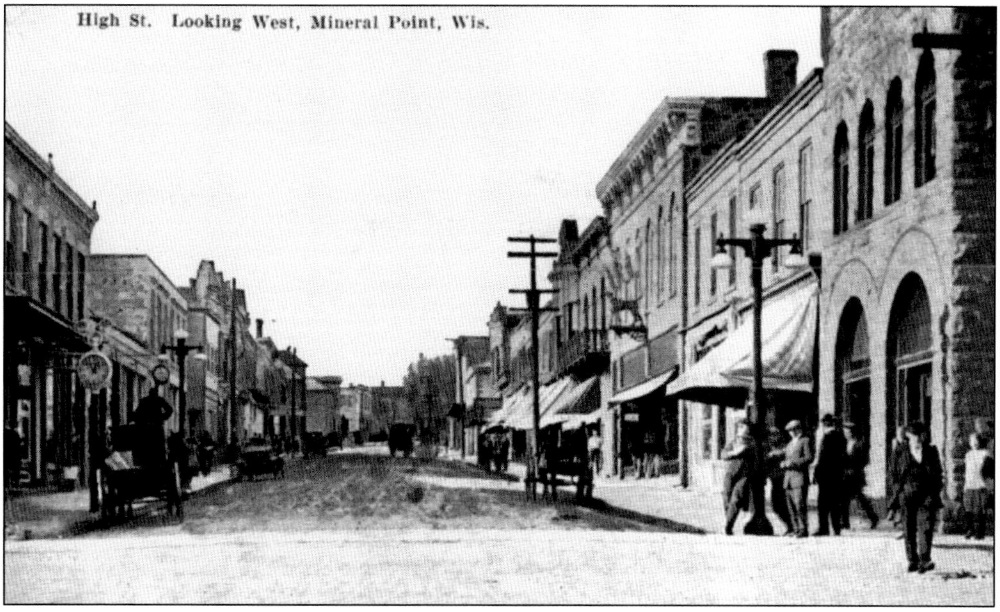

Looking west on High Street, well-dressed people are out and about. Light posts have been installed on the street, and business is prospering.

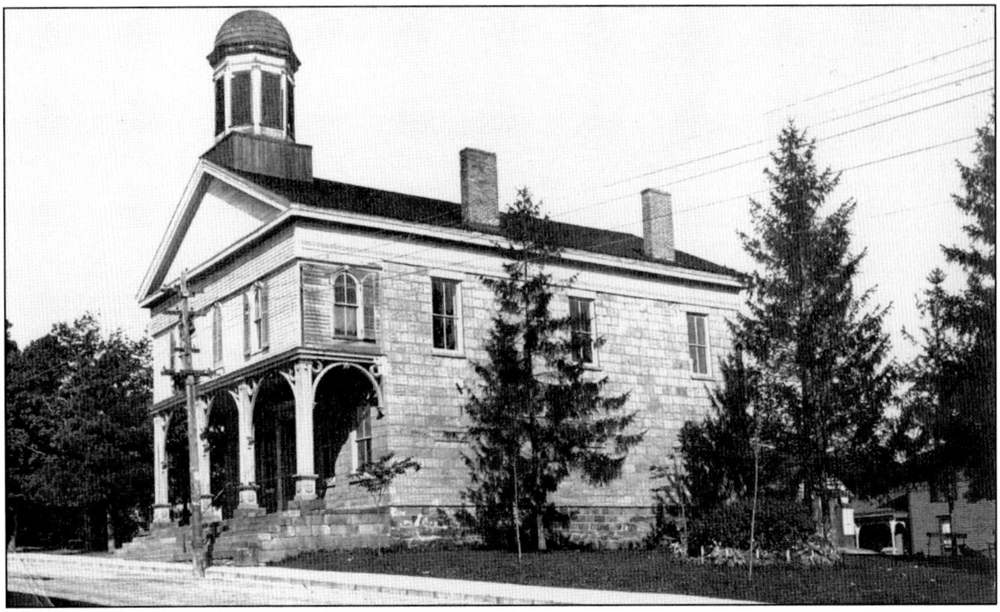

Mineral Point built a grand courthouse for a cost of $7,468 and constructed it of locally quarried limestone. It included a jail made of hewn timbers lined with iron plates, a courtroom, and offices. In 1846, the territorial legislature passed an act to divide for the last time what was left of Iowa County, thus creating Lafayette County. The county was reduced to a fraction of its original size, and this left Mineral Point at the bottom of the county, not the center. The people in Dodgeville were unhappy. They wanted the county seat moved to a more central location—Dodgeville.

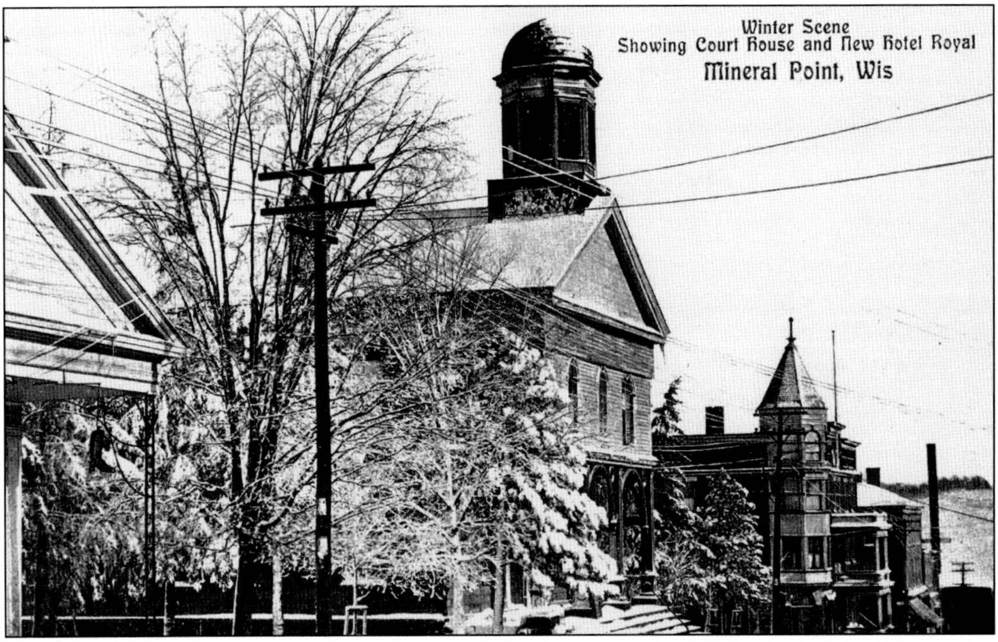

In November 1858, the county voted by 350 votes to move the courthouse to Dodgeville. Due to a technicality in publishing the notice, the election was contested. In 1859, the Wisconsin Supreme Court ruled in favor of Mineral Point, thus sending the courthouse back to its origin.

The *Mineral Point Tribune* wrote concerning this event: "County Seat Question Settled! Mineral Point Ahead! Dodgeville Gone Under! The 'Pointers' Jubilant! Hurrah! Hurrah! Hurrah! It did not last long." Two years later the legislature again passed another law to vote on the question; they voted to move the county seat to Dodgeville, where it is to this day.

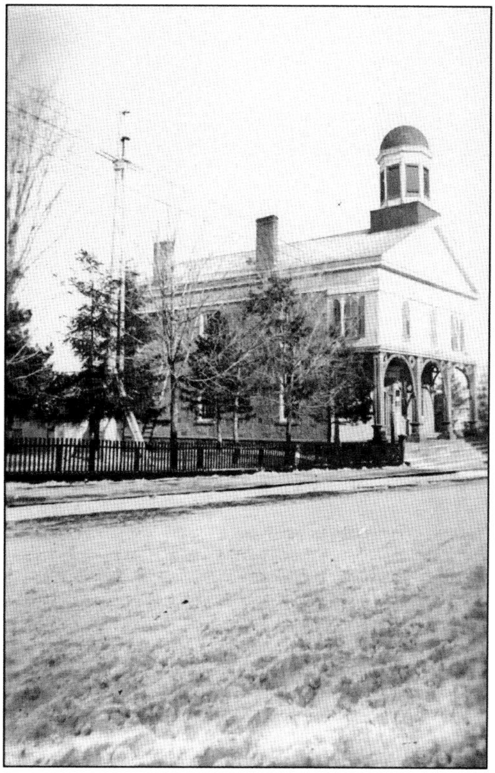

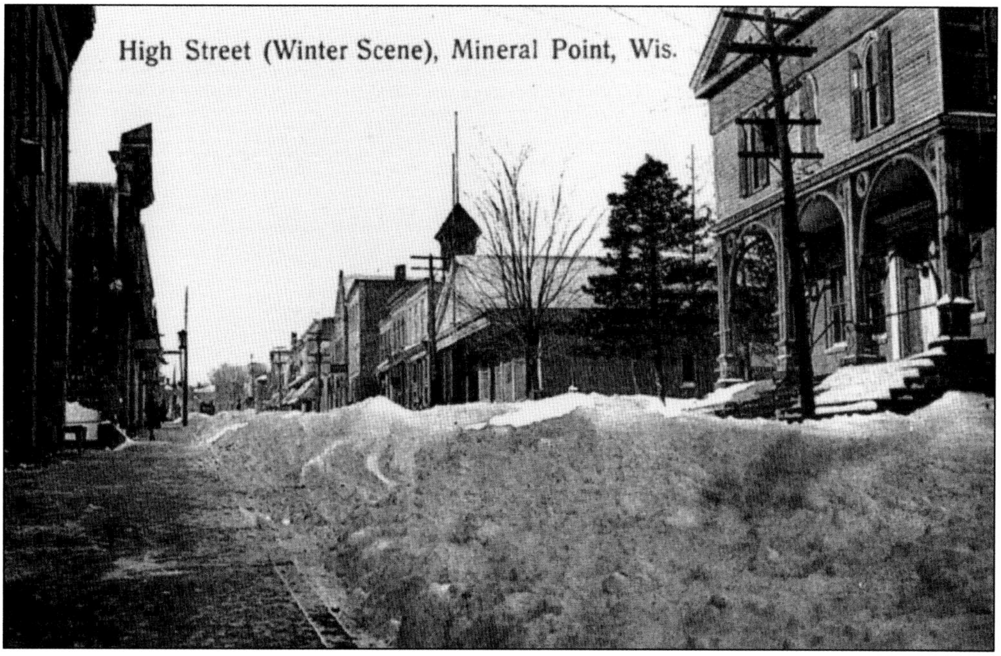

The courthouse building, which was left vacant after the county seat was moved to Dodgeville in 1861, was remodeled to house the Mineral Point City Hall. The old county courthouse served the city of Mineral Point until it was demolished to make way for the construction of the present municipal building in 1914.

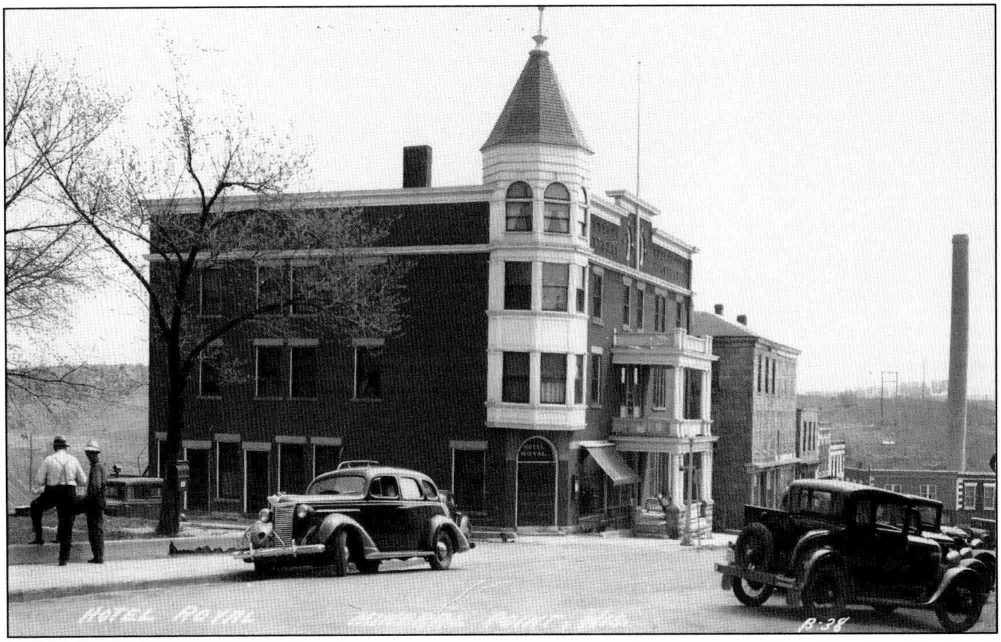

The Hotel Royal is a Classical Revival/Queen Anne–style structure listed in the National Register of Historic Preservation. When built in 1900 at a cost of $25,000, it was one of the most luxurious hotels in southwestern Wisconsin. The red brick was an extravagant choice over local native limestone, as were the plush furnishings from Chicago Marshall Fields. Some of the original ceilings, wainscoting, and metal-embossed walls have endured through numerous renovations over the years.

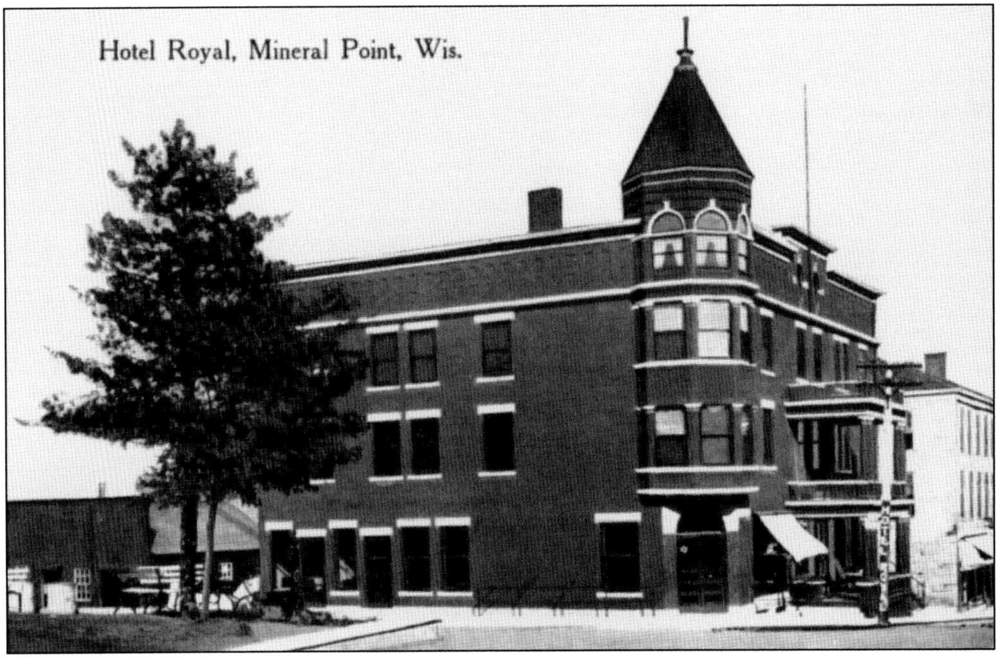

A special train from Chicago brought some of the 190 dinner guests present for the gala grand opening of the Royal Hotel on Easter Sunday in April 1901.

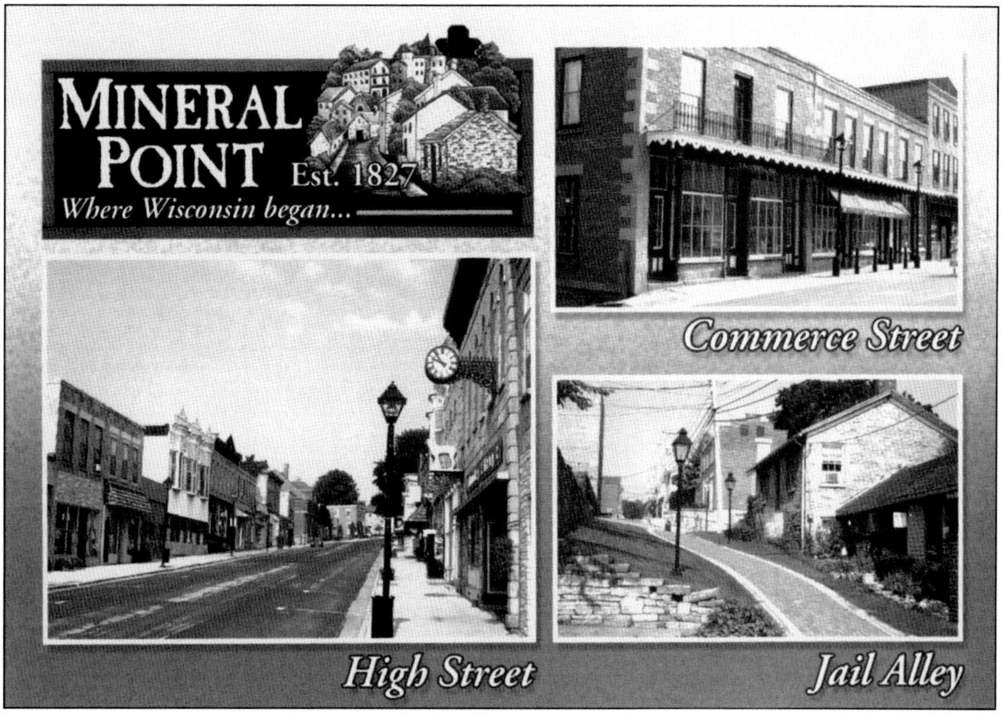

The three streets where most of the Mineral Point businesses are to be found in the downtown area are High Street, Commerce Street, and Jail Alley. From its beginning as a mining settlement it has evolved into a charming community—a unique combination of small-town friendliness, artistic influences, architectural significance, and historic value. It is midway between Madison, Wisconsin, and Dubuque, Iowa, off Highway 151. (Photograph by Gari Walz.)

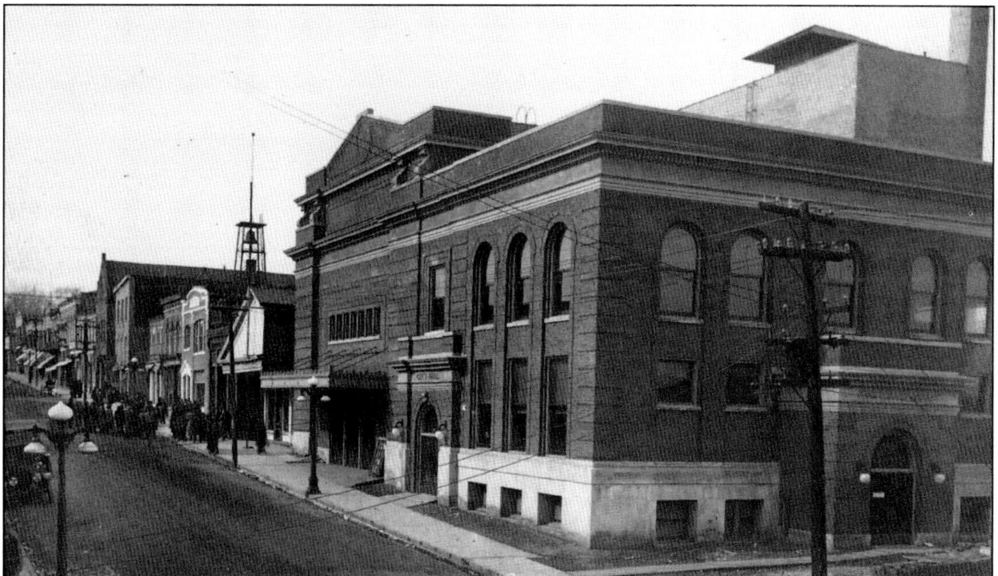

The new Mineral Point Municipal Building replaced the old courthouse. Initially it housed the city hall offices, an opera house, a jail, and the library. Later the jail moved to Dodgeville. The building never lost its popularity. It is presently used as a library, archival room, and theater.

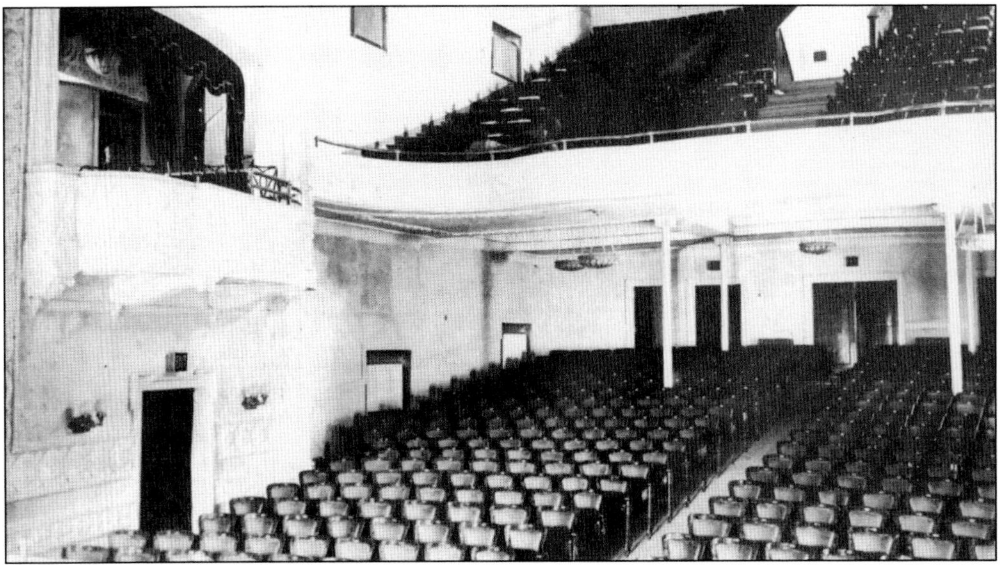

The Mineral Point Opera House was built in 1914 as the "Theatre for All the People." Its beauty rivaled that of theaters in New York and Chicago. During its early days, it was a vaudeville and performing arts house that attracted some of the country's outstanding artists and productions of live drama, grand opera, and symphonic music. The original seating accommodated 700 people on the main floor, in the balcony, and in two boxes.

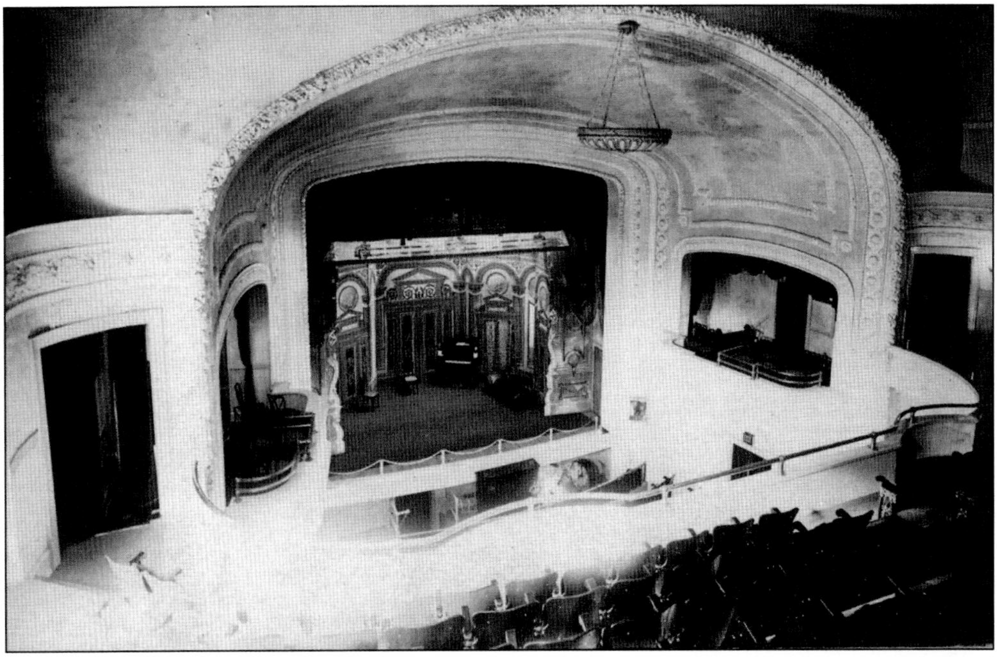

During the 1920s when silent movies became popular, interest in stage productions faded and the opera house became primarily a movie theater. Today the theater continues to provide the area with movies, live concerts, and performances by the local theater group called the Shake Rag Players. They have been performing at the opera house for over 40 years. The theater has been in a continuous state of restoration since 2003. Plans continue to restore it to its original state of grandeur.

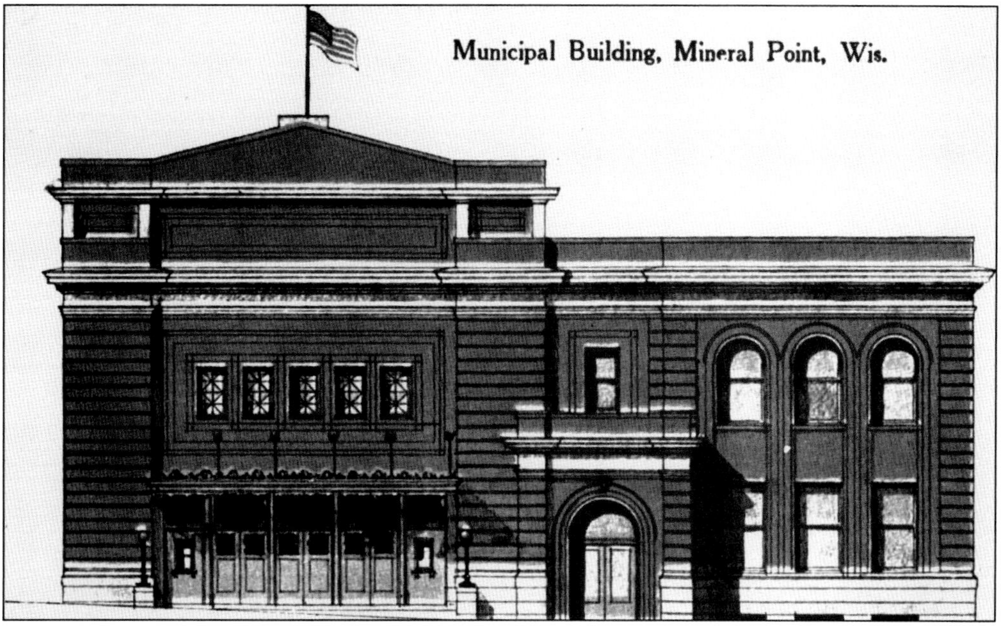

The Mineral Point Municipal Building houses the library, which has outgrown its space. It is currently planning an expansion to the back and up to the second floor. The Mineral Point Archives is tucked in the basement of the Mineral Point library. Barred windows are reminders that this once housed the city jail. They now protect the valuable treasures found within. The collection of materials includes books, maps, photographs, newspaper files, letters, and other documents pertaining to the history of Mineral Point and the region.

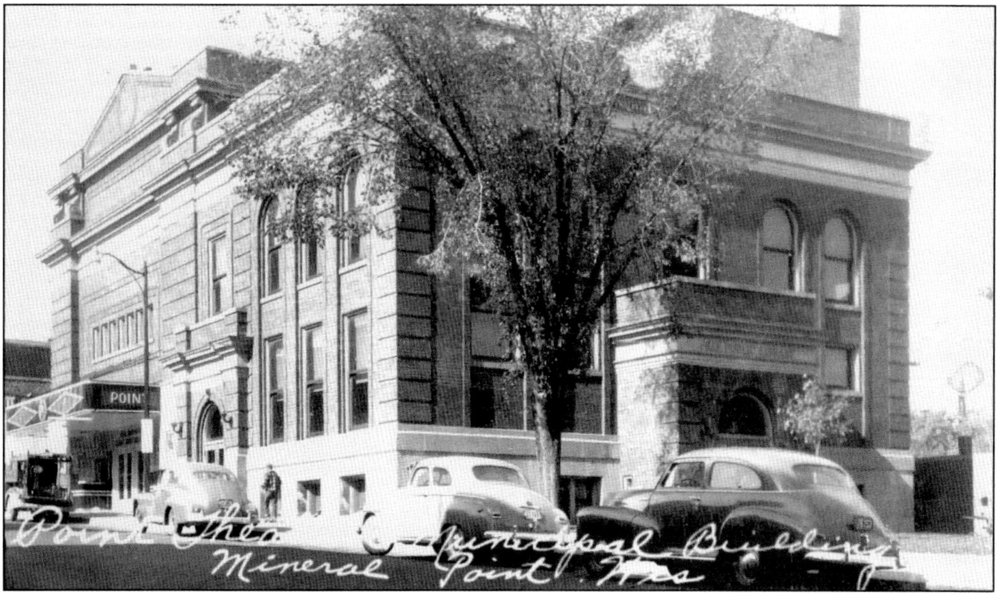

The collection in the Mineral Point Room was originated with a generous donation of materials from Robert Neal in 1981. Personal papers include a series of letters between Pres. Woodrow Wilson and his friend David Jones, a Mineral Pointer. Betty White, actress and widow of another native son, Allen Ludden, has donated some of her husband's papers to the collection. Ludden was a well-known television personality who hosted the show *Password*.

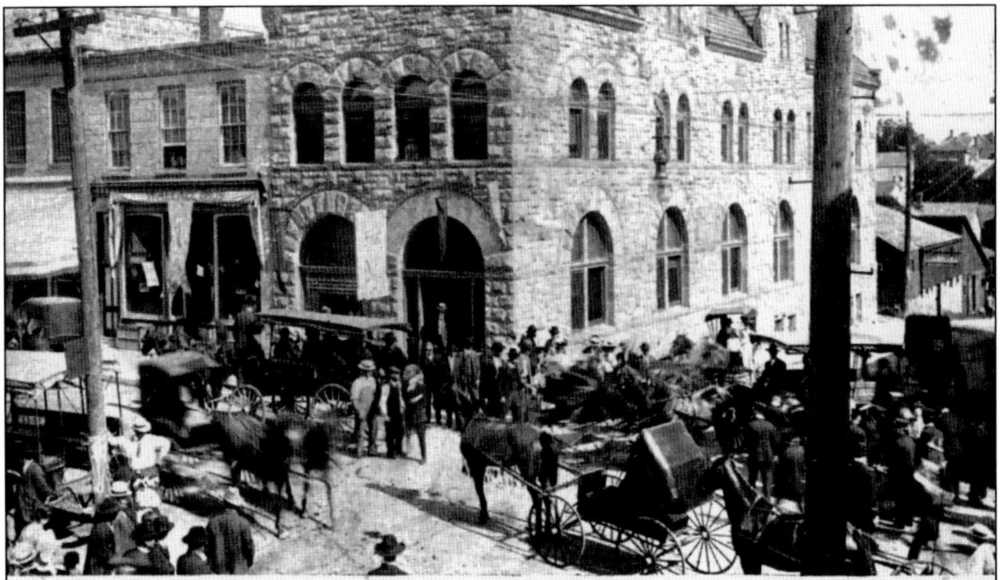

Mineral Point, Wis., on a busy day.

Mineral Point had three bank failures. The one that everyone remembers and still talks about happened in 1909. The vice president of the First National Bank of Mineral Point was Phillip Allen Jr. He was a pillar of the church and a Sunday school superintendent. And he stole over $700,000, which would be worth millions of dollars in today's world. In this photograph people are gathered at the front of the bank. Are they coming to check on their money?

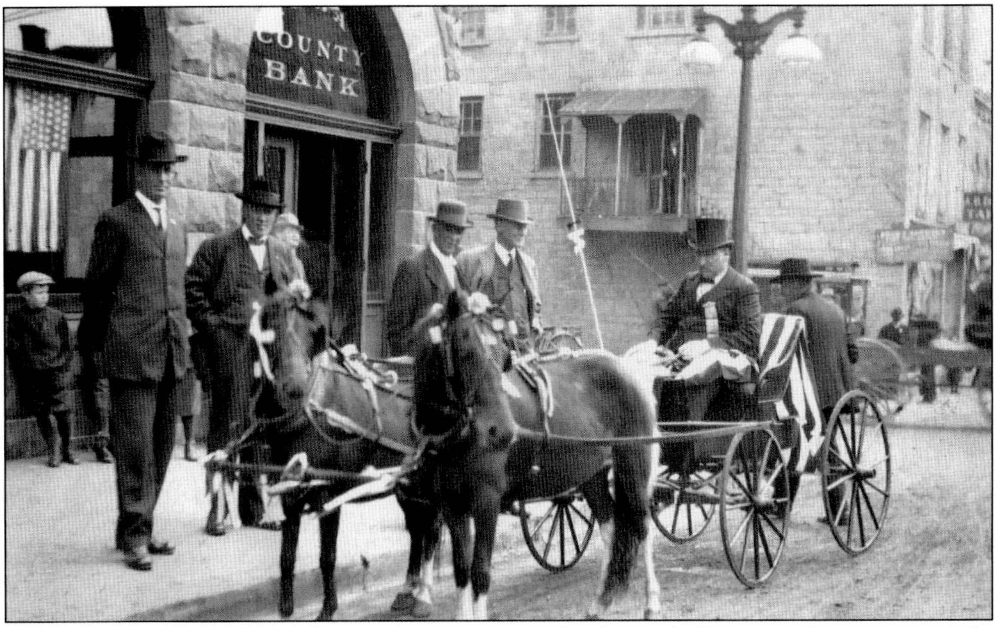

These distinguished-looking businessmen may well be the bank directors who were sued for not stopping Allen, although they knew nothing about his forgeries. Widows and orphans who trusted Allen with their financial matters were hit hard. Newspapers detailed how people around the nation shared in the disbelief found in Mineral Point. In this 1924 photograph the bank's name above the door says Iowa County Savings Bank.

The First National Bank still sits proudly on the corner of Chestnut and High Streets. It is presently vacant but the open vault can be seen through the window. The bank name changed once again, this time to Farmers Savings Bank, and eventually it built a new bank at 305 Doty Street.

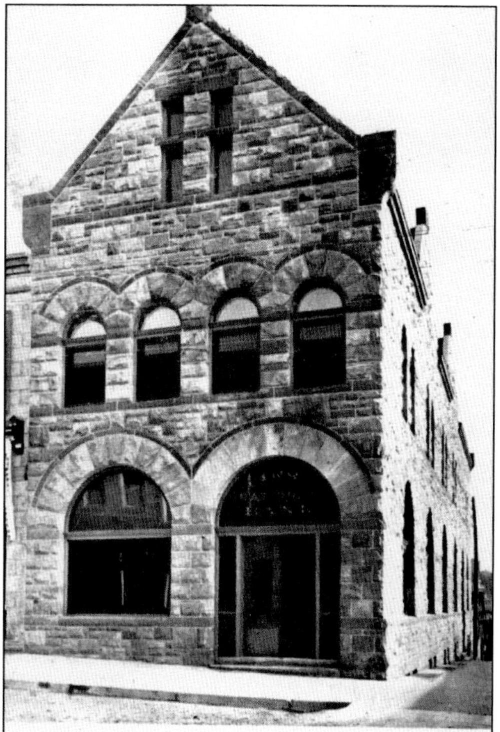

First National Bank, Mineral Point, Wis.

A. W. THOMA, MINERAL POINT, WIS.

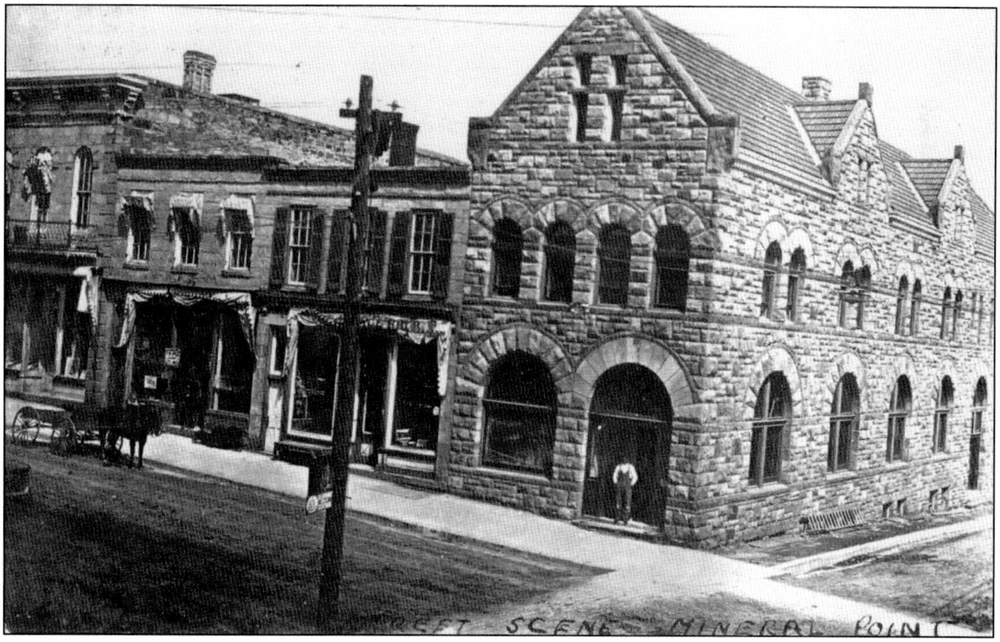

The back of this 1909 card says, "This is the bank that broke and left us all in the soak." After being convicted of embezzlement, Phillip Allen went off to serve 10 years at the federal prison at Fort Leavenworth, Kansas.

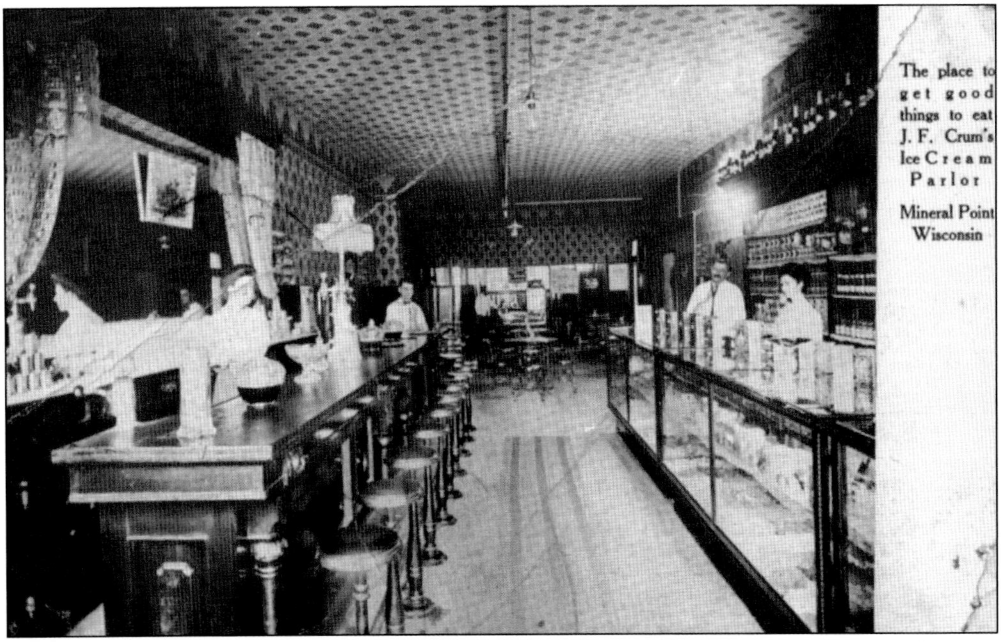

This 1909 card shows the place to eat good things is J. F. Crum's ice-cream parlor. An old-fashioned soda fountain on the left invites the public to partake. On the right can be found canned goods and wine on the shelves. Notice the wine is on a high top shelf, probably so young people cannot get at it. Adding to the character of the room is the embossed tin ceiling.

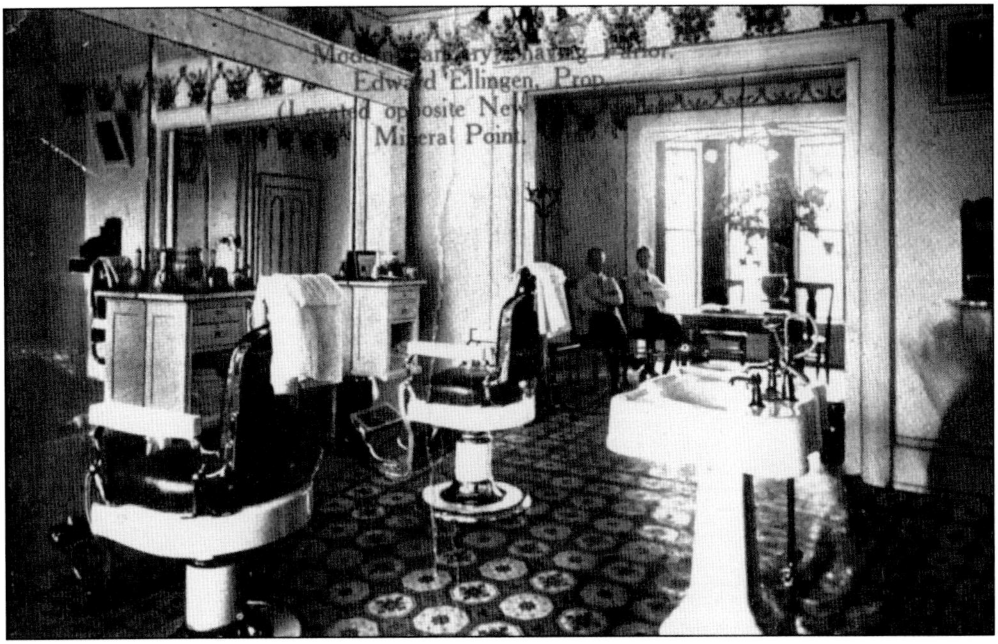

This was called a "Modern Sanitary Shaving Parlor," with Edward Ellingen listed as the proprietor. No doubt both of these popular businesses were located on High Street.

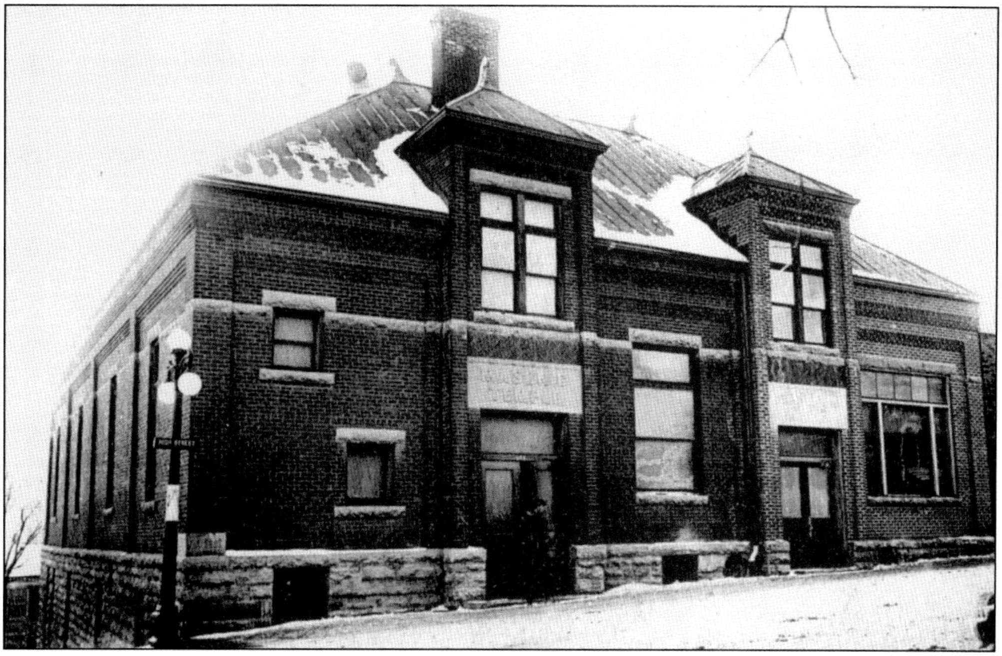

The Masonic temple is the oldest surviving Masonic lodge in Wisconsin. The cornerstone was laid in 1897. Several members of this lodge helped form the original Wisconsin state government. The present building, designed by John Charles, a Cornish immigrant and architect of statewide repute, was constructed after the original meeting rooms were destroyed by fire. A brick addition was constructed in 1920.

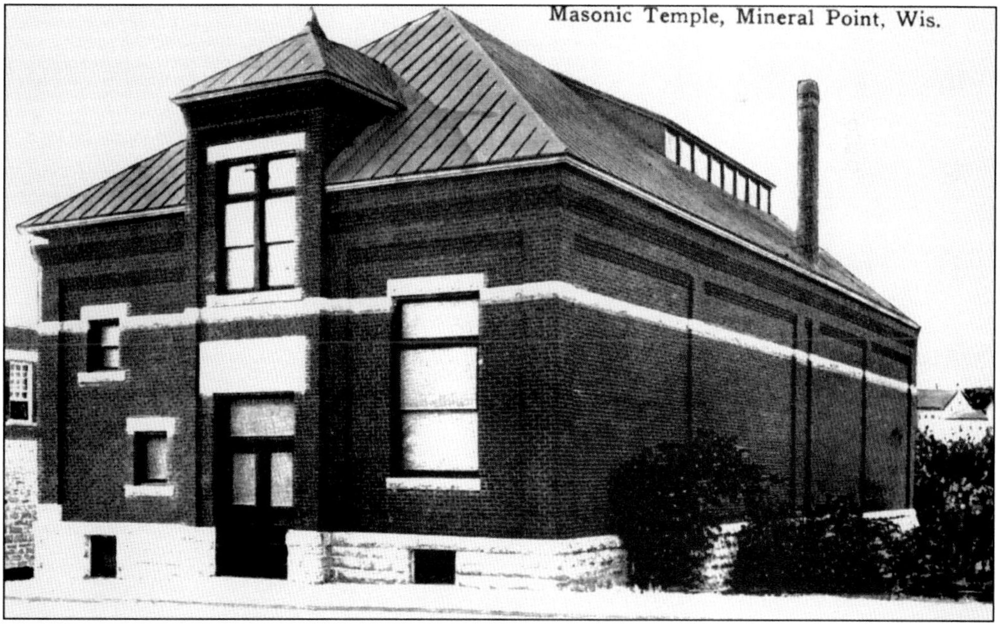

Inside the Masonic lodge was a large meeting room auditorium and also a dance hall. When author Marian Hendricks was in high school her class went to this lodge to hear the first radio in Mineral Point. The teachers wanted the students to hear the inaugural address of Pres. Herbert Hoover. It was 1928, and this was a monumental occasion.

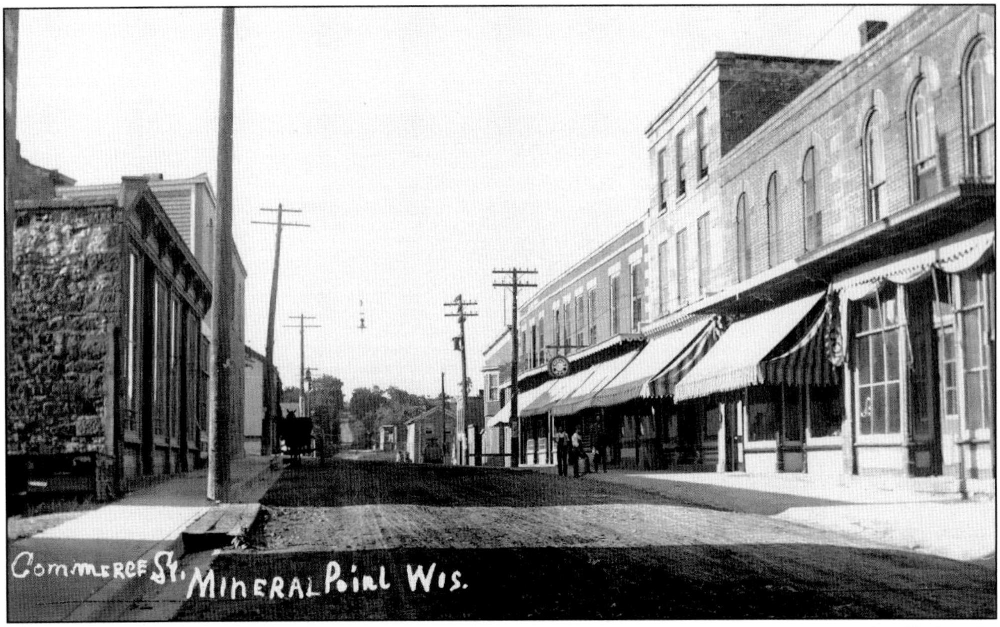

This view looks to the north on Commerce Street. According to George Bechtel's book, *Would've, Could've, Should've*, Mineral Point experienced one disaster after another—a decline in mining, discontinuation of railroad service, closing of banks, a downtown fire, a tornado, and the Depression. The strongest of men would have been devastated, yet the Cornish we-can-do-anything attitude prevailed.

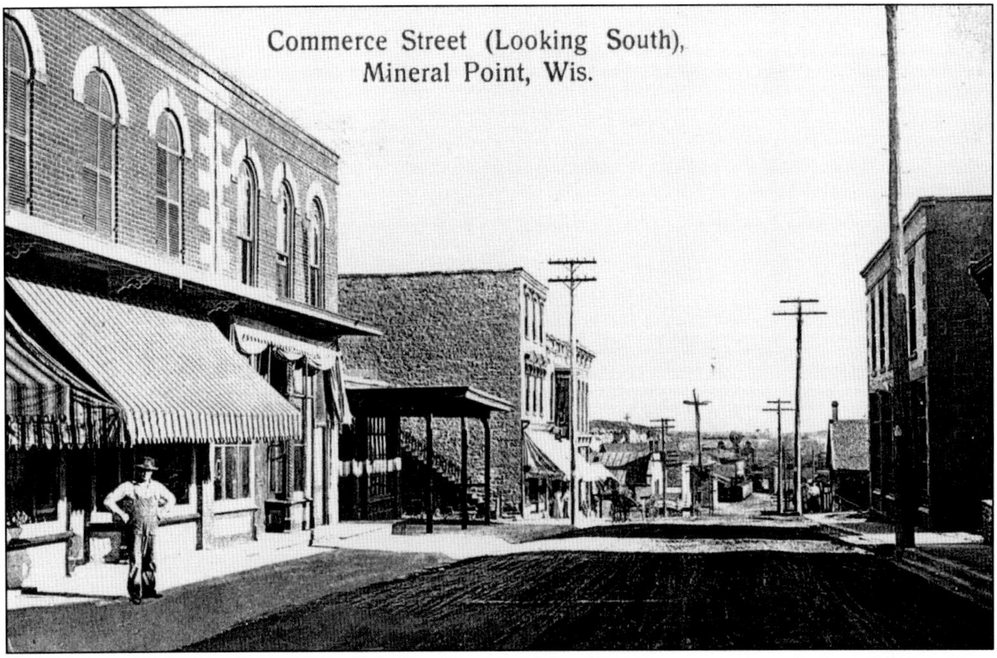

This card is looking south on Commerce Street, where businesses came and went. There were years when the street looked deserted and others when it appeared to thrive. At the bottom of the street can be seen a train at the depot. Beyond that was the location of the Mineral Point Zinc Works. Today the street is alive with artists, craftsmen, and tourists.

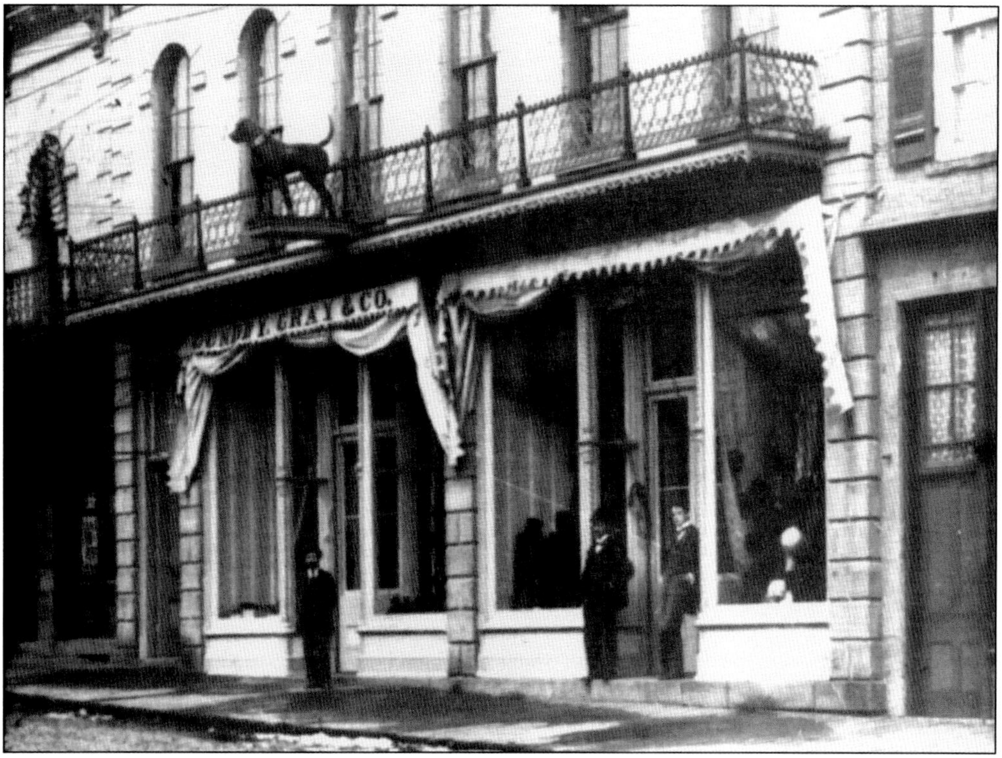

The Gundry and Gray Store with its trademark pointer dog was the most successful dry goods store in the area. The dog was the beacon that drew the customer in.

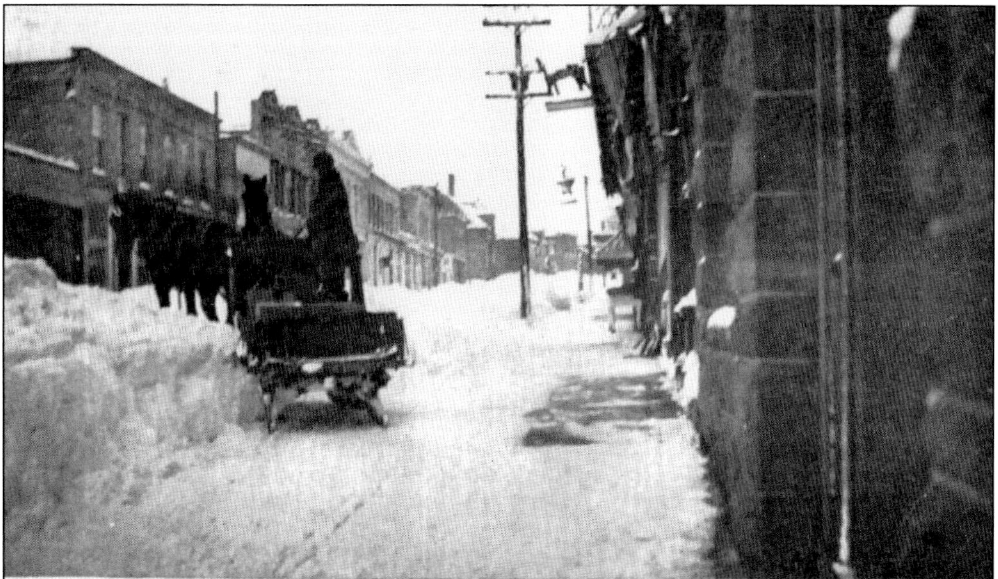

HIGH STREET, WINTER SCENE, MINERAL POINT, WIS.

This winter scene shows the street piled high with snow. Before the days when plows were available, people tried to clear the sidewalks and left the streets filled with snow. The horses and sleighs used the snow down the middle of the road.

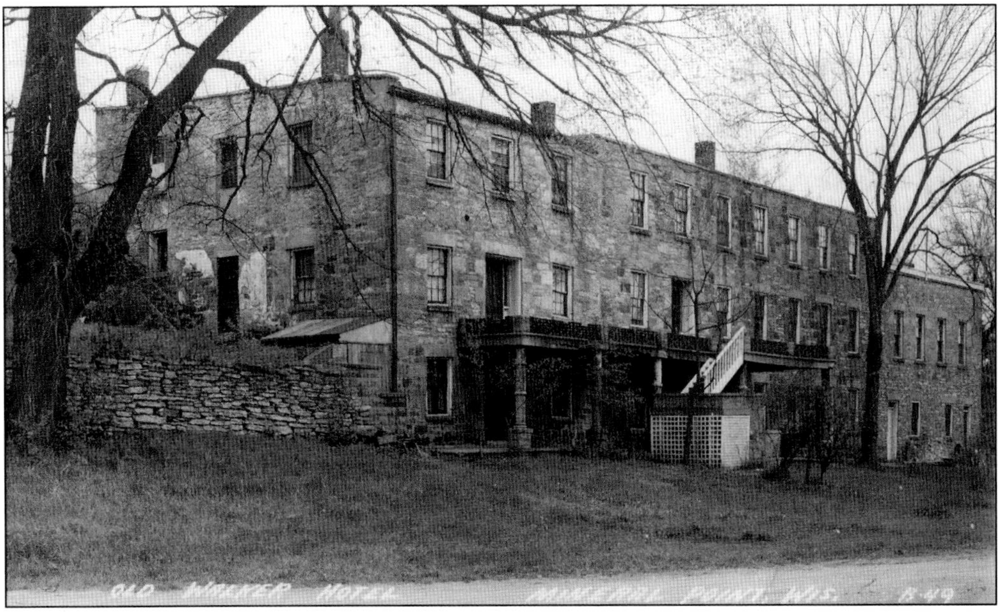

The Walker House, located at 1 Water Street, across from the depot, is a huge railroad hotel that was built in the mid-1900s. It was converted to a popular restaurant in 1960. The food served was based on old Cornish recipes such as their famous meat and potato pasty. The property remained endangered because it had been vacant and neglected for many years. It is located in a National Register District. It has recently been purchased and is being restored.

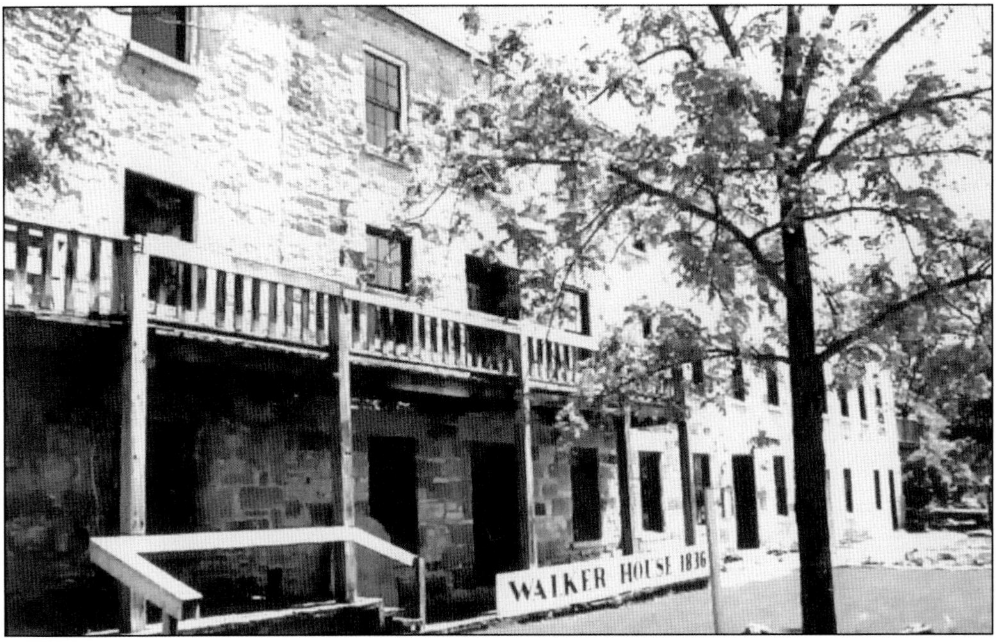

During the early 1800s, the inn served as a stopover for immigrants and peddlers traveling through the western territories to the Dakotas. In 1841, the notorious outlaw Edward Caffee was caught in the hotel and hanged at the south end of the building. Five thousand people came with their picnic baskets and camped overnight. A gaudy parade was planned. His ghost and other spirits are still said to be seen from time to time. (Photograph by Betty France.)

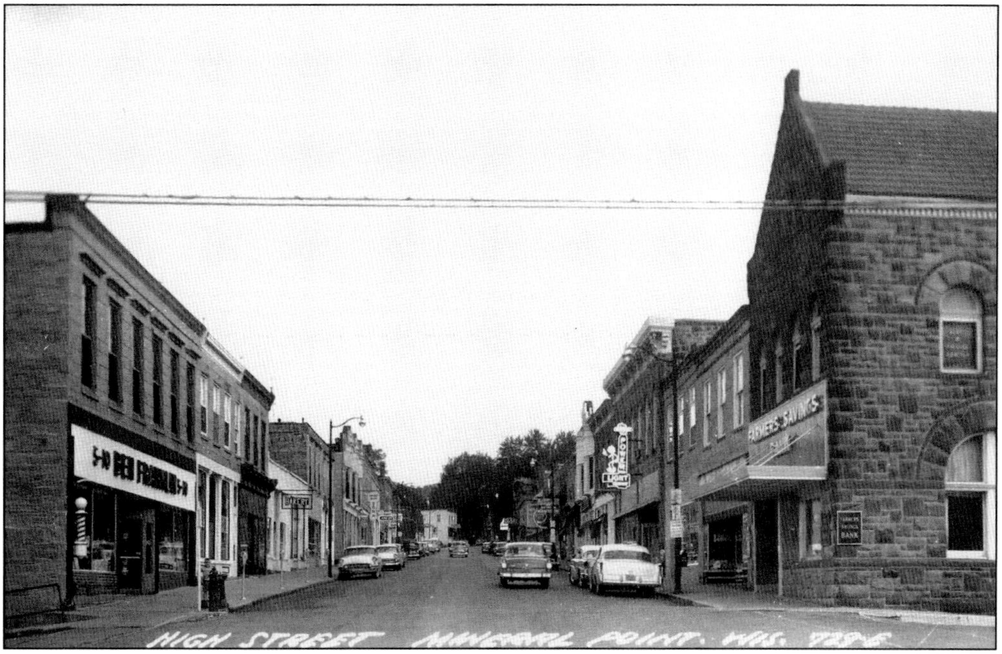

In the 1950s, the miners are gone. Now there is Ben Franklin and the Farmers Savings Bank. Life is good, and the city is starting to boom again.

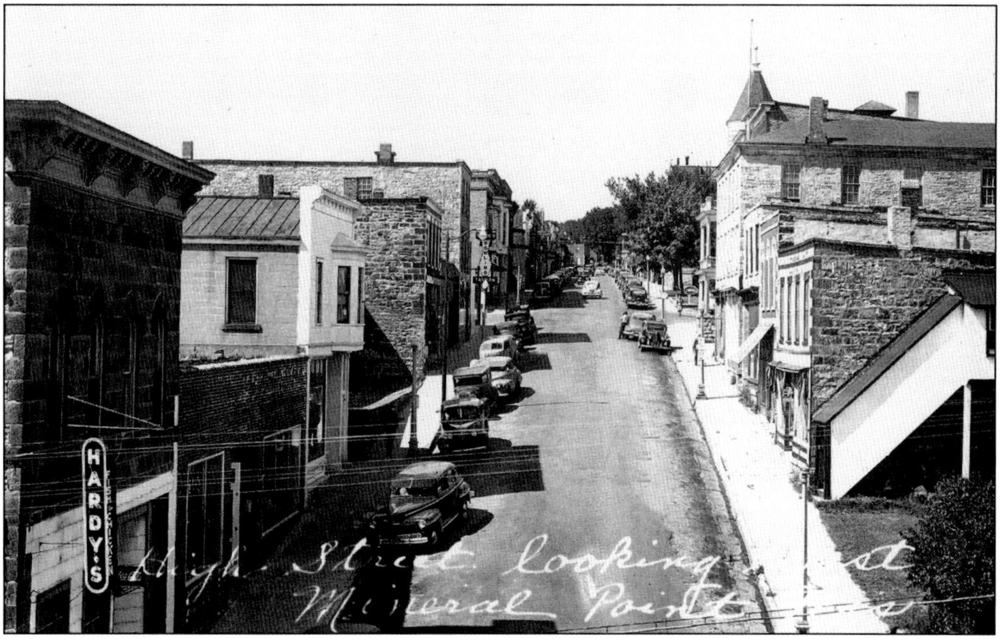

In 1949, the city was struggling. The main street needed resurfacing. The artists had not yet arrived to rejuvenate the city. The first newspaper in the community was the *Miners' Free Press*, founded in 1837. Other papers came and went through the years, including the *Wisconsin Tribune*, the *Mineral Point Tribune*, the *Iowa County Democrat*, and the *Democrat Tribune*.

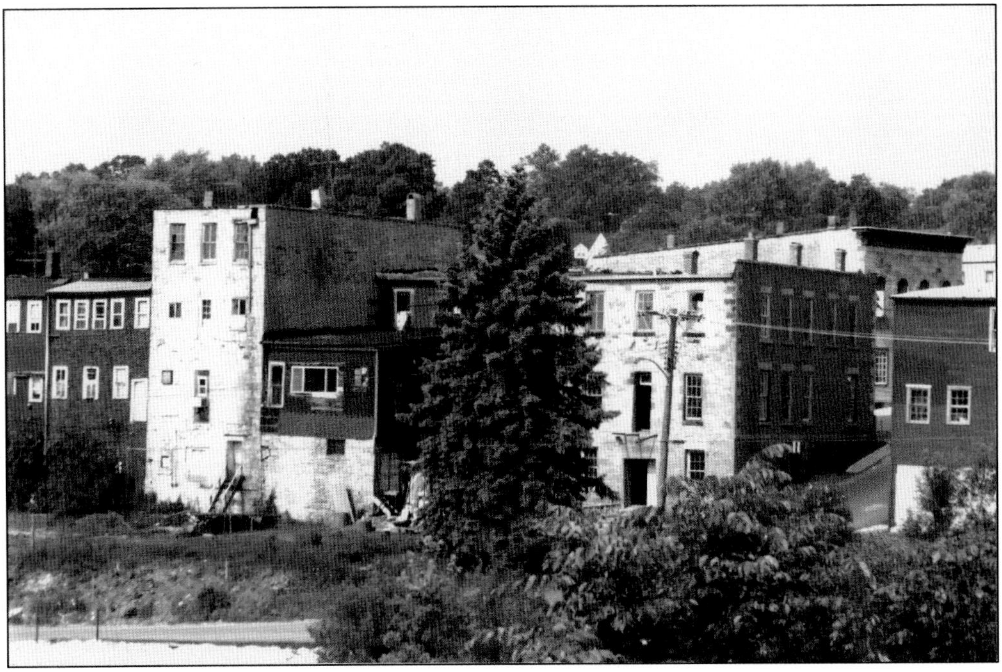

The back side of Commerce Street buildings suggests that one is in a European city. Or maybe it is Cornwall. It is not typical for Wisconsin architecture. (Photograph by of Betty France.)

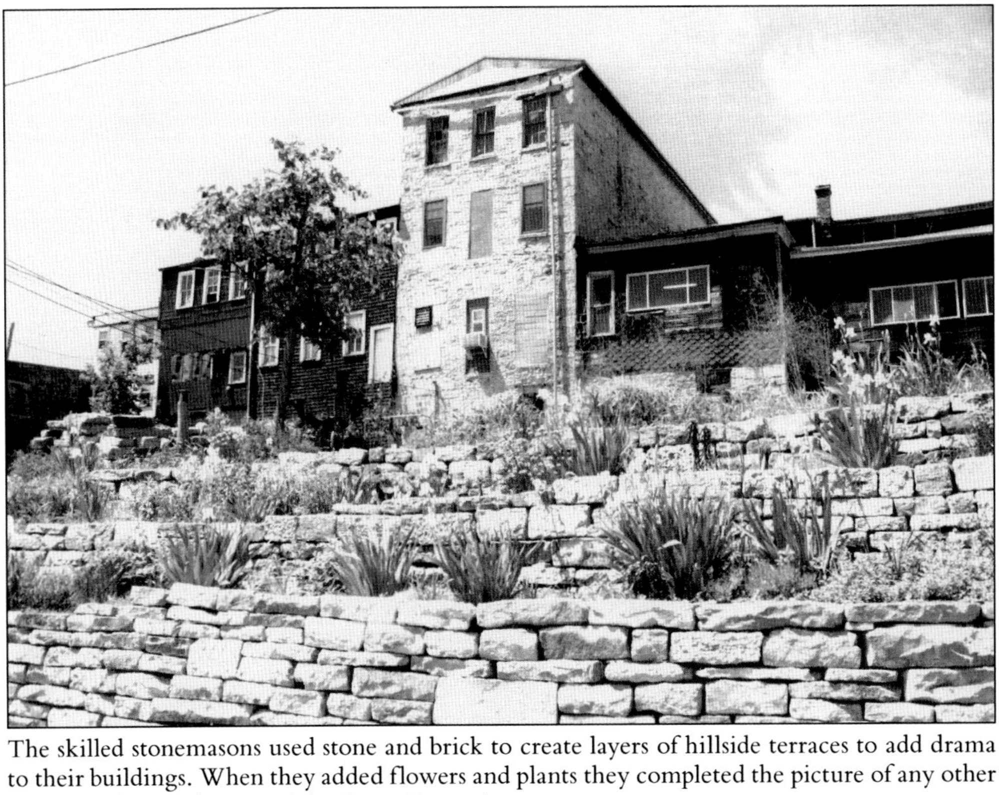

The skilled stonemasons used stone and brick to create layers of hillside terraces to add drama to their buildings. When they added flowers and plants they completed the picture of any other time and place. (Photograph by Betty France.)

Seven

EARLIEST BEGINNINGS

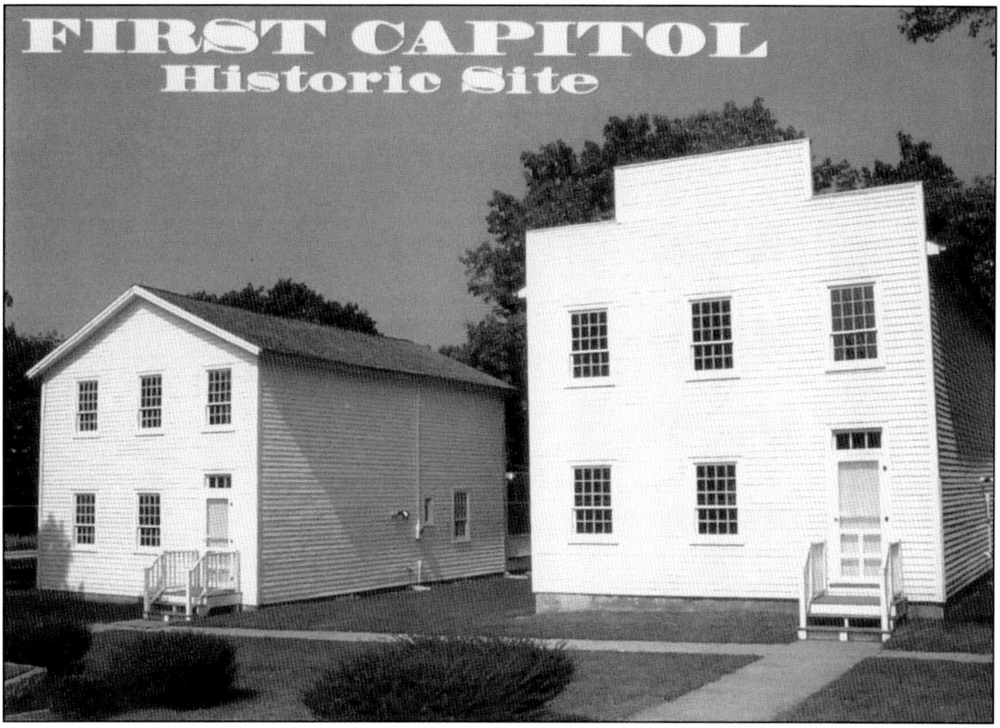

On April 20, 1836, Congress passed an act establishing the Wisconsin Territory, composed of the present states of Wisconsin, Iowa, Minnesota, and the eastern halves of North Dakota and South Dakota. Pres. Andrew Jackson signed the bill immediately and a week later nominated fellow democrat Henry Dodge as governor of the new territory. The first legislature of Wisconsin Territory convened in these buildings at Belmont, a briefly booming village on a high hill covered with prairie grasses a few miles outside of Mineral Point. (Photograph by Gari Walz.)

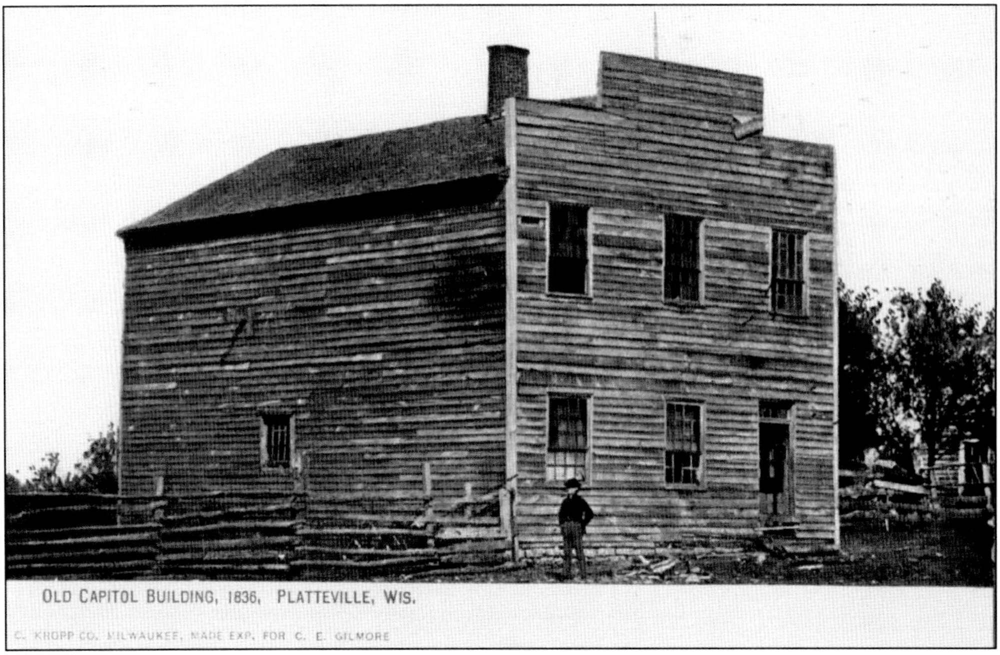

There was so much criticism of Gov. Henry Dodge's choice of Belmont for the first territorial capital that a bitter contest developed. In 1849, Mineral Point was supposed to be the first capital of the state. Eventually, after much fighting, Madison was chosen as the site for the state capital. Belmont's businesses moved, and the village declined. Mineral Point is a few miles from these buildings at what is now the First Capitol State Park. This card is incorrectly labeled being at Platteville, which is another town not far from Belmont.

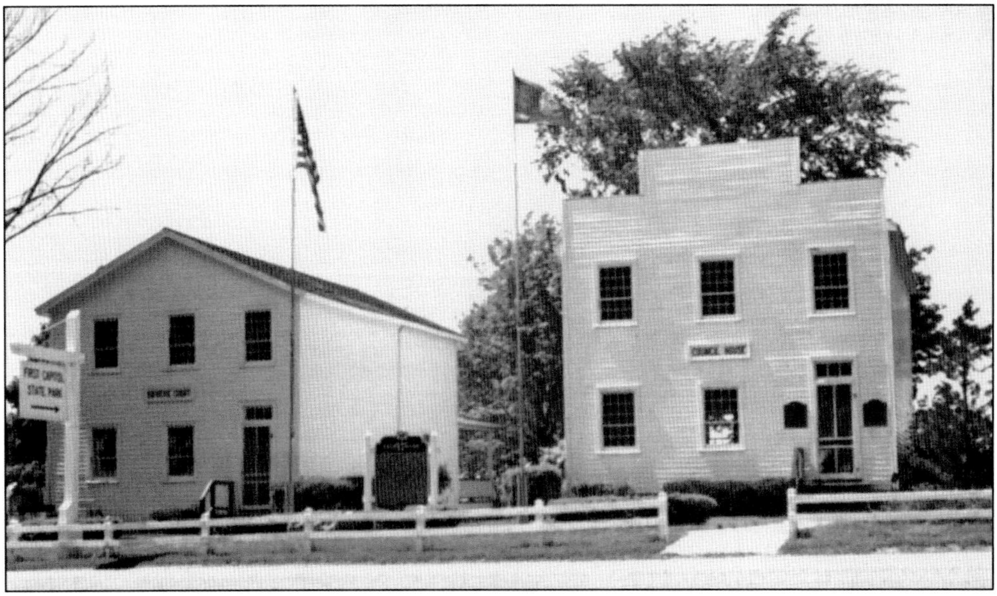

These buildings stand surrounded by cornfields and cows, well off the main road. One would never guess how far important men of the times came to get to this place. Important decisions were made in these humble dwellings, decisions that affected all of Wisconsin's future history. (Photograph by Michael Mewis.)

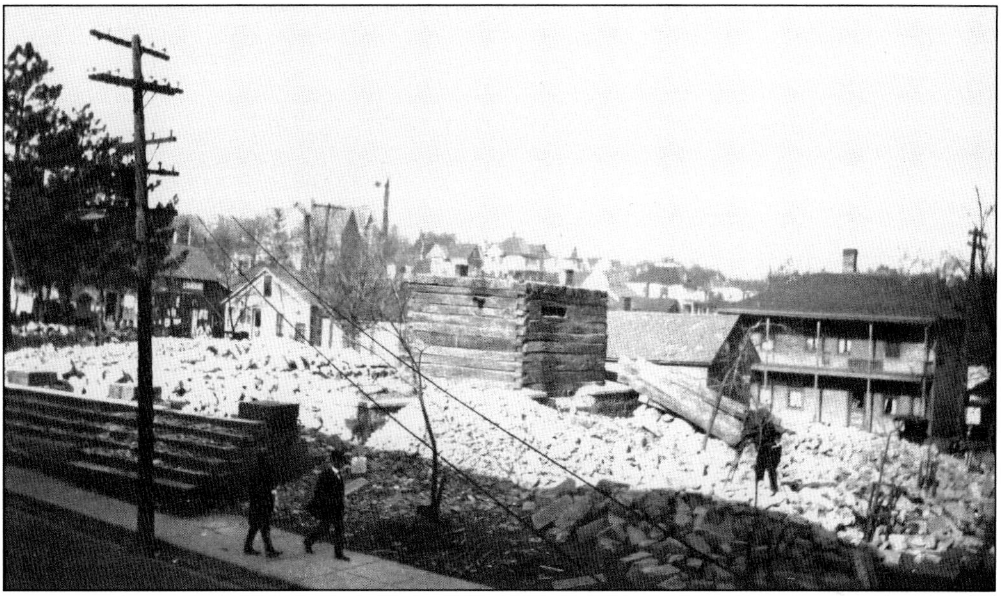

When the first courthouse was demolished, it revealed the original Mineral Point Jail that was in the basement of the courthouse. Made out of rough logs, it had a small window for air and a door. The jail was located in the rear of the courthouse building and was accessible by a narrow street, which, logically, became known as Jail Alley.

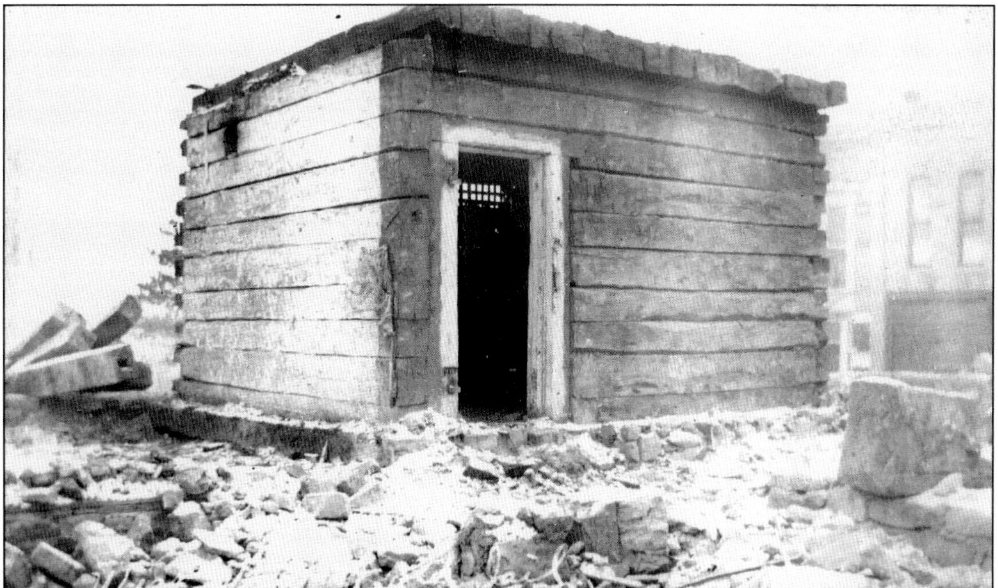

A close-up shot of the west side of the Mineral Point Jail shows a bare-bones log room. This log jail was built by James Gordon in 1838. He used roughly hewn logs to build the first jail in southwestern Wisconsin. Being practical, municipal employees, attorneys, and tradespeople built homes along the Jail Alley ridge, which provided an easy walking distance from the courthouse and High Street where they earned their livings.

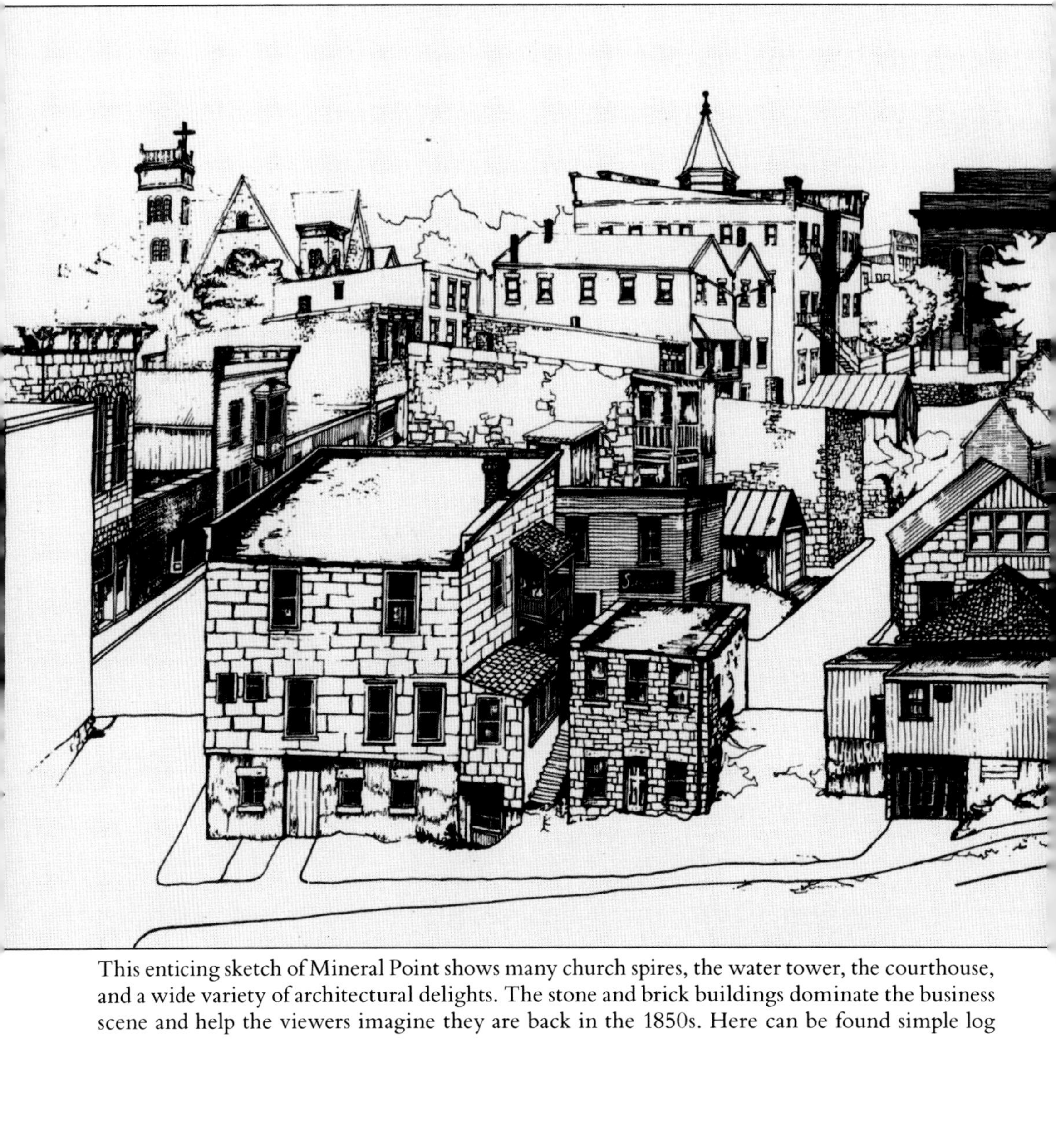

This enticing sketch of Mineral Point shows many church spires, the water tower, the courthouse, and a wide variety of architectural delights. The stone and brick buildings dominate the business scene and help the viewers imagine they are back in the 1850s. Here can be found simple log

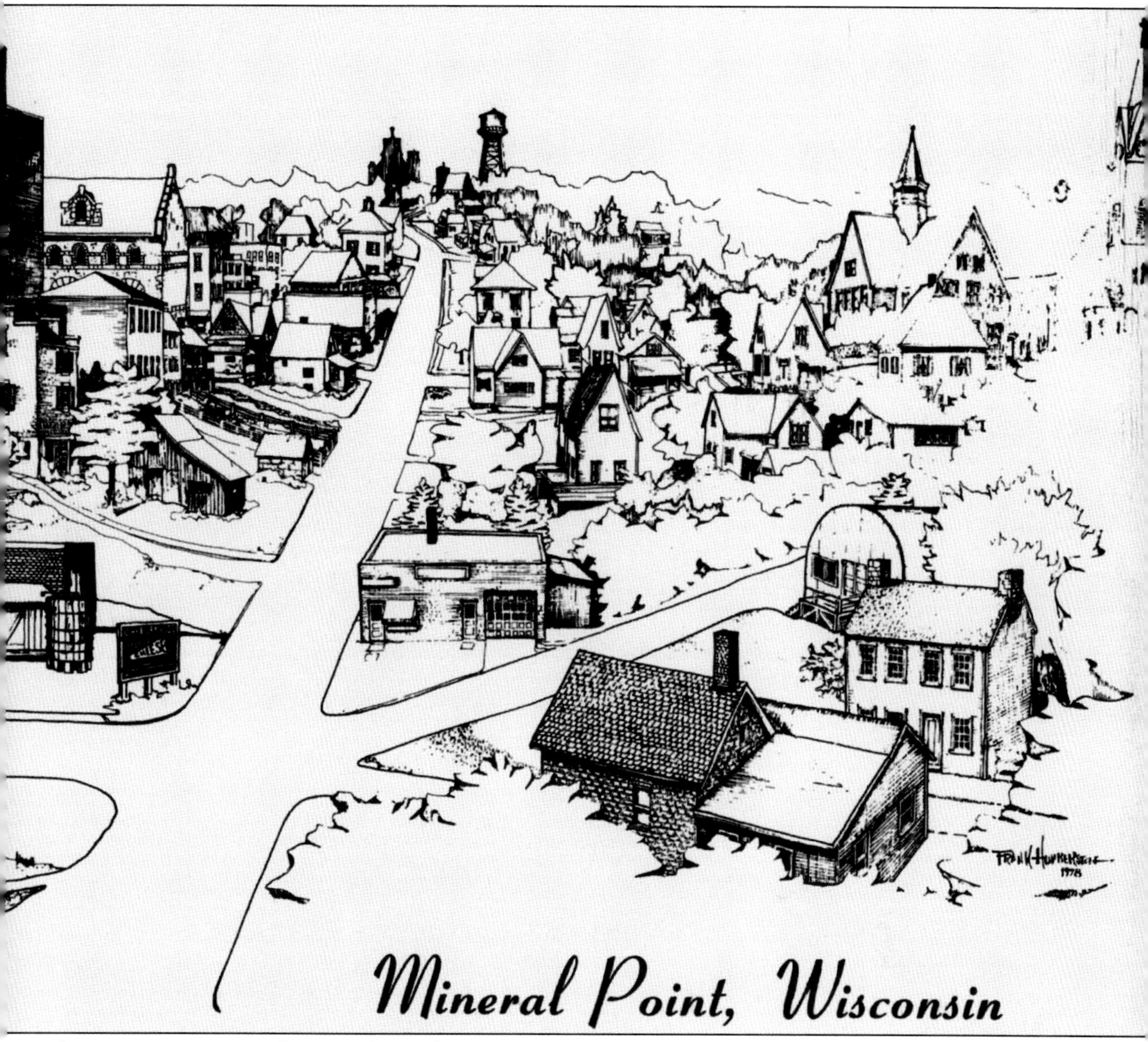

huts, stone mining cabins, and grand Victorian mansions. Native pottery, original jewelry, and homemade items fill the quaint shops in this artists' haven.

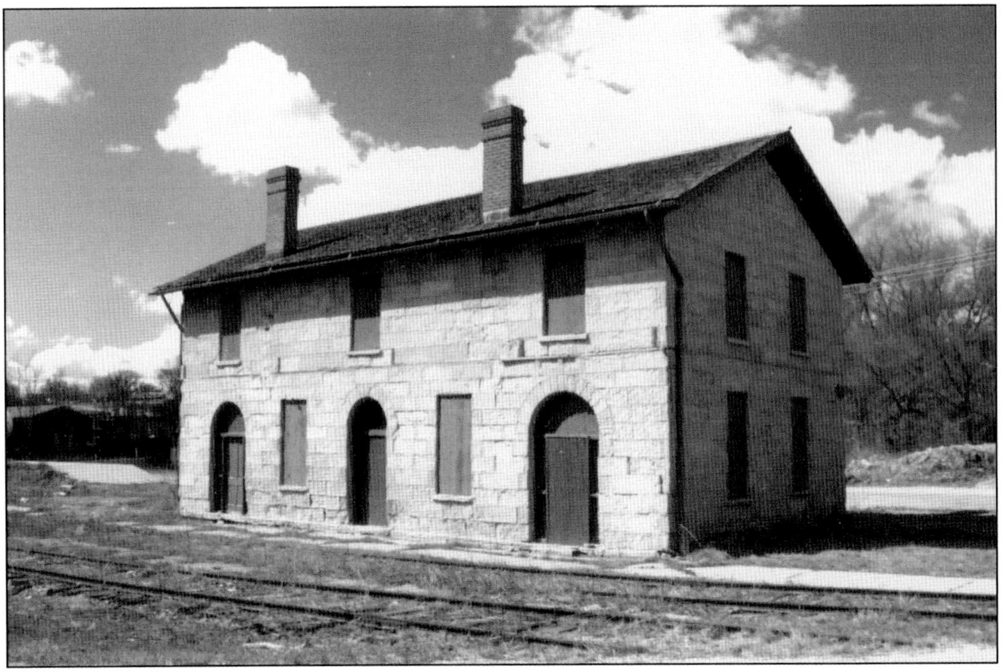

Built by Cornish stonemasons in 1856 of locally quarried limestone, the stately vernacular-style Mineral Point railroad depot is one of the few surviving pre–Civil War depots in the United States. It is the oldest depot in Wisconsin and the oldest surviving structure of the Milwaukee Road. It is the only Wisconsin depot constructed of stone. (Photograph by Betty France.)

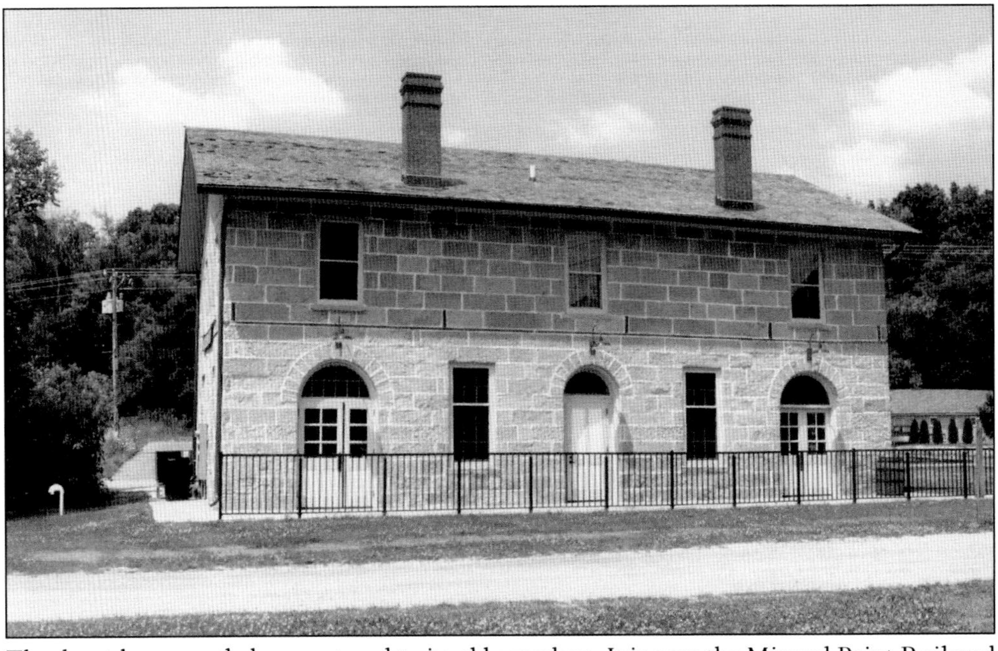

The depot has recently been restored to its old grandeur. It is now the Mineral Point Railroad Museum where exhibits honor the depot's rich railroad heritage. This depot serves as home to the Mineral Point Railroad, the Mineral Point and Northern Railway, and the Mineral Point Zinc Company. (Photograph by Betty France.)

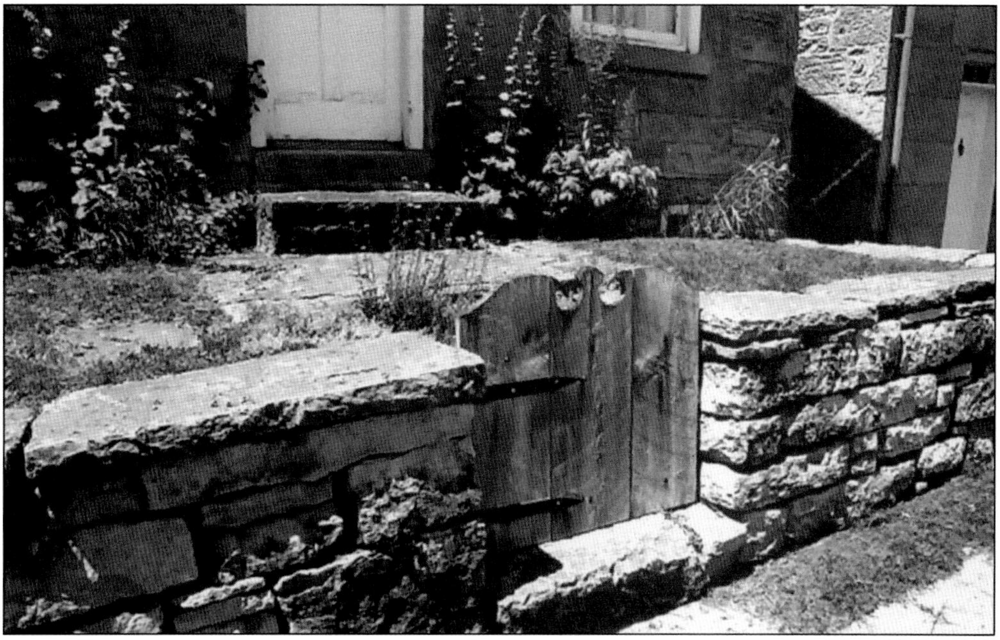

The Cornish miners laid stone fences and crooked stone paths along terraced hillsides. Their expert knowledge of stone masonry added to the old-world charm of the village. (Photograph by Betty France.)

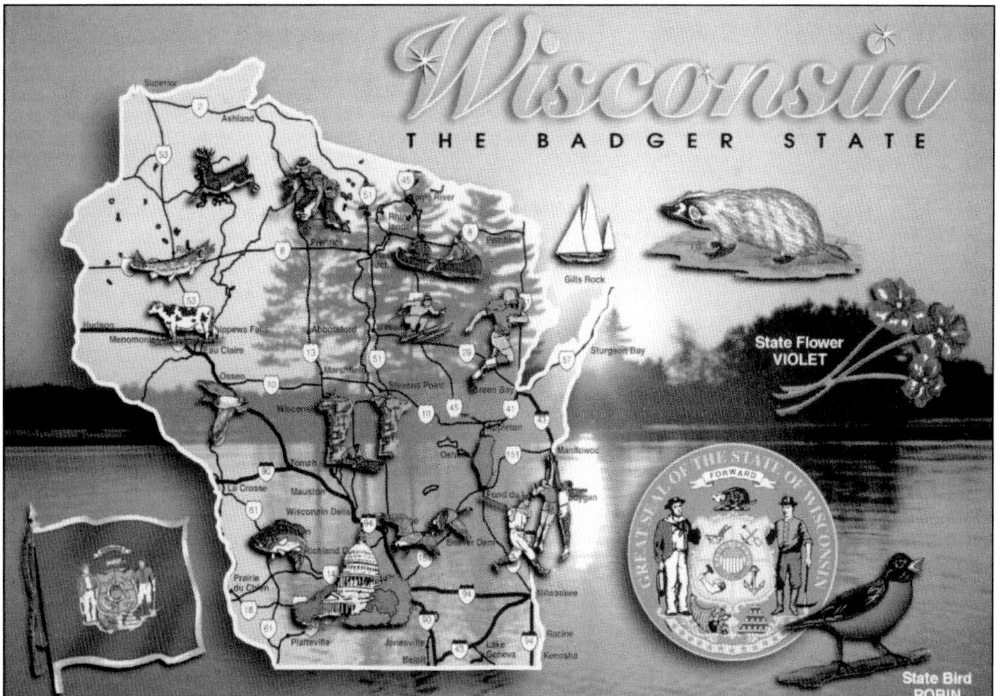

The early beginning of Wisconsin started here in this Cornish lead-mining region. The business of mining and the formation of the Wisconsin Territory are intertwined in the southwest portion of the state.

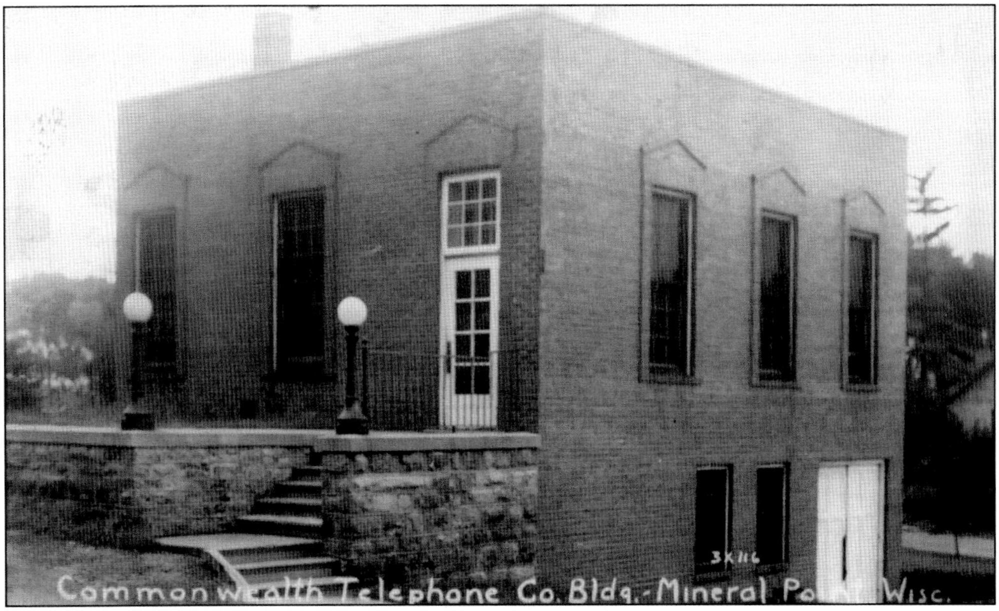

In 1883, Mineral Point's city council approved a plan for the Wisconsin Telephone Company to construct a telephone line in the city. By 1895 telephone service was ready to start with 16 subscribers for service. By 1908 the telephone exchange was housed in the First National Bank Building. Later the Commonwealth Telephone Company built this building directly behind the bank. It became General Telephone and is now Verizon.

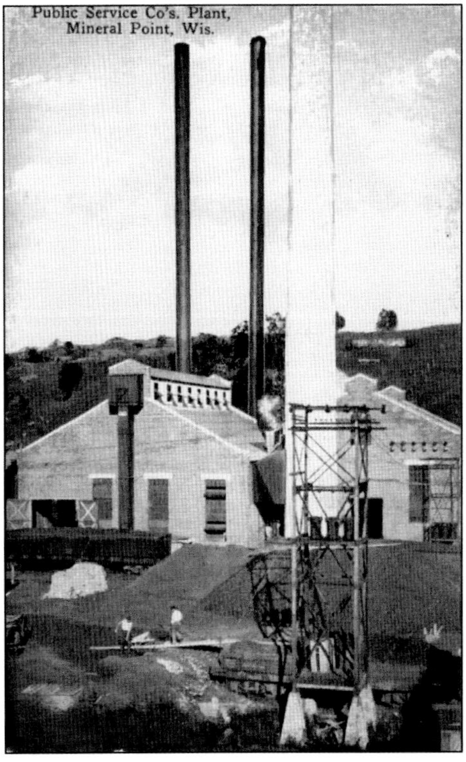

The boom arrived, and Mineral Pointers made a lot of money during 1891. They spent much of it developing their city. They laid new sidewalks, redid miles of streets, enlarged the Ward School, and replaced the old kerosene streetlamps with electric lights. Electricity lit up the zinc works plant and the village, much to the delight of the villagers. This is the Public Service Company plant, which was the first electrical company in town. It was located at 124 Water Street. It was bought by the Wisconsin Power and Light Company in 1924.

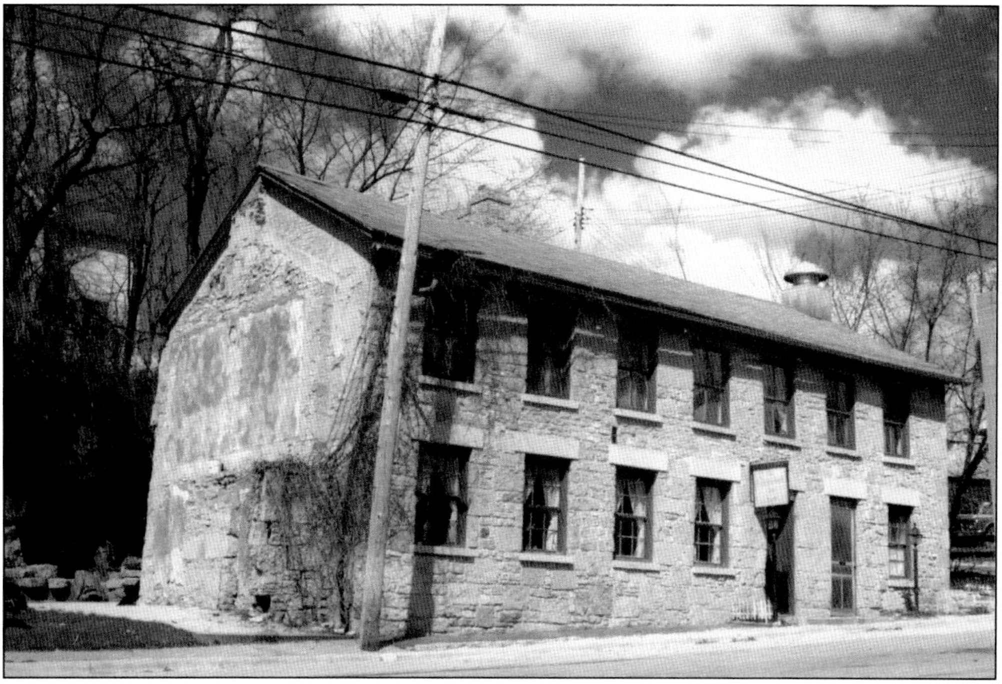

The Chesterfield Inn is currently one of Mineral Point's favorite eating spots. The rooms above the restaurant are available for rent. The outdoor eating area is especially appealing because it abuts a large stone wall, like those commonly found in this hilly area. (Photograph by Betty France.)

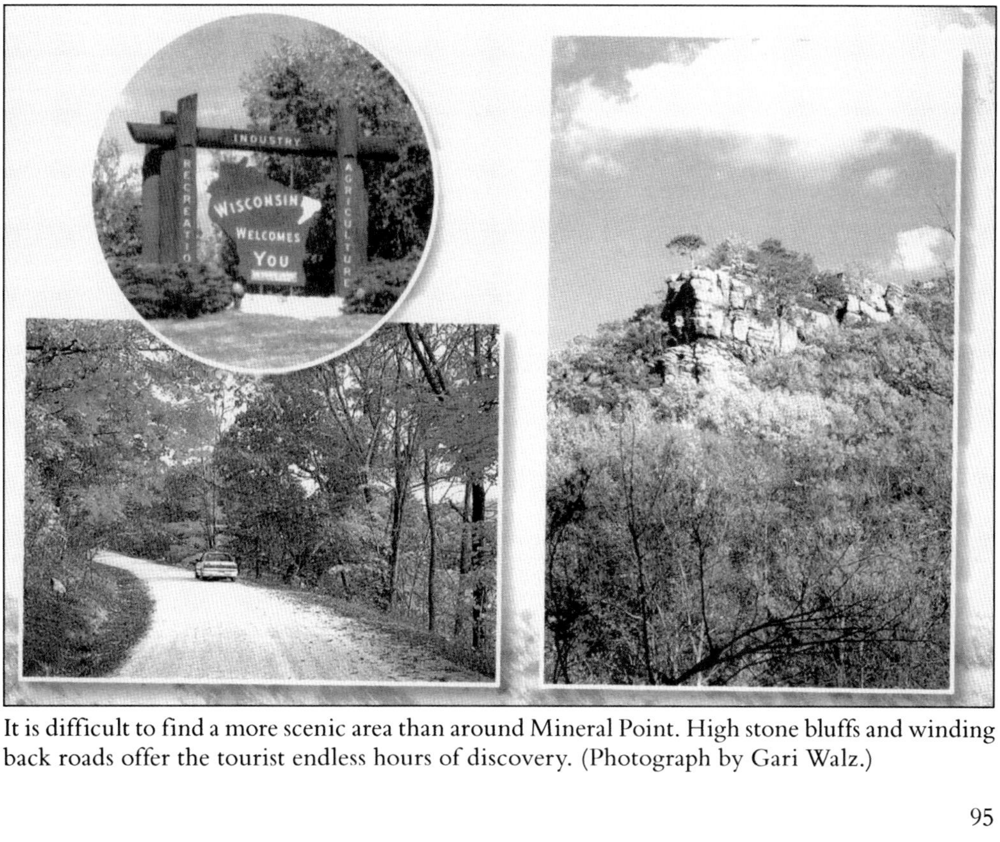

It is difficult to find a more scenic area than around Mineral Point. High stone bluffs and winding back roads offer the tourist endless hours of discovery. (Photograph by Gari Walz.)

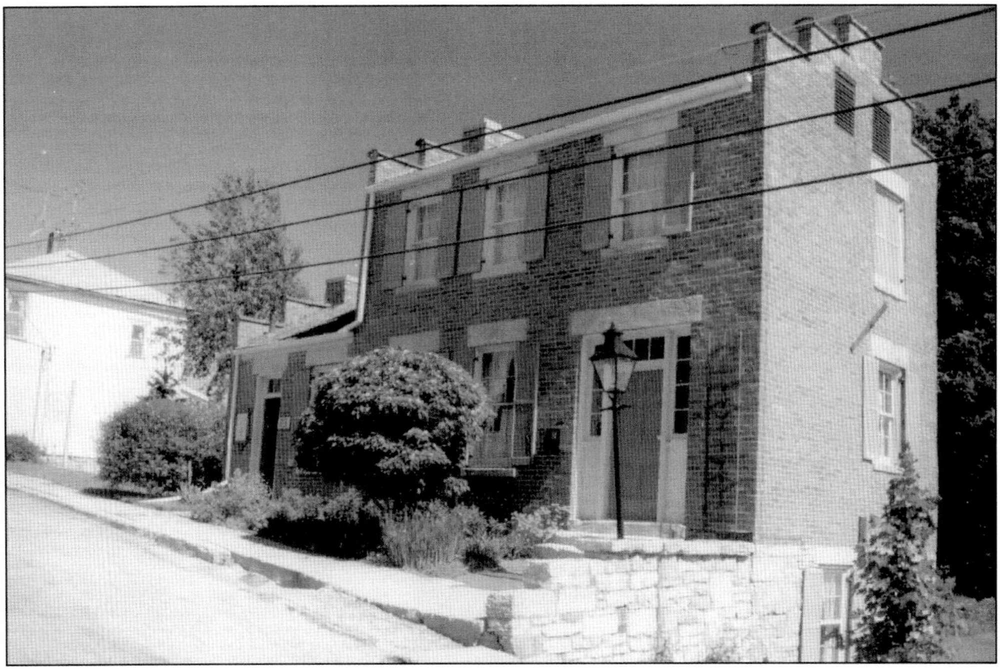

This home is called the Parley Eaton House, which was constructed during the 1840s and stands today as an excellent example of restoration and preservation. It is a fine example of the Cornish skill used to create stone basements and walls holding up a brick house. Their homes were not only practical, but they were beautiful.

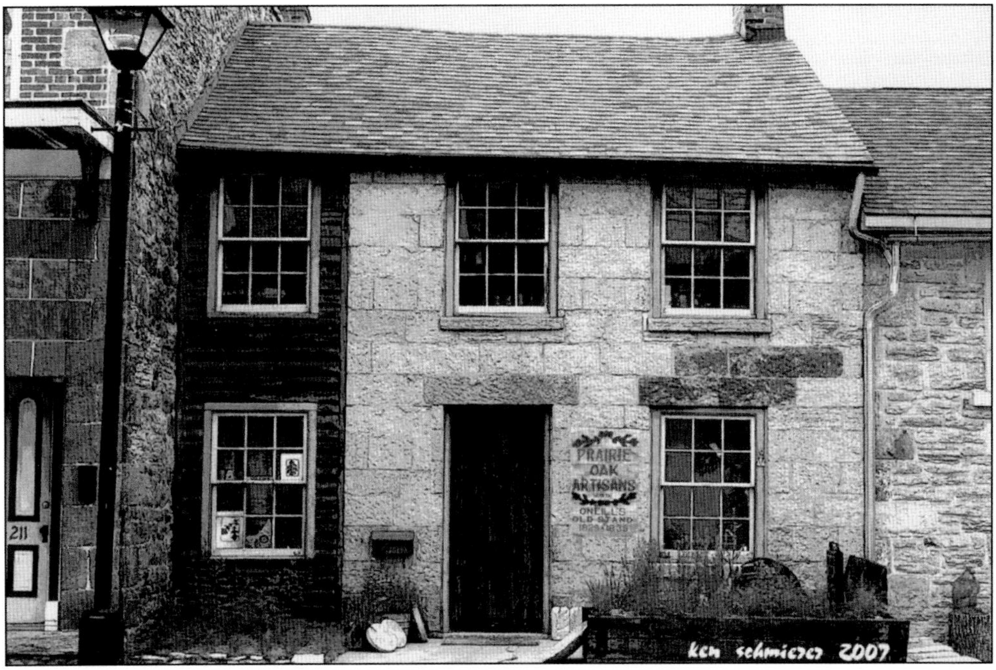

What was once an old house is now renewed as the Prairie Oak Artisans Shop. These old homes lend themselves to restoration that creates interesting and appealing shops. (Photograph by Ken Schmioo.)

Eight

Picturesque Pecatonica

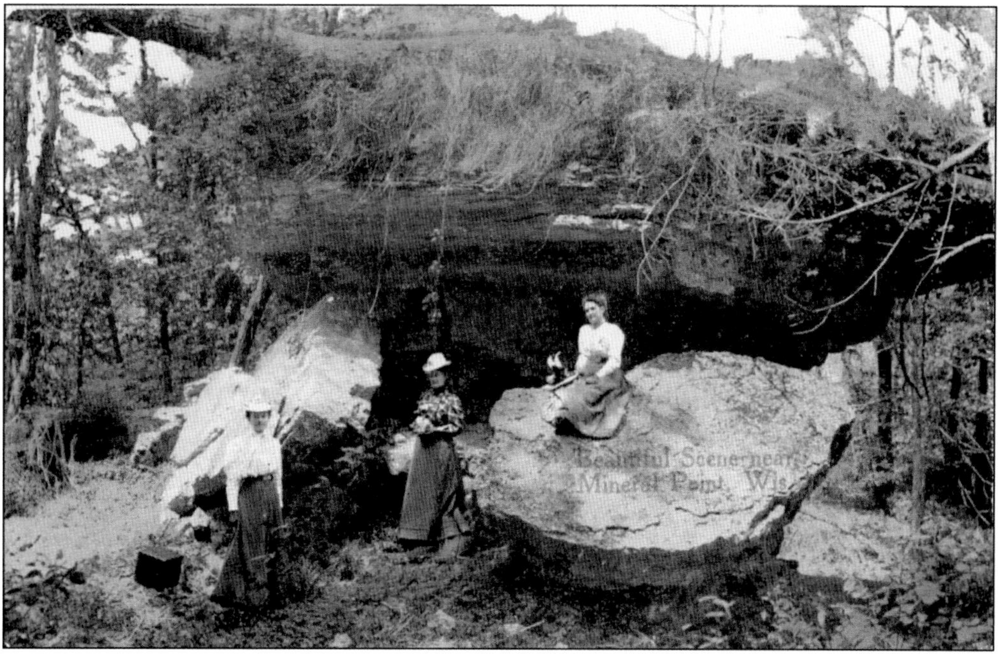

In this early view of the Mineral Point area, three women are beautifully dressed. They are wearing hats and long skirts as if they just came from Sunday church. This is a far cry from the blue jeans worn today. They appear to be enjoying this scenic spot, which shows a large boulder. They may be sitting before the entrance to a cave or an old lead ore mine.

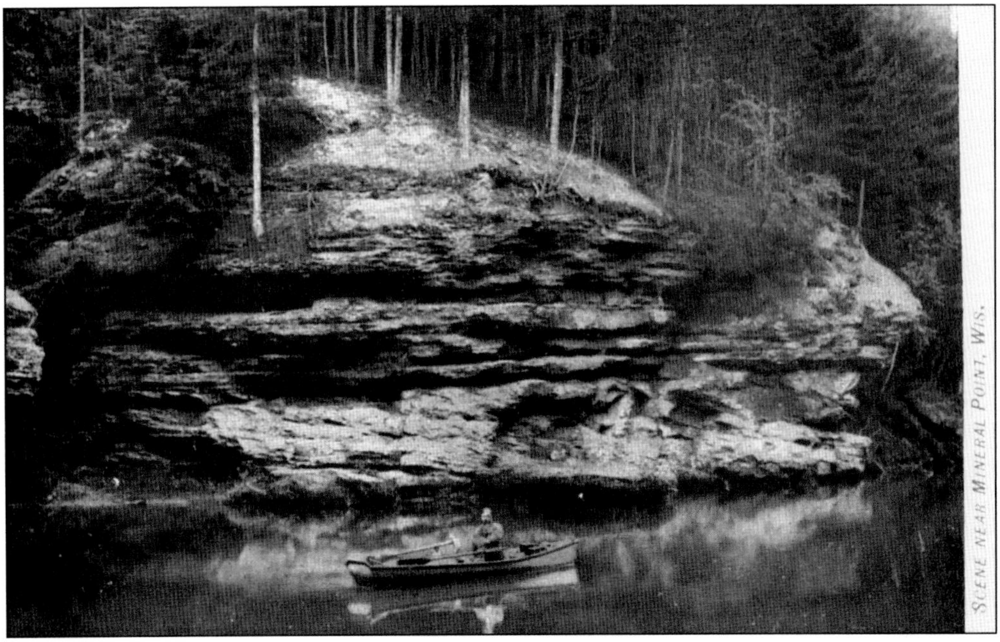

This boater is probably on the Pecatonica River paddling his rowboat past a stratified rock formation of the hillside. Such formations are typical of the driftless area in southwest Wisconsin. The driftless area escaped the advancement of the early glacier. As the glacier moved southward it divided and left this area untouched as God originally created it. That is why one often hears the local residents use the phrase, "This is God's country."

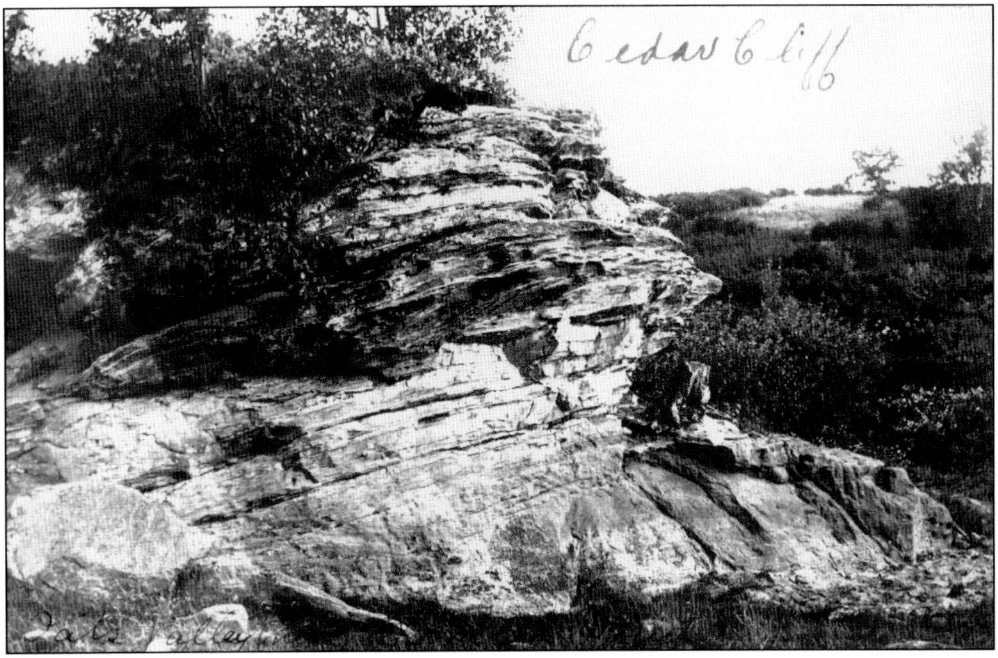

This similar picture shows stratified rock at somewhat of an angle. This is titled Cedar Cliff, which was located somewhere near Mineral Point.

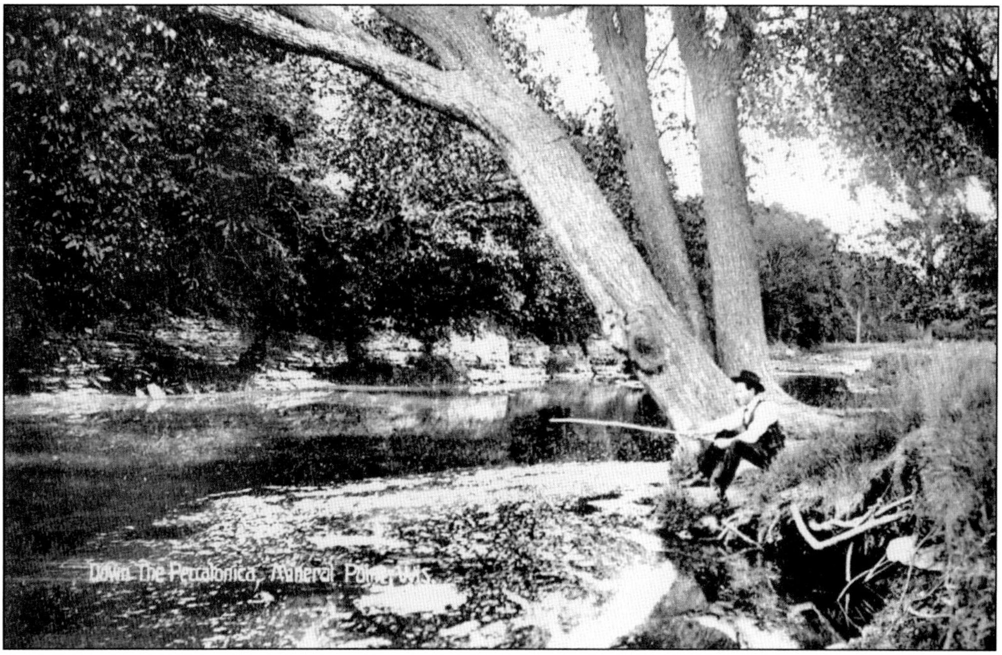

A fisherman on the Pecatonica River wears a white shirt. Think of the hard work it must have taken to wash and iron all these white shirts that people wore for everyday.

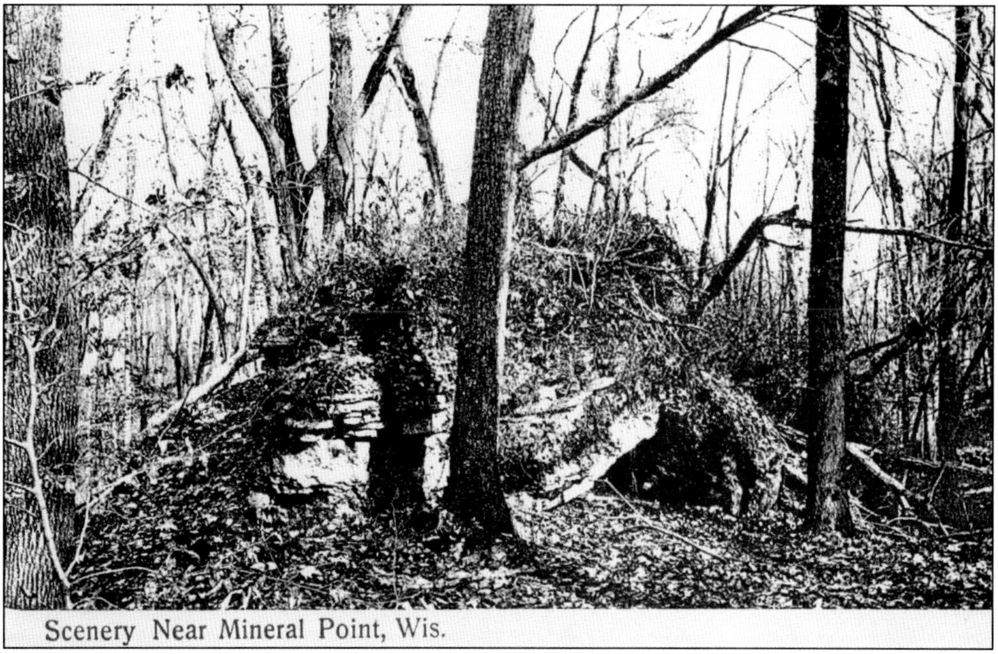

Caves dotted the whole area. Some were entrances to lead ore mines where the miners hoped they would find galena, lead of their dreams.

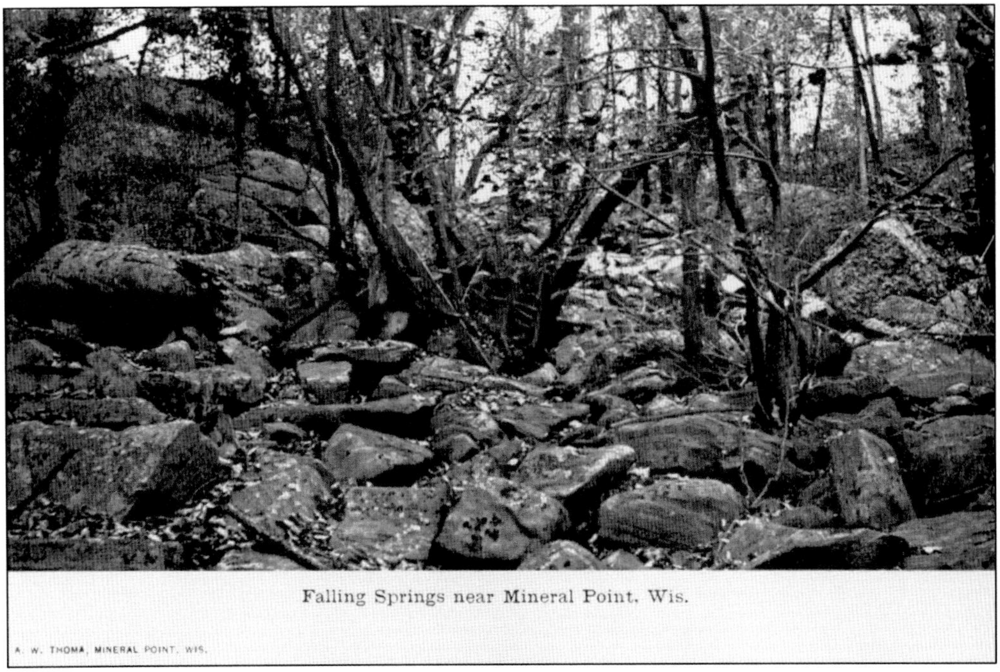

This card is called "Falling Springs near Mineral Point." There were many springs in and around the village. Some were used to create beer; others were used for drinking water. Many converged to become the Pecatonica River.

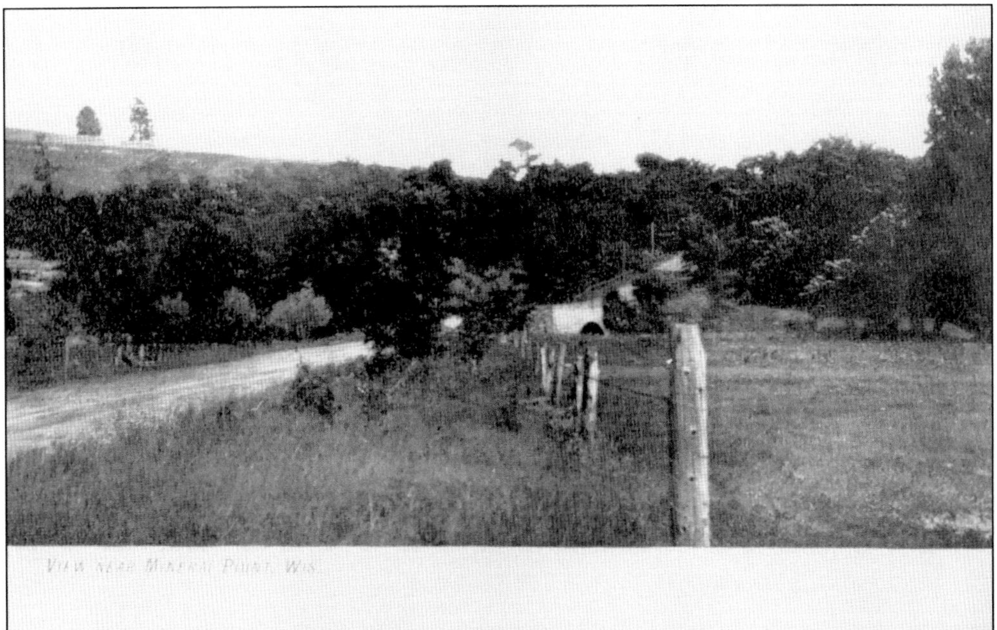

This country road near the edge of Mineral Point leads to a small bridge that crosses a branch of the Pecatonica River. A fence line bordering the road shows that cattle and farms were now a way of life. Many miners took up farming and continued to prospect for lead on their farms.

Hyde's Mill is located a short distance northeast of Mineral Point. This scenic spot is another example of the uplands due to its unglaciated landscape. This area reminded the early settlers of their homeland. (Photograph by Gari Walz.)

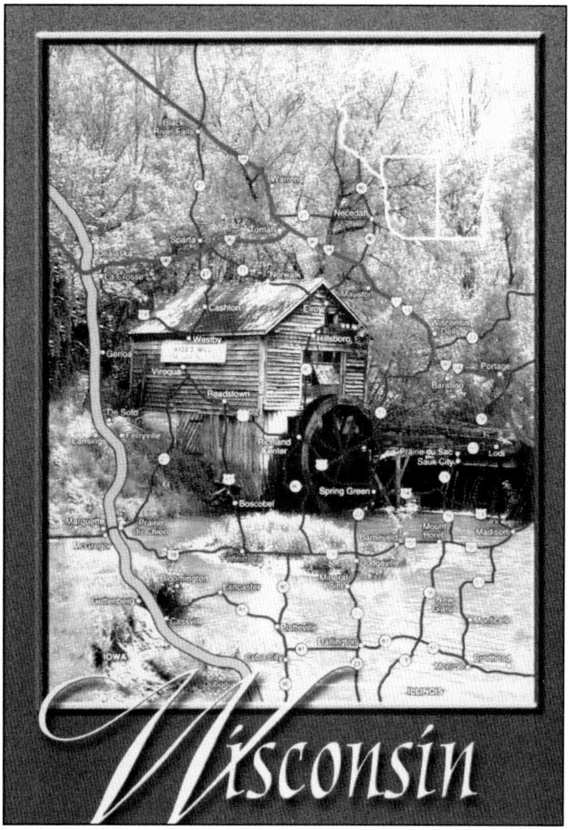

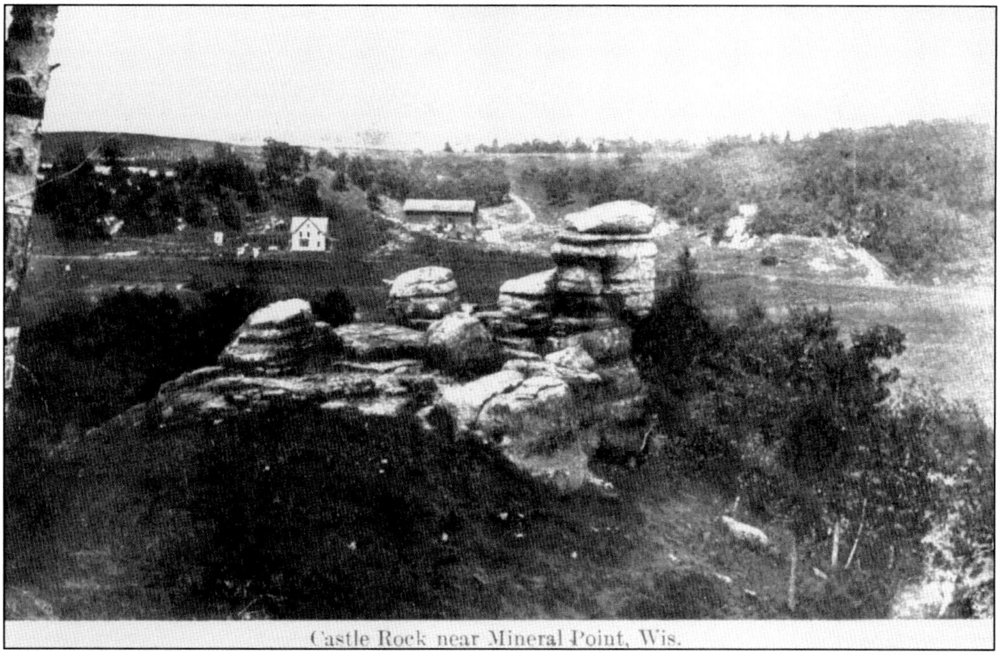

Wisconsin author August Derleth wrote a book about this scenic area called *The Hills Stand Watch.* He said part of the appeal of the area is that no matter where one goes the hills stand watch.

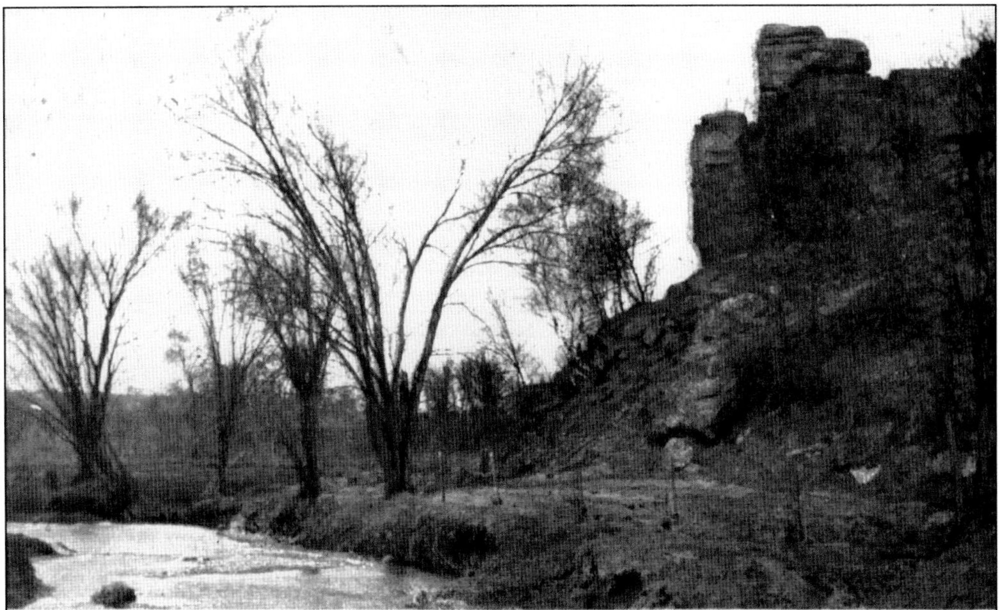

Castle Rock and Pecatonica River, Mineral Point, Wis. Pub. by A. W. Thoma, Mineral Point, Wis.

This view shows both the Pecatonica River and the majestic Castle Rock. The topography of this particular part of the driftless area is that of a high ridge, intersecting at varying angles with hills and valleys and streams all heading south toward the Pecatonica River, which flows into the Rock River, which flows into the Mississippi River, which finally flows into the Gulf and the open sea.

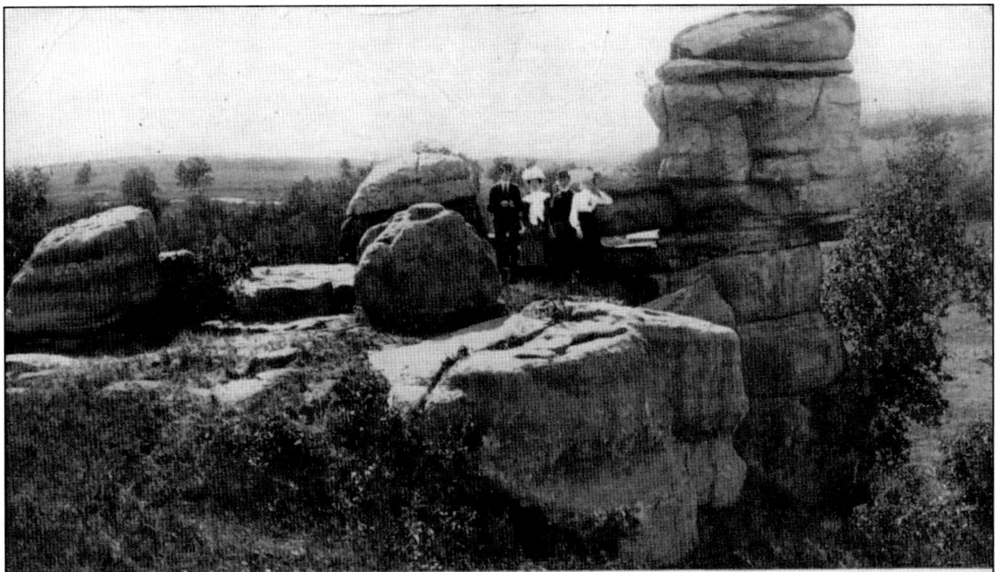

CASTLE ROCK, MINERAL POINT, WIS.

Women wore their big Sunday hats, and men wore their black suits and hats to climb the Castle Rock. Castle Rock was the most popular of all rock formations of the area. It was a favorite Sunday pastime to pack a picnic lunch and while away the hours at this scenic spot.

Early sunbathers dressed in formal Victorian attire enjoy their visit to Castle Rock. People took pride in being dressed up for even the most informal occasions.

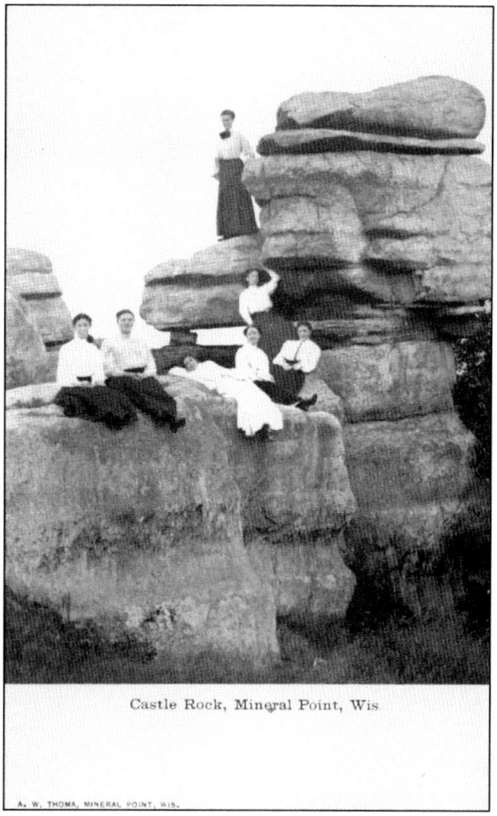

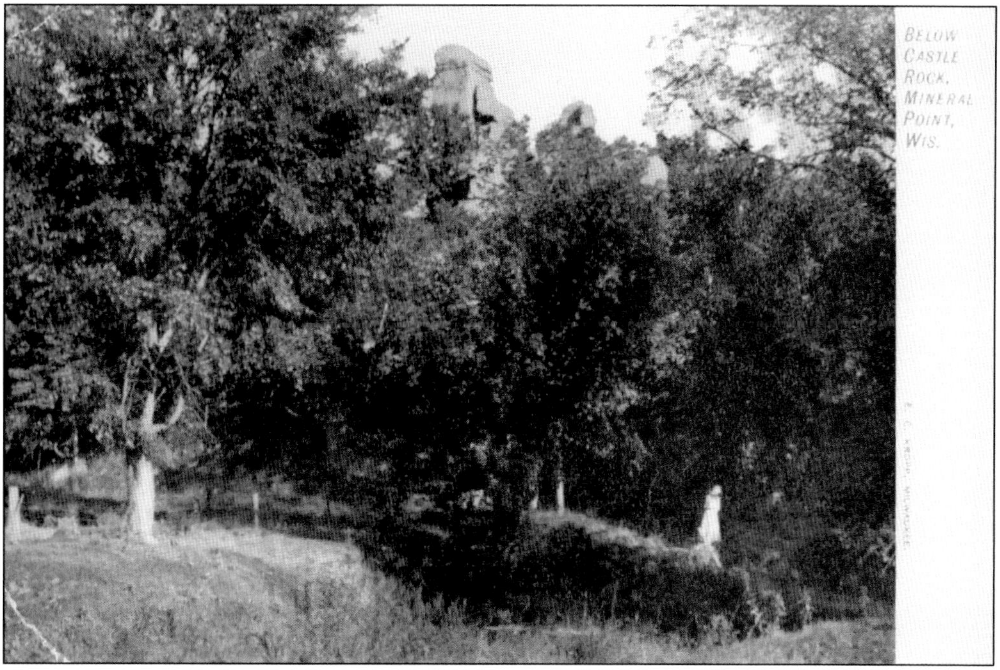

This 1907 card shows a woman dressed in white walking along the riverbank. In the center of the picture Castle Rock is towering overhead.

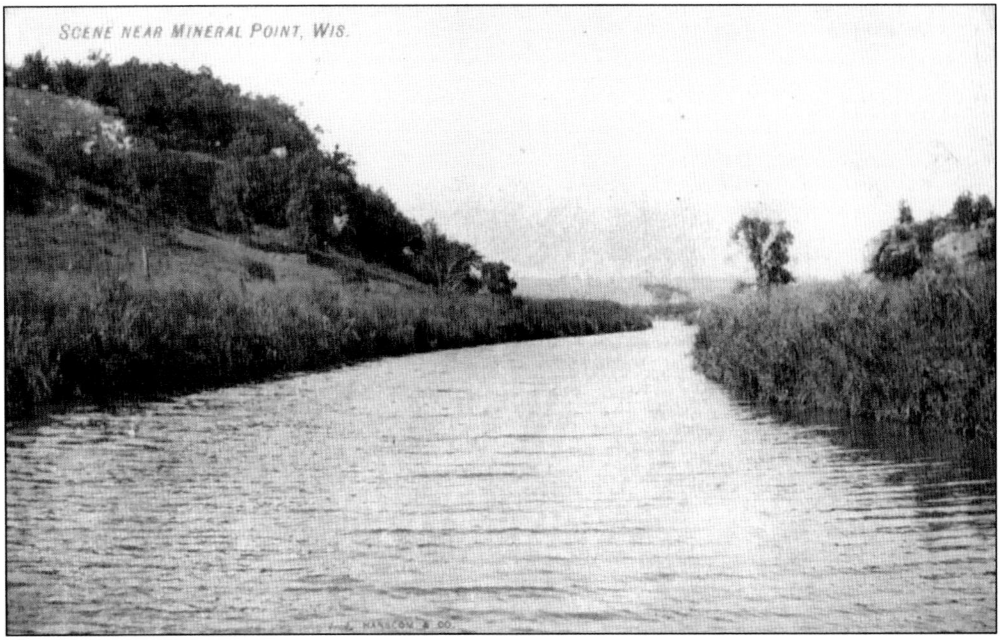

In 1908, the Pecatonica River was easily accessible to the people. Today most of the land is privately owned and not available to the public.

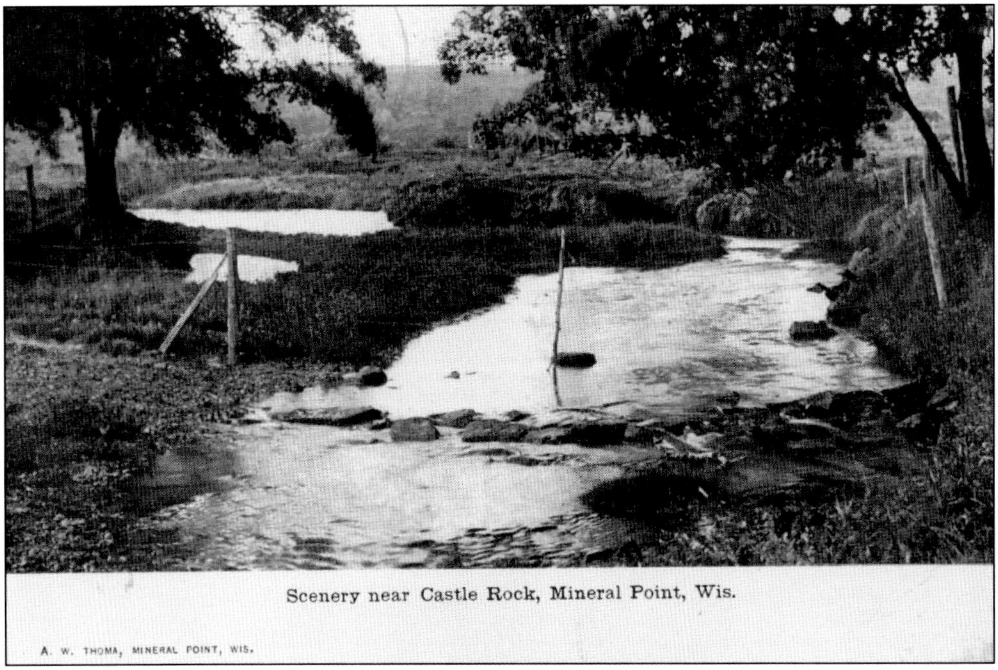

At the base of Castle Rock the Pecatonica River weaves through the countryside. As land was sold to individuals, property rights were defined by wire fencing, as can be seen here crossing the Pecatonica.

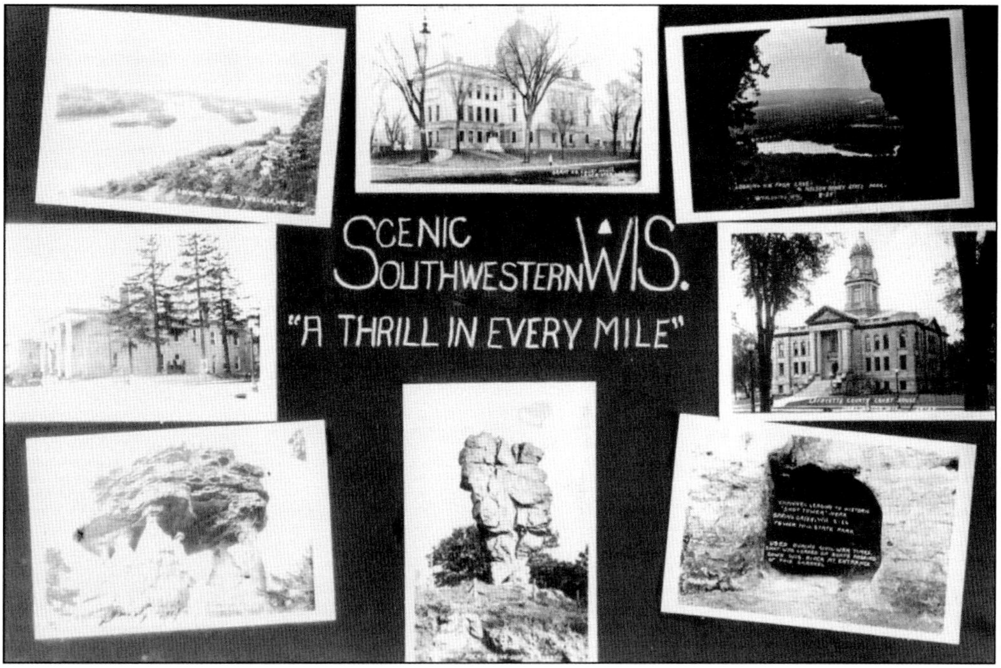

The variety of early life in southwestern Wisconsin is depicted in this miniature photograph collage. Life was low-key in these rural areas, but the locals did not think so, as seen from the heading on this card, "A Thrill in Every Mile."

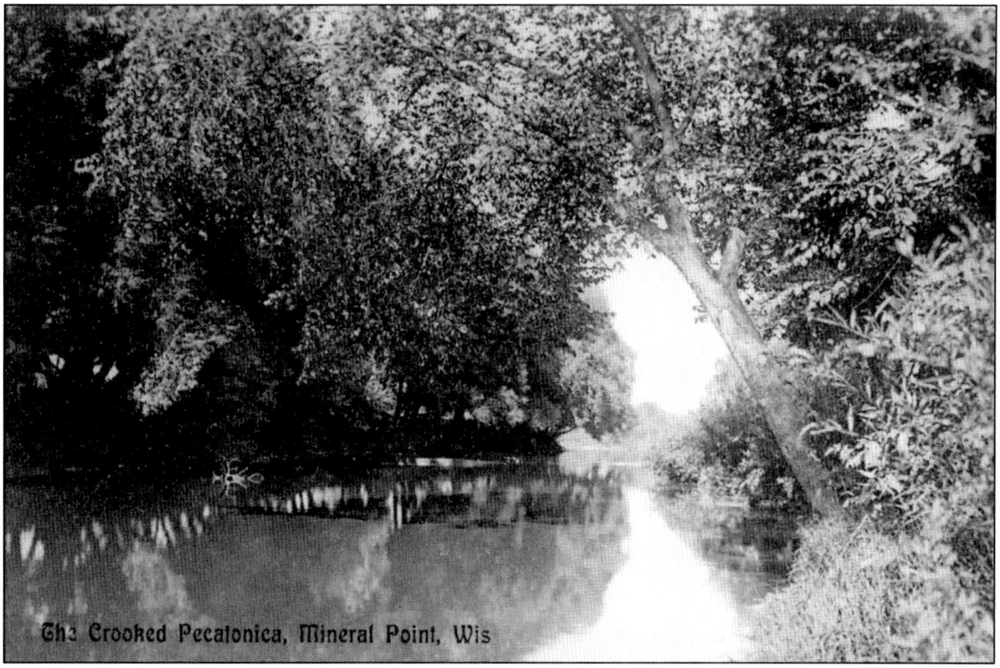

The crooked Pecatonica River was a fisherman's delight. They always made enough time to go fishing because the river offered a welcome respite from the dreary mining environment. Besides that, food was scarce for the miners and a fish dinner was appreciated.

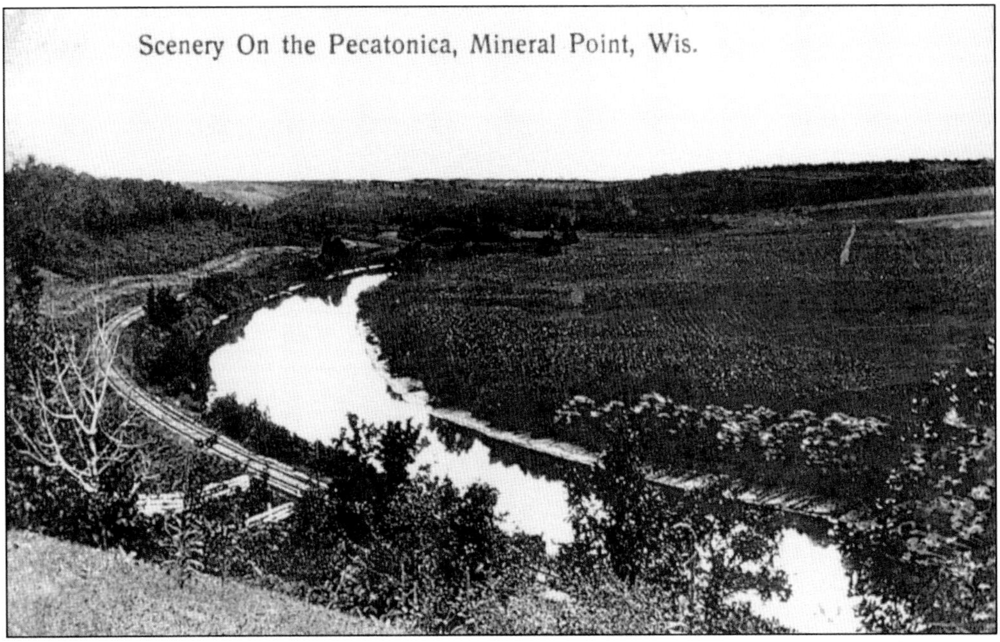

The Mineral Point Railroad tracks were laid along the edge of the Pecatonica River because it was more level land.

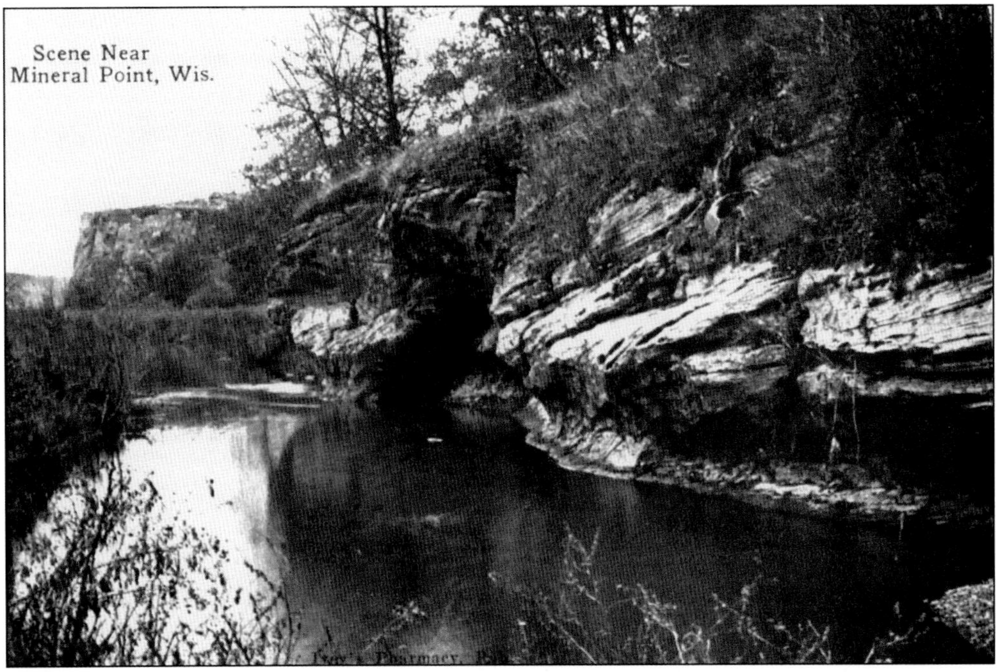

Rock and river join to form an interesting and scenic riverbank. The rock formations are sedimentary, deposited ages ago, long before the glaciers, which bypassed this area. These fixed formations are of various kinds of limestone and sandstone.

Cedar Cliff was especially steep. It provided a challenge for hardy rock climbers who used long sticks to steady their feet as they climbed upward.

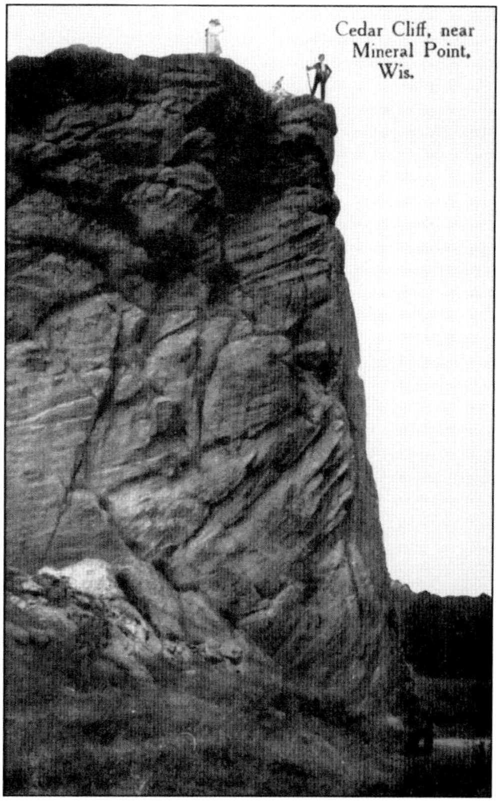

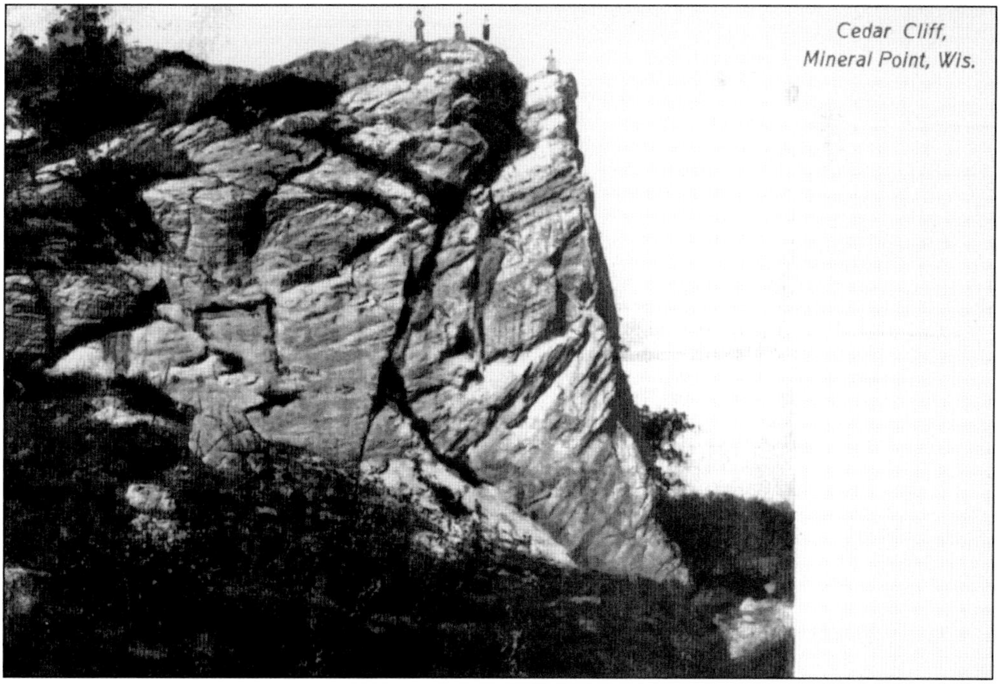

The view from the top was breathtaking enough to make the climb. This small driftless area is certainly the oldest thing on the face of the earth.

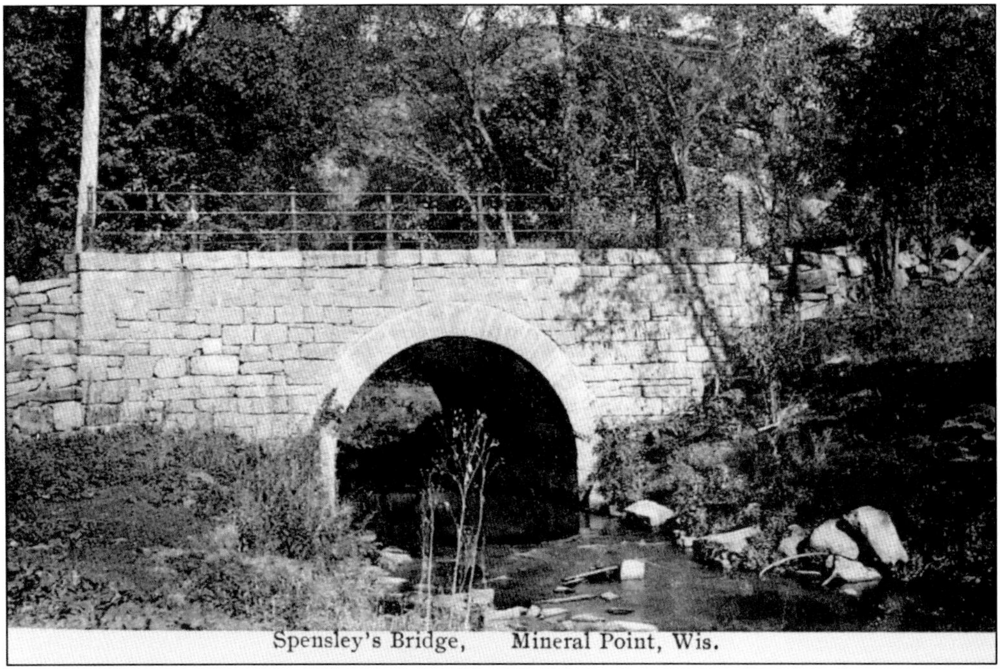

Spensley's Bridge was on the edge of town. It crossed the Pecatonica River on the land owned by James Spensley, a prominent Mineral Point farmer and smelter. Spensley was a representative of the state legislature in 1866. He probably had enough money to build this fine bridge. He needed it to get to the lead mine that was on his farm.

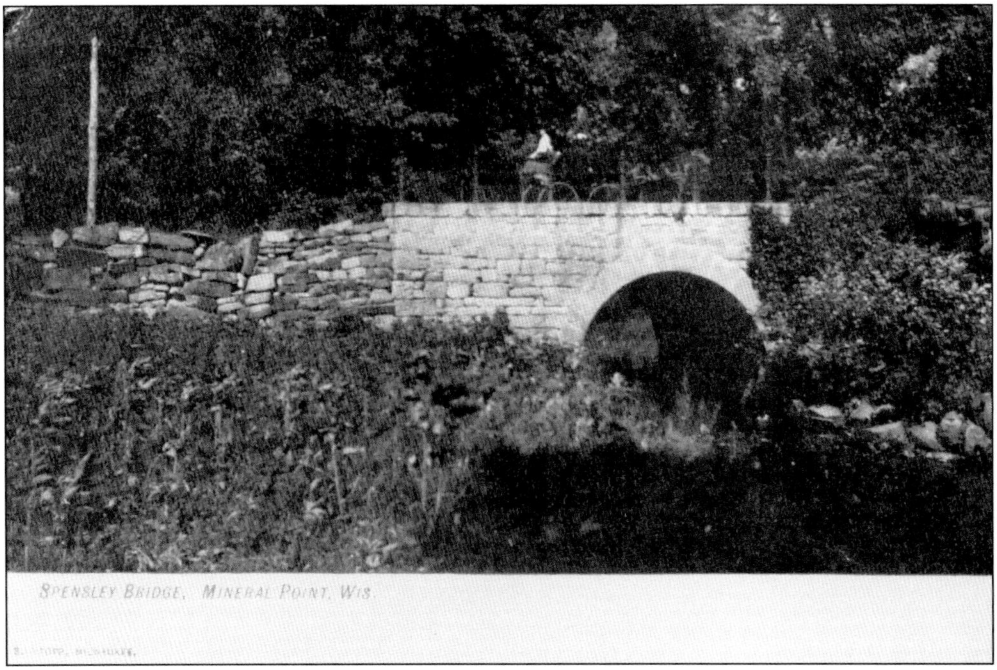

There were few bridges in the area, and this one was a favorite for buggy rides. It has lasted since the mid-1800s.

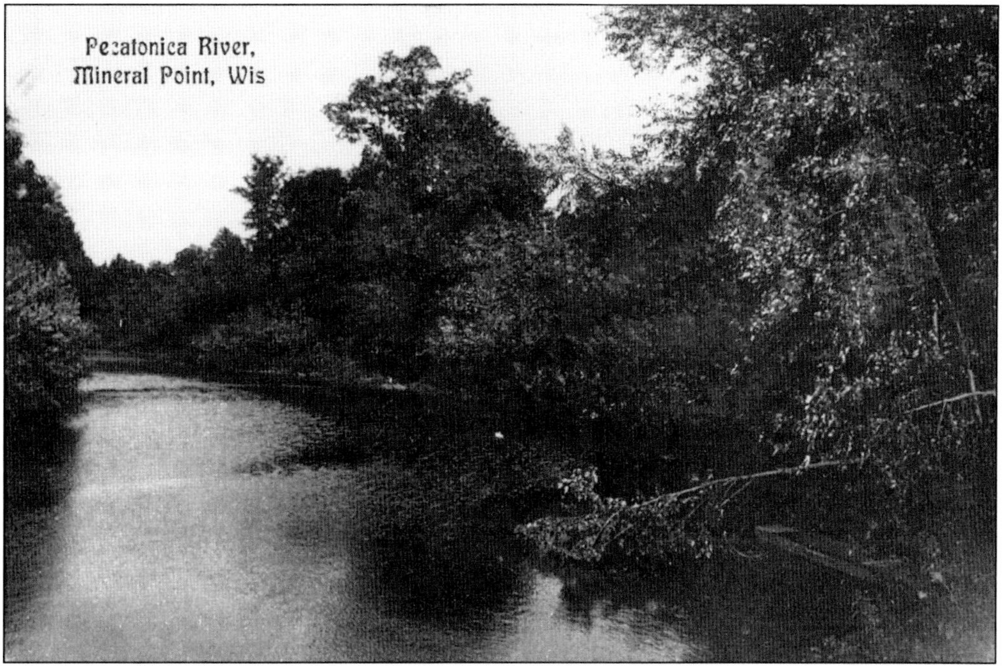

Once much wider, today the Pecatonica River has partially silted in. The early miners cut down many of the trees along the riverbank to fuel their lead ore smelters. The soil eroded and filled in the river.

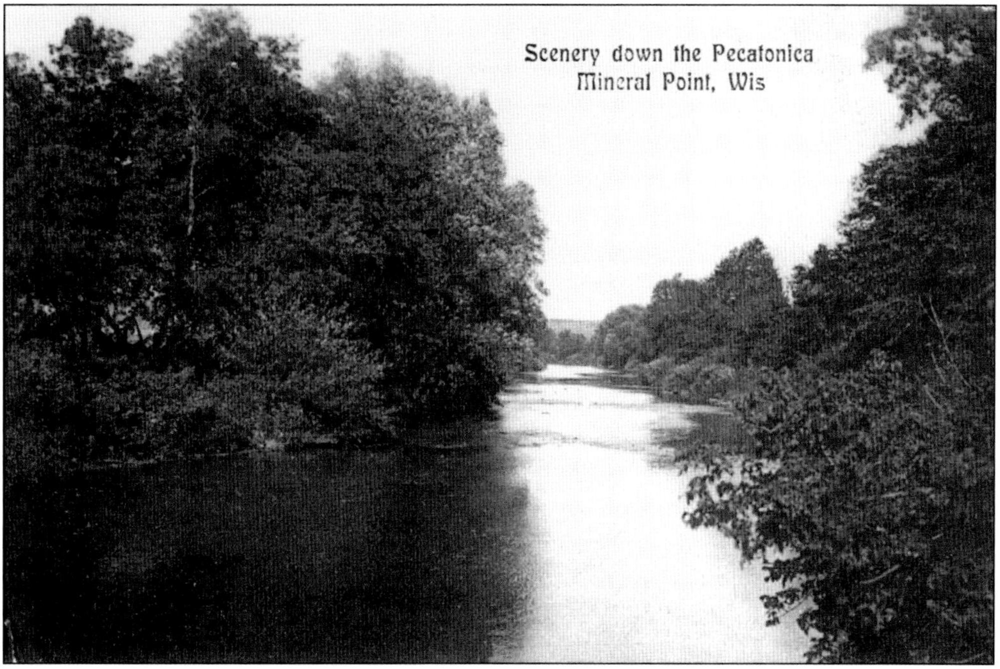

A 1909 view of the Pecatonica River is reminiscent of a lazy summer day.

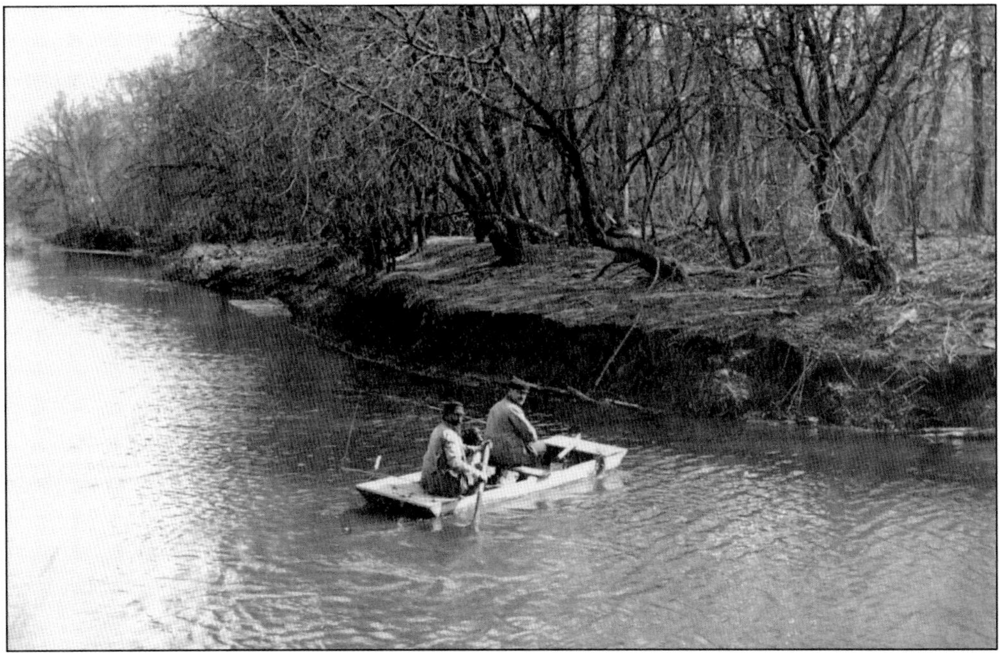

Two miners take a break to fish from their flat-bottom boat on the picturesque Pecatonica River.

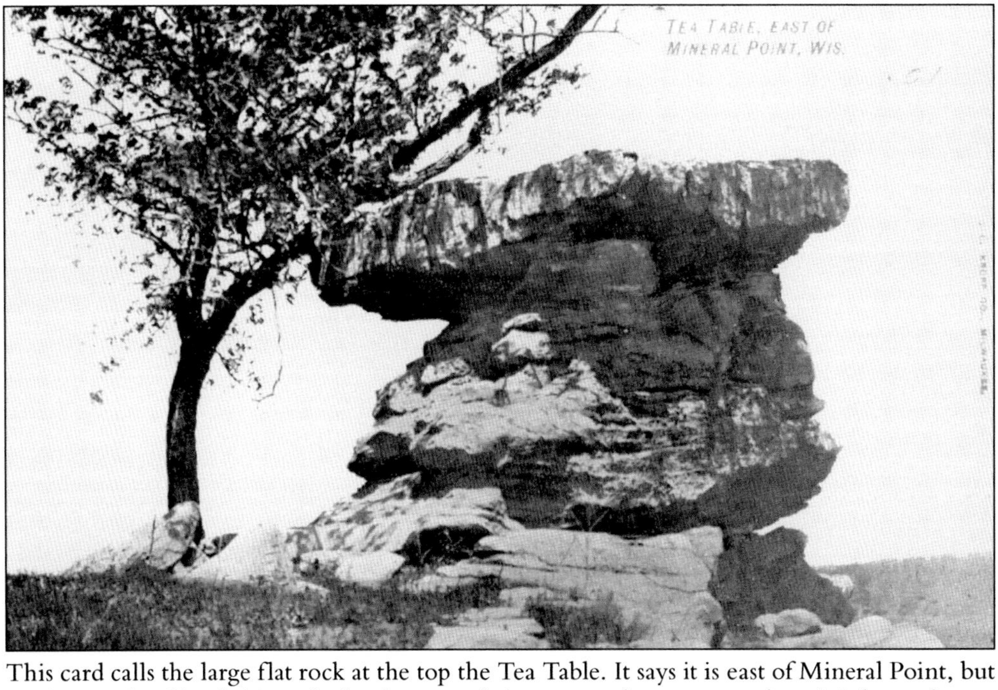

This card calls the large flat rock at the top the Tea Table. It says it is east of Mineral Point, but locals say it has blended into the landscape and they are no longer sure where it is located.

Nine

Bird's-Eye View

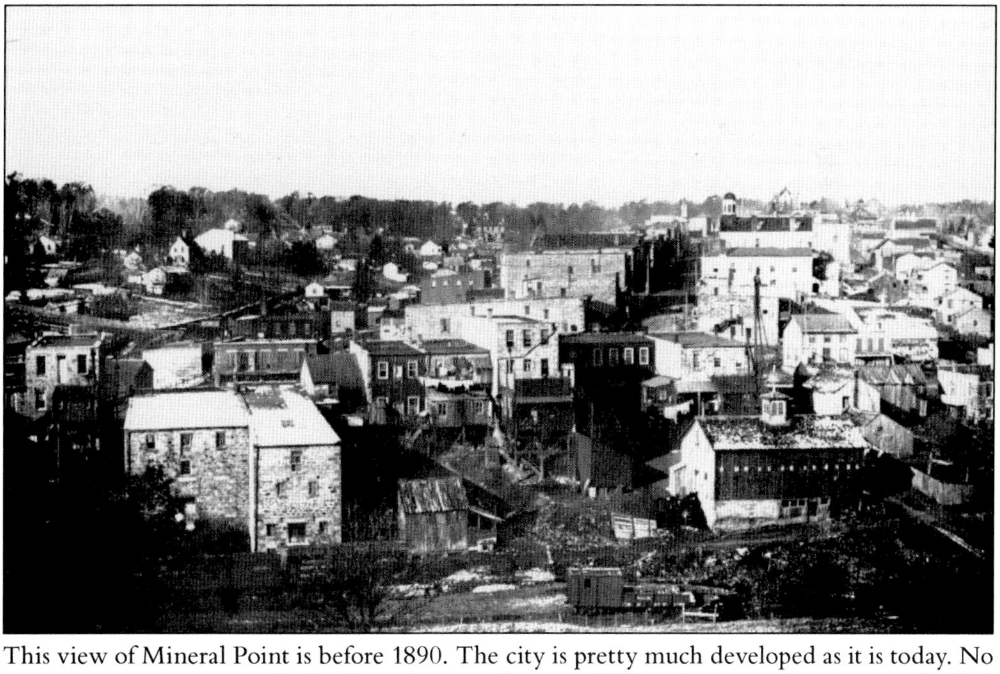

This view of Mineral Point is before 1890. The city is pretty much developed as it is today. No trees are seen, except on the horizon, because they would have been cut down to use for fuel for the smelters. The first miners came here to literally pick the lead ore up off the ground in 1827. Today Mineral Point has a strong retail district, service to the area farmers, several small industries, and a strong tourist appeal. Buildings have been restored, and business is brisk.

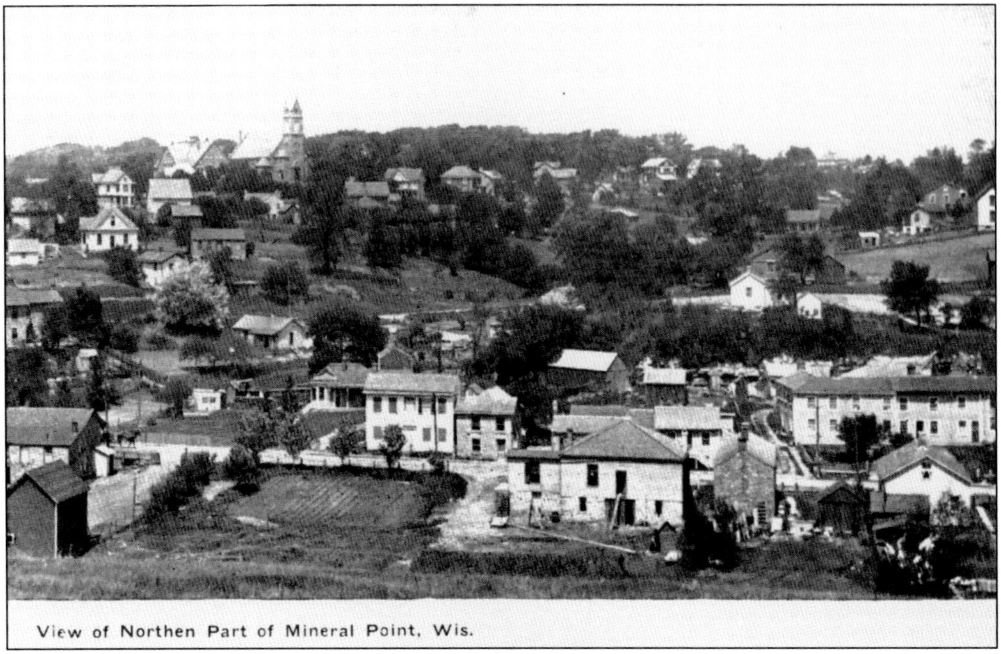

This 1909 view of the northern part of Mineral Point highlights the St. Mary's Catholic Church and school in the upper left corner. This solid brick Romanesque-style church was the focal point for the German immigrants who came here in the 1870s.

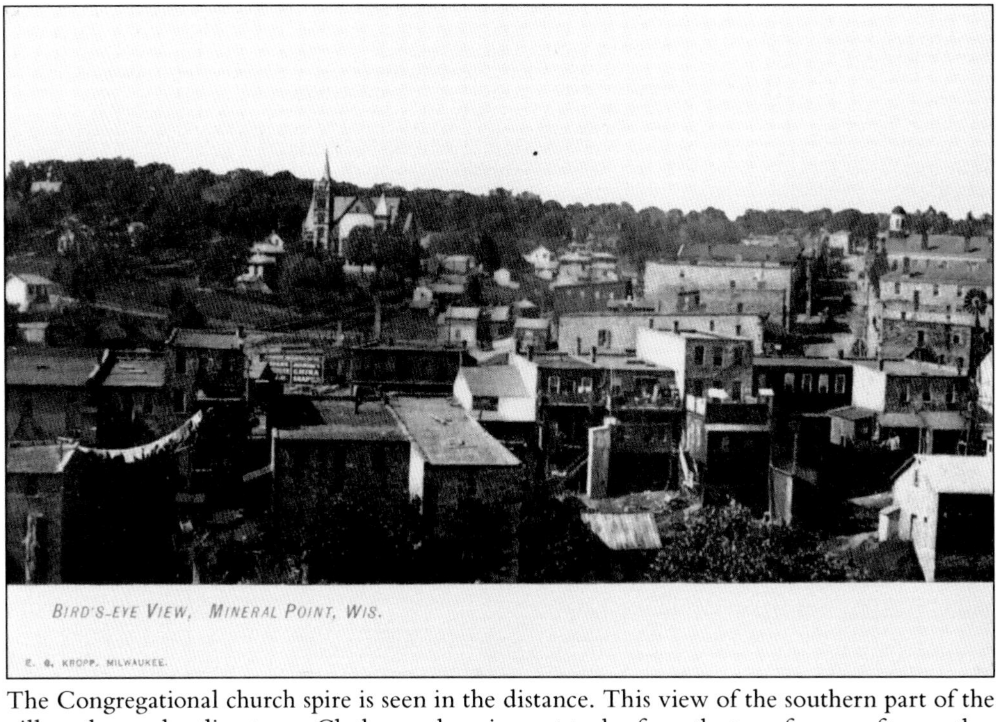

The Congregational church spire is seen in the distance. This view of the southern part of the village shows a bustling town. Clothes are hanging out to dry from the top of one roof to another building, using a pulley to get them "forth and back," as the Cornish would say.

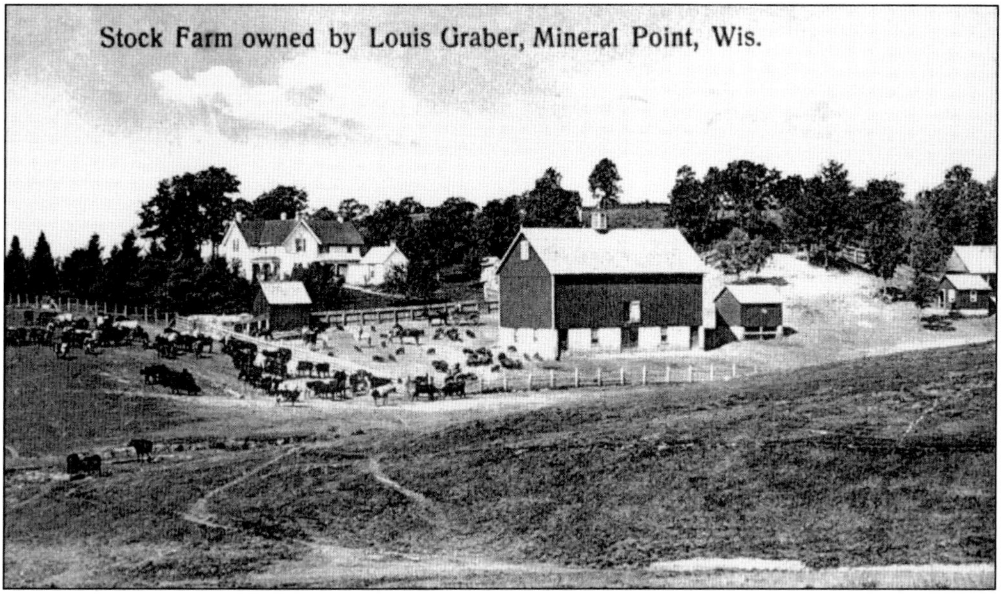

As mining became less profitable, the miners either moved on to look for California gold or they settled down to farming. Many of them farmed while still working small mines on their property. The soil was fertile, and food no longer had to be brought in from far distances. Stock farms raised cattle for beef. They continue to thrive in the Mineral Point rural area.

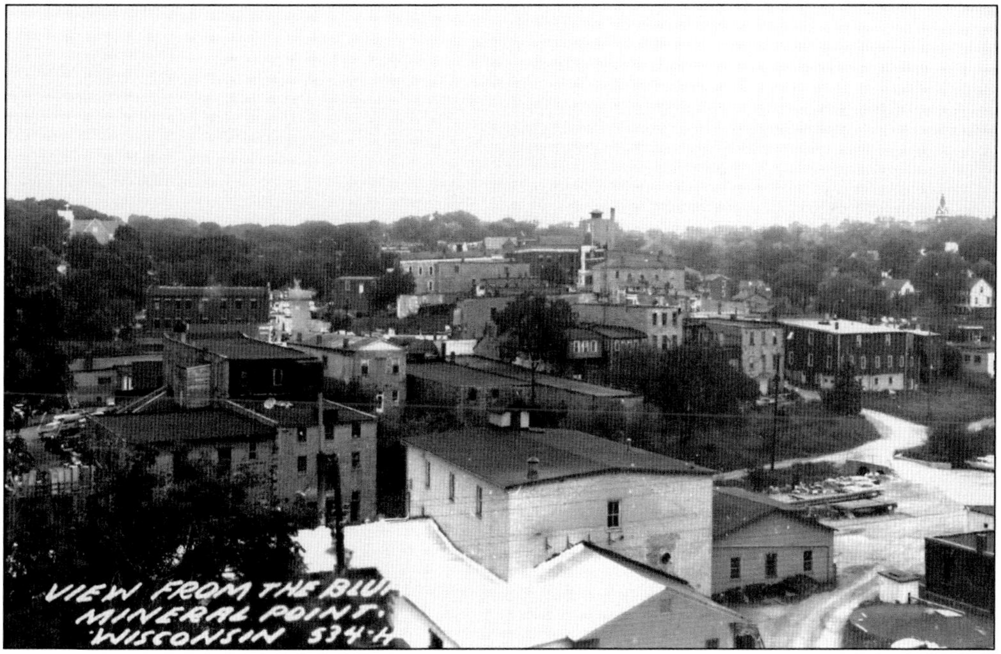

This is an early view of Mineral Point as seen from the bluff above the city. While the town looks bleak, it had progressed from the times when sanitation in the village was nonexistent. In early days there was no indoor plumbing. The methods of disposing of human wastes were of the crudest, and many houses did not even have outdoor privies. There were no screens on windows and doors, and flies would flit from filth in one house to food on the table in the next. People fled from the plague, spreading it even wider.

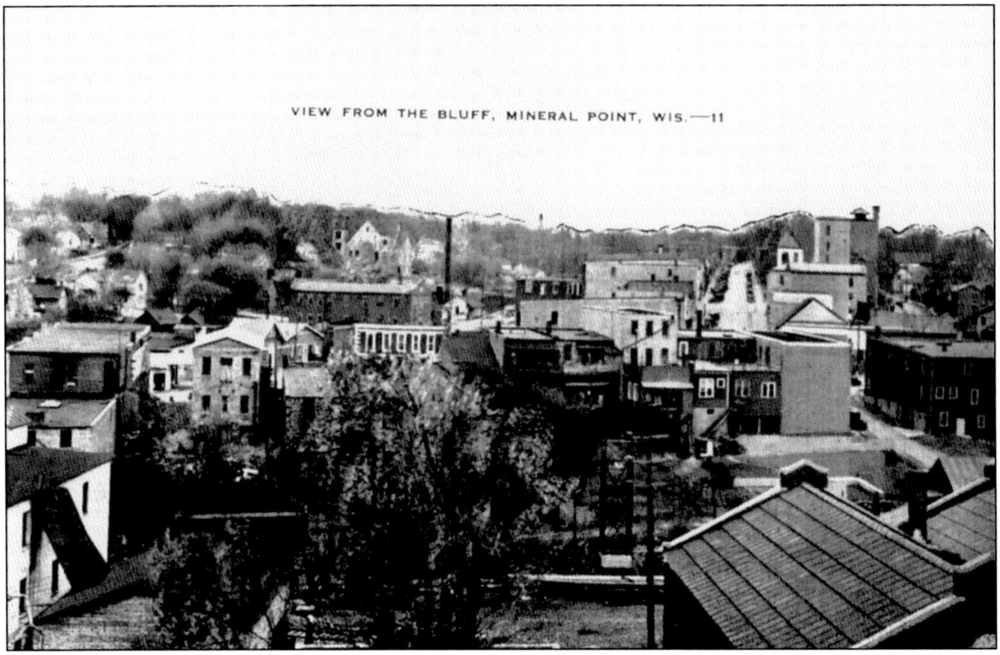

In Mineral Point the plague of cholera was a dreaded scourge. Some residents camped on a hillside during the epidemic of 1849. They wrote notes saying that for a couple of months there were four or five deaths per week. Doctors at that time still resorted to bleeding and advised against giving the patient any water to drink even though one of the symptoms of cholera was an insatiable thirst.

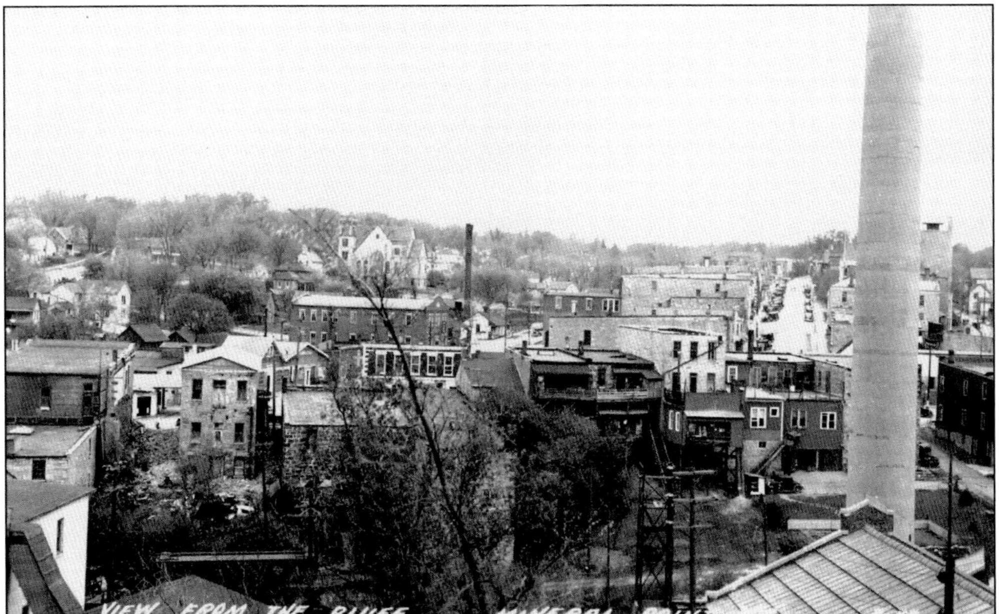

It was a time of medical quackery. Eventually the doctors learned not to dehydrate by bleeding and not to refuse water to a patient with an insatiable thirst. In 1851, the local doctors organized a board of health and things started to greatly improve.

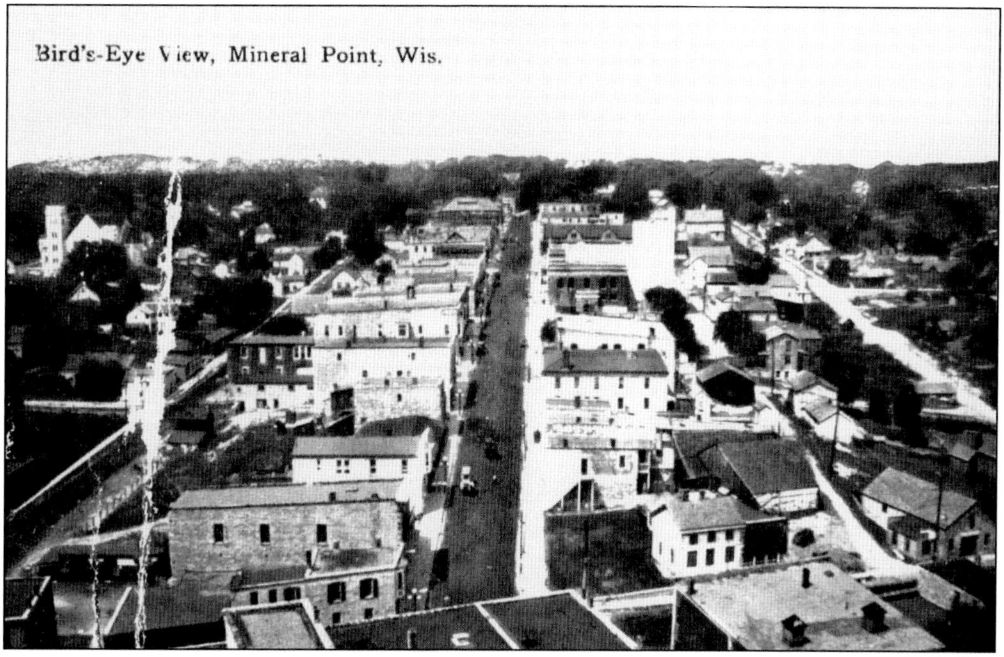

Some daring individual climbed to the top of the ice plant smokestack to get these 1905 images of the town. The middle of the picture is of High Street. Off to the left was the Congregational church, and the road off the far right was Doty Street.

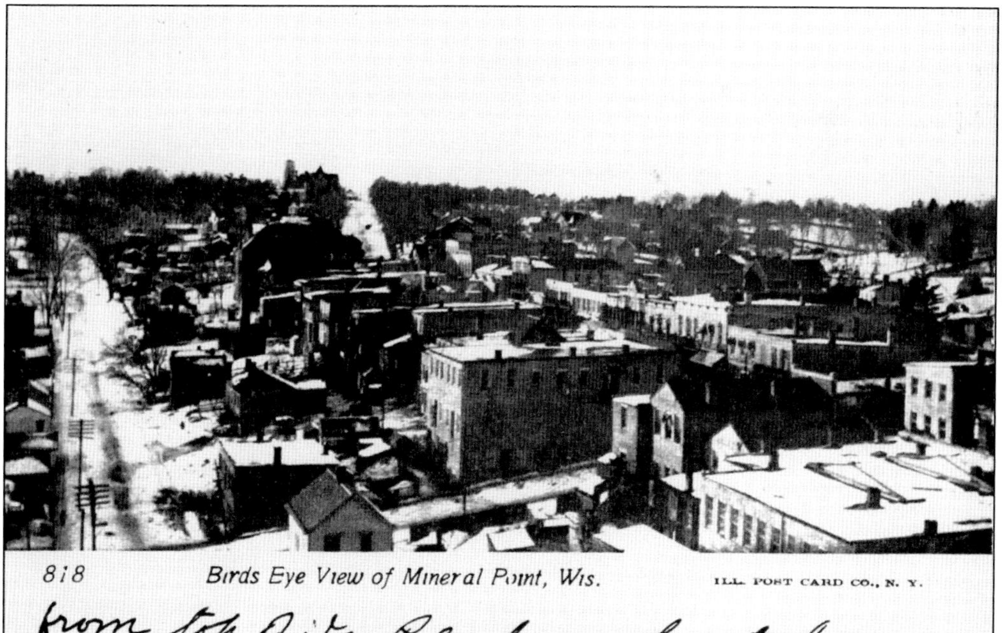

The population of Mineral Point in the early 20th century was 2,991. A new high school had been built of hand-cut limestone blocks. Local houses were built of quarried limestone and sandstone, which were readily available in the surrounding area.

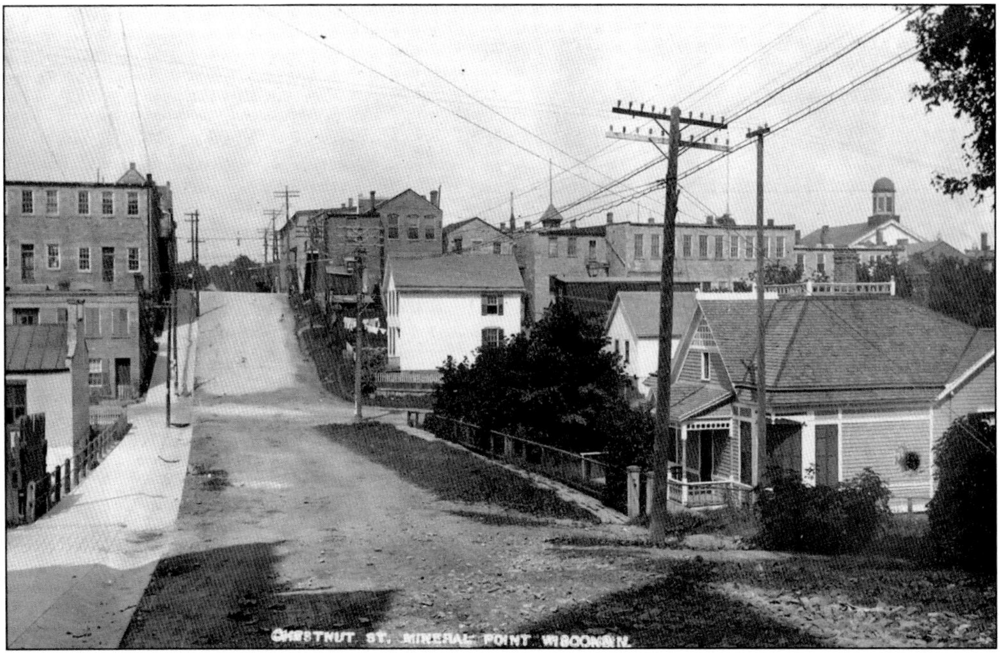

Looking north on Chestnut Street, the buildings look sturdy and secure. By the early 20th century, life had improved; streets and roads were laid out to give a sense of order and allow for a better road system to get around the town.

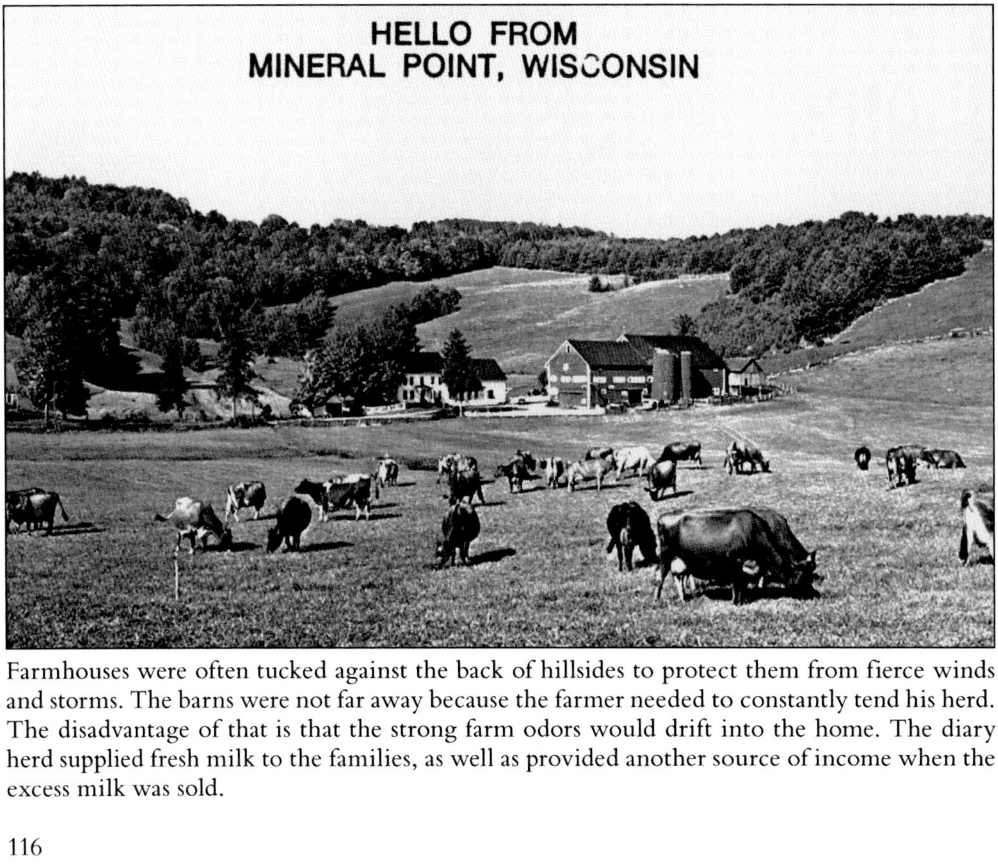

Farmhouses were often tucked against the back of hillsides to protect them from fierce winds and storms. The barns were not far away because the farmer needed to constantly tend his herd. The disadvantage of that is that the strong farm odors would drift into the home. The diary herd supplied fresh milk to the families, as well as provided another source of income when the excess milk was sold.

Ten

Recreational Activities

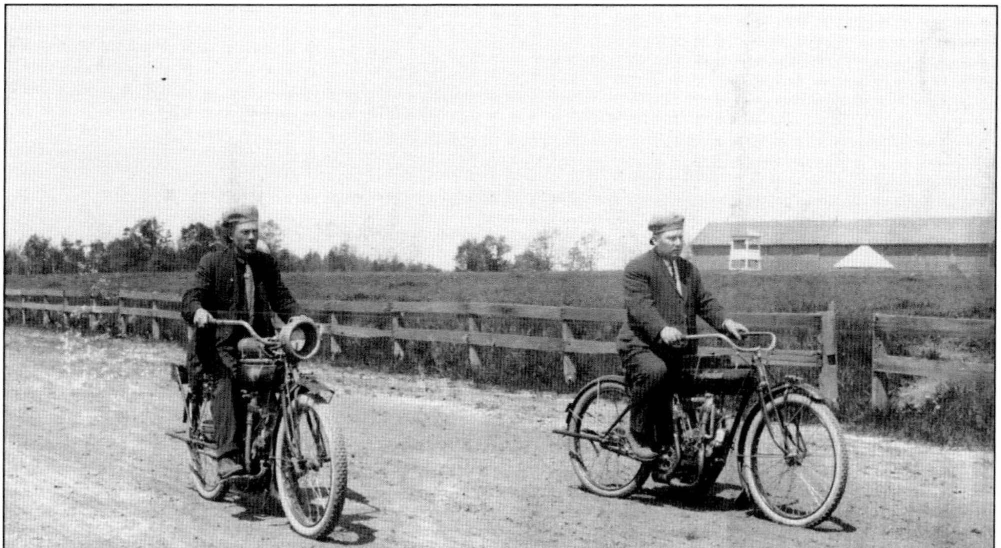

Like any small town, Mineral Point had a variety of outdoor activities that the local citizens enjoyed. Biking was popular on the hilly countryside, as was riding these early versions of motorcycles. Softball and track teams in high school brought out most everyone to cheer them on to victory, especially if the games were against Dodgeville, their long time rival. Marching bands drew people to see the festive parades.

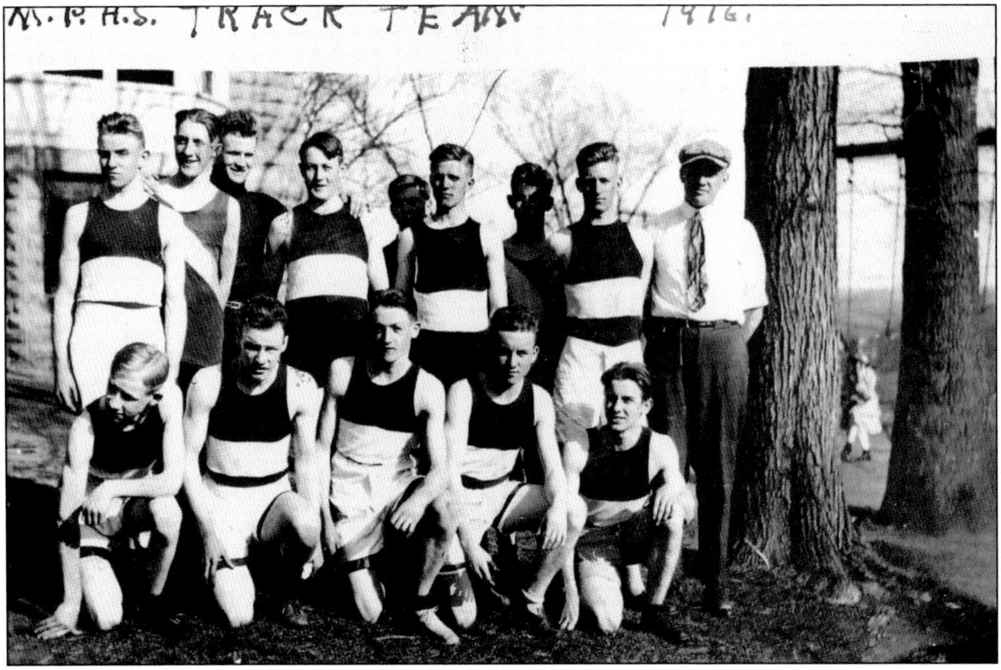

The Mineral Point High School track team is shown here in 1916. Track and boxing were both popular sports of the time.

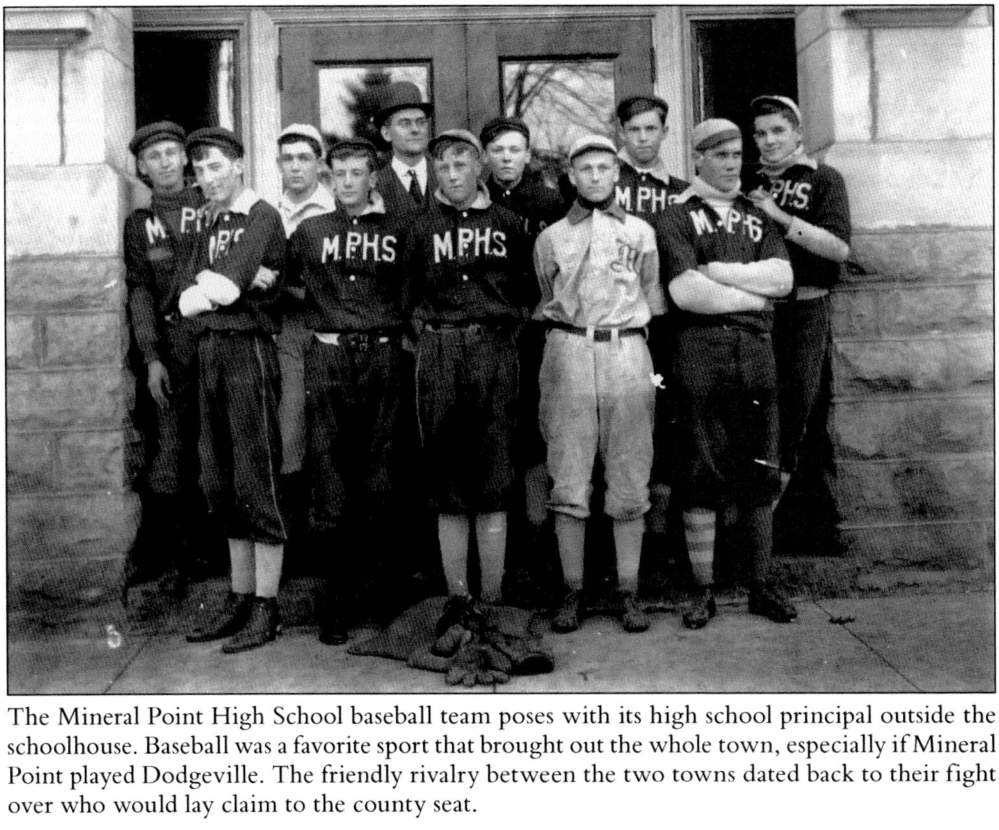

The Mineral Point High School baseball team poses with its high school principal outside the schoolhouse. Baseball was a favorite sport that brought out the whole town, especially if Mineral Point played Dodgeville. The friendly rivalry between the two towns dated back to their fight over who would lay claim to the county seat.

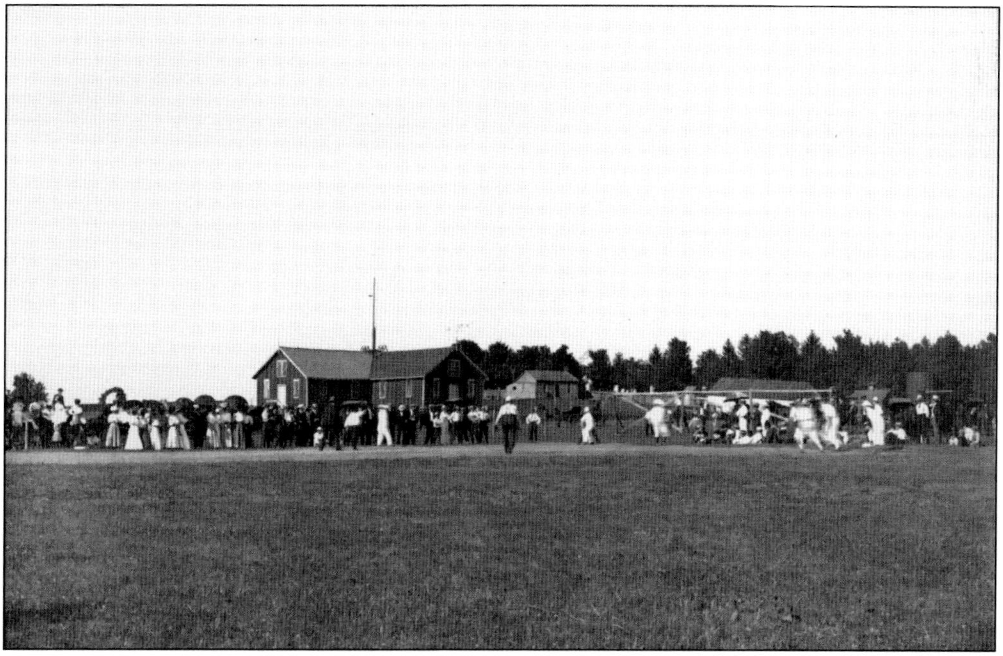

Mineral Point plays Darlington at this baseball game. The cheerleaders are wearing long dresses.

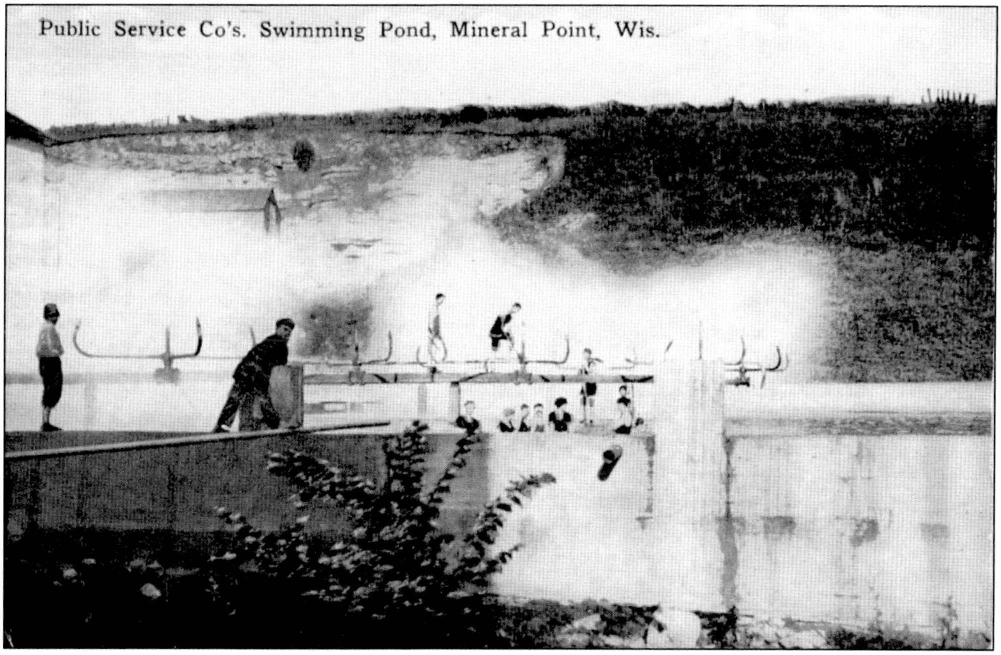

The Public Service Company's swimming pond is located on Commerce Street around 1916. It looks like they successfully rigged up a diving board that is being enjoyed by both the divers and the onlookers. One boy has brought a tire, which was probably used like an inner tube for floating.

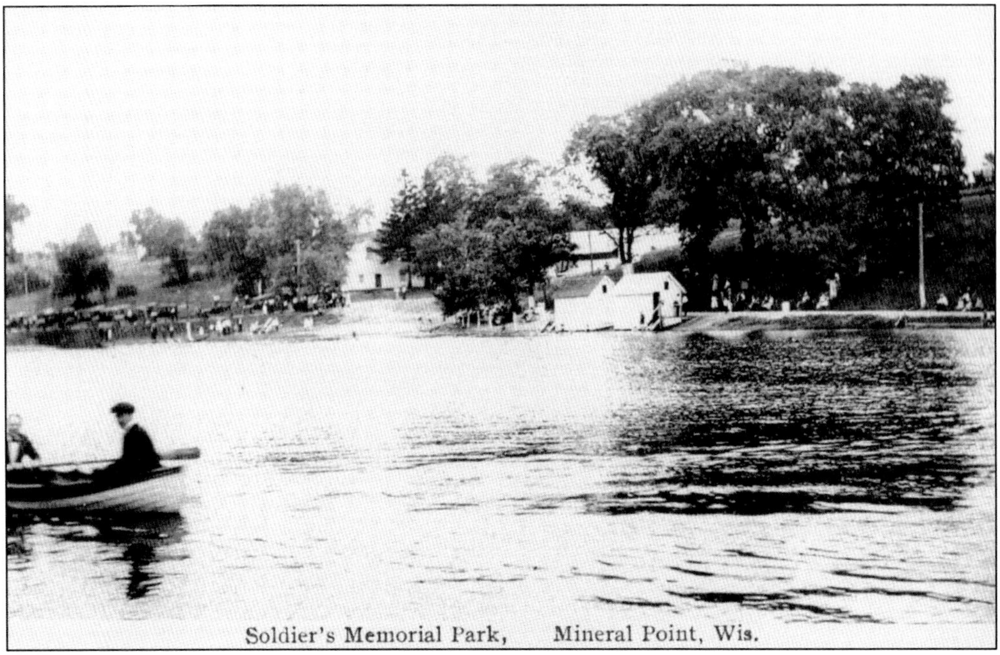

A rowboat floats along the deep end of the Soldiers' Memorial Park in 1923.

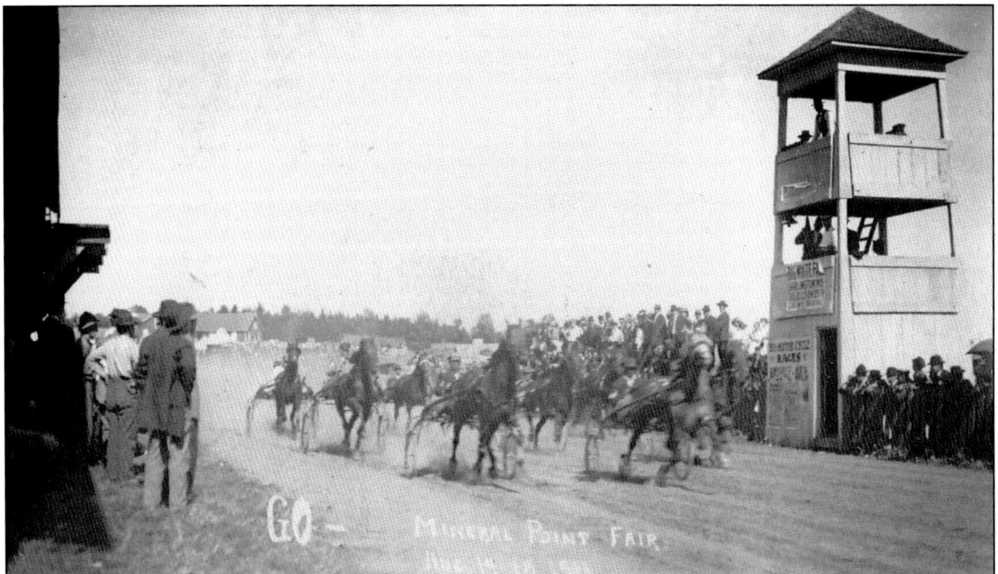

Men bet large wagers on these horse races. The judge's booth was filled with officials who called the winners.

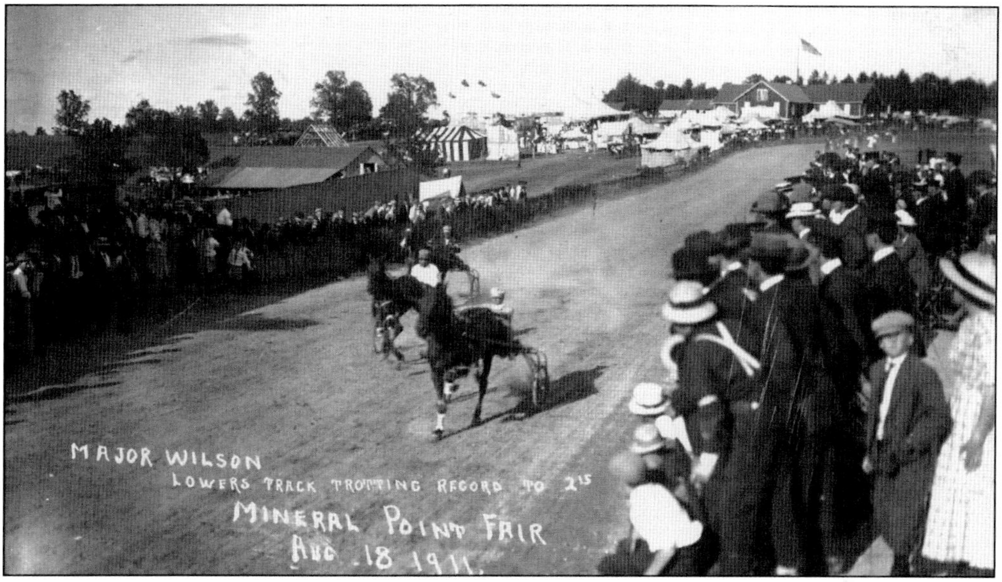

Horse racing was the favorite event at the Mineral Point Fair. Mobs cheered on Major Wilson to victory. The fair still uses its original slogan, "It's Your Fair! Be There!" The Iowa County Fair celebrated its 150 year anniversary in 2006.

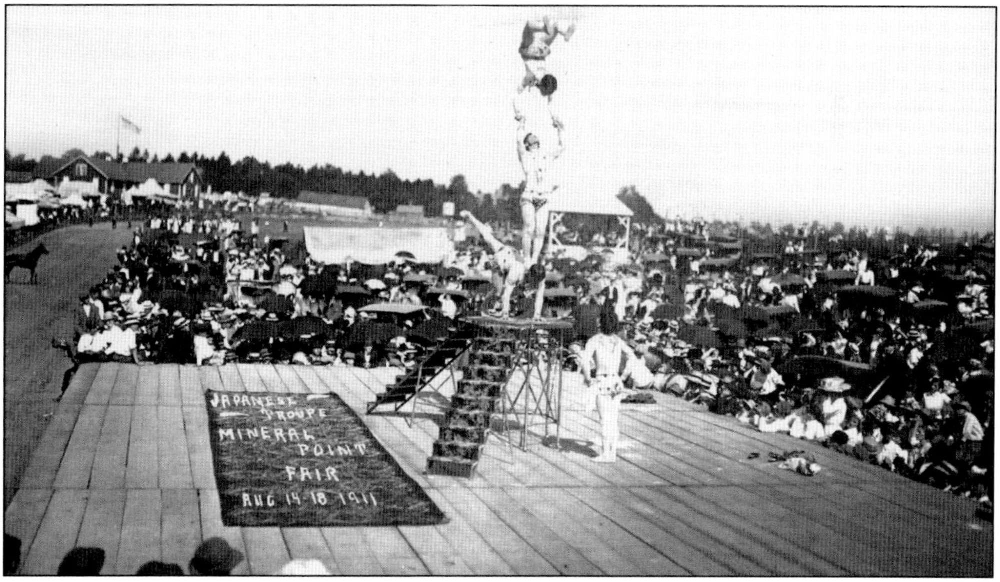

Pictured above is a scene from the August 14–18 Iowa County Fair of 1911. The performers are a Japanese troupe the fair used for entertainment that year. The top total attendance on record for the fair was 20,592 in 1950. Livestock shows and youth exhibits have held the fair together as it has been recognized as having one of the top cattle exhibits in Wisconsin. Large prize money helps promote agriculture and 4-H in Iowa County.

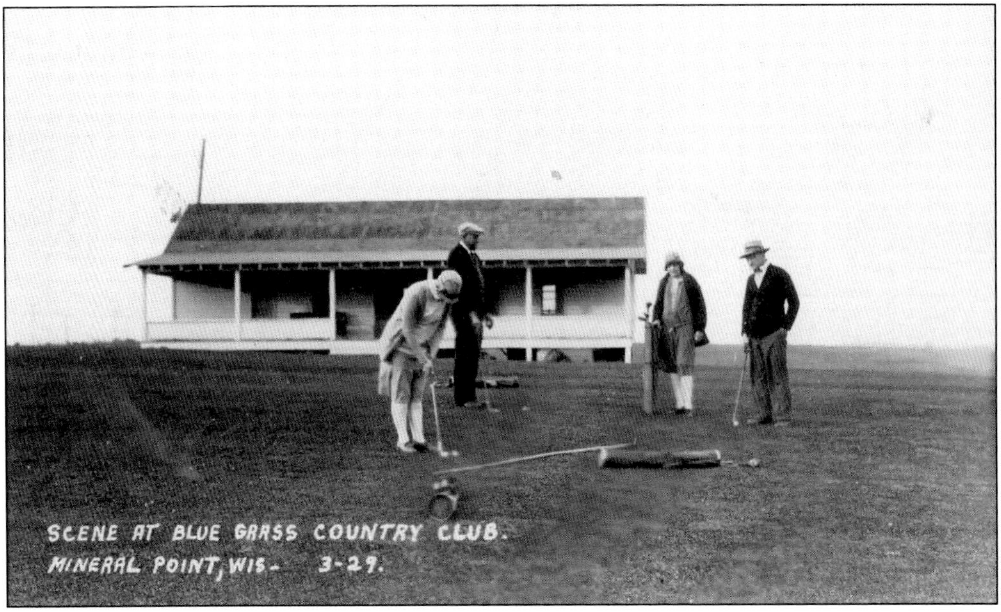

These golfers were not waiting for summer when they bundled up in March 1929 to play in front of the Blue Grass Country Club. The golf course and club opened in April 1923 with 75 distinguished citizens as members. Membership was $40 a year if one lived in town and $15 if one lived out of town. It was located approximately where Goodweiler Veteran Services and Alliant Energy now stand. The Dodge-Point Golf Club was organized in 1947 with 230 members.

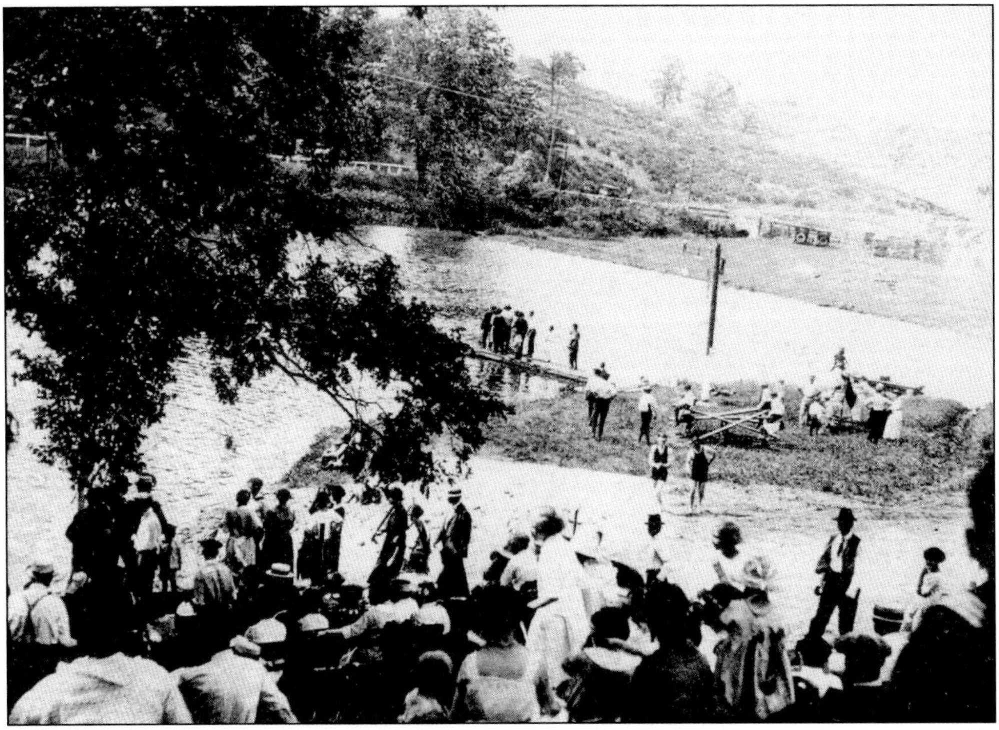

People gather at the edge of the lake at Soldiers' Memorial Park to watch a swimming meet. The park is a beautiful spot and a center for many types of recreation in Mineral Point.

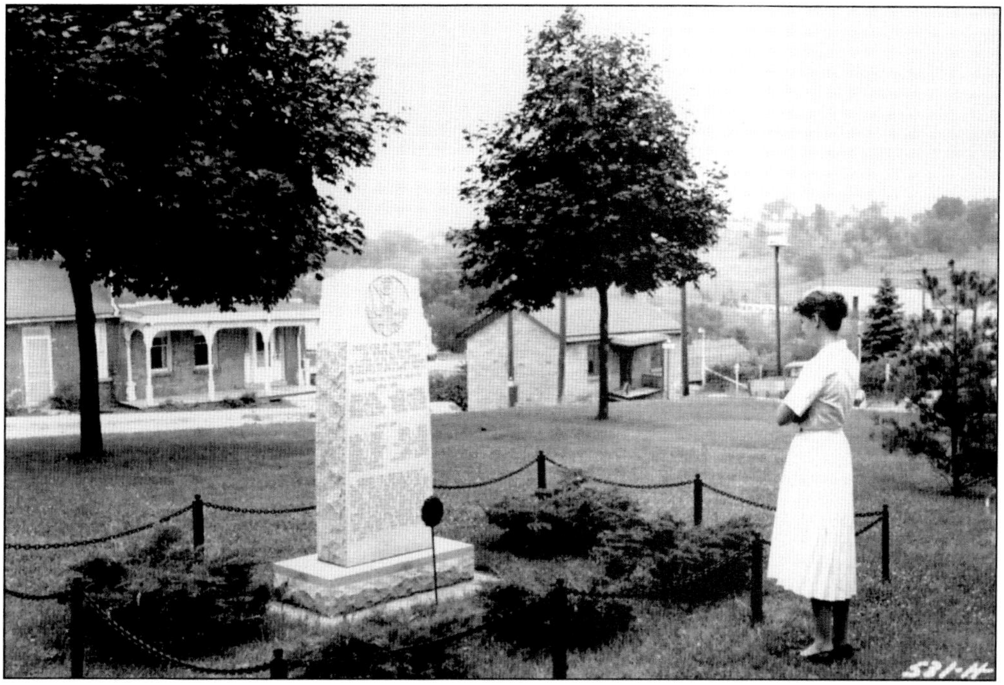

Library Memorial Park is located on High Street next to the library. It was here that the first courthouse stood. A veteran's memorial monument stands in this park.

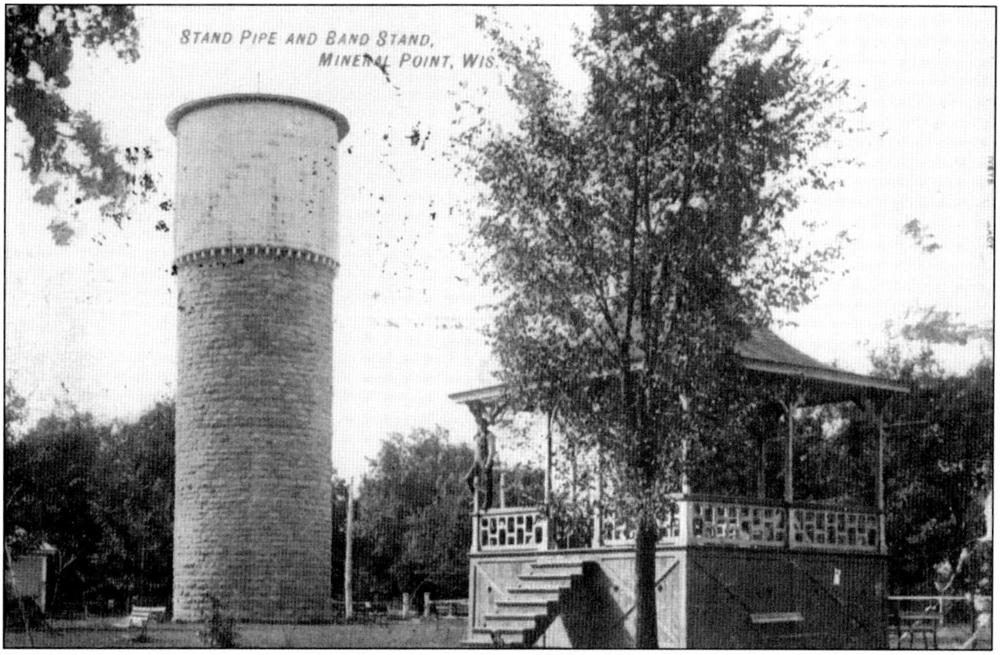

Water Tower Park in this 1913 view shows a bandstand and a large tower that held the city water. There was another water tower before the current one. The present city water tower of unusual design has won several awards for its uniqueness. The bandstand is no longer standing.

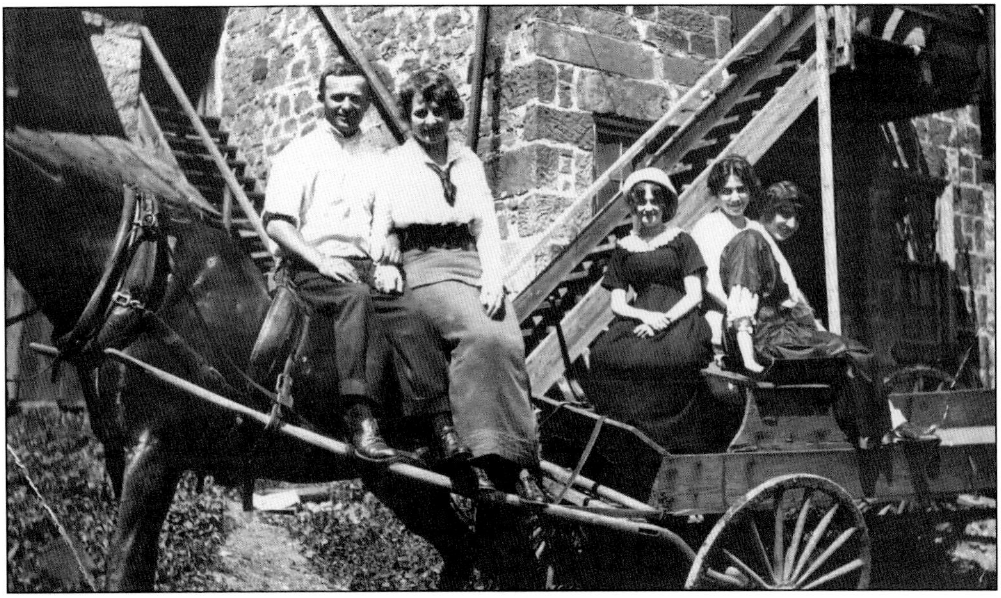

One lucky guy with four women is out for a wagon ride in 1915.

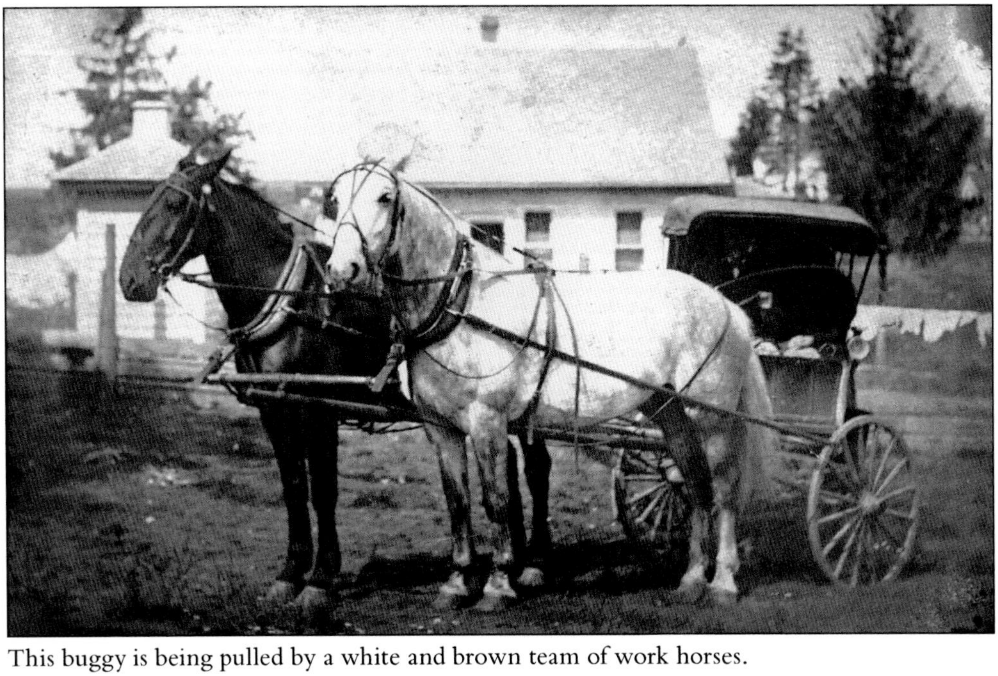

This buggy is being pulled by a white and brown team of work horses.

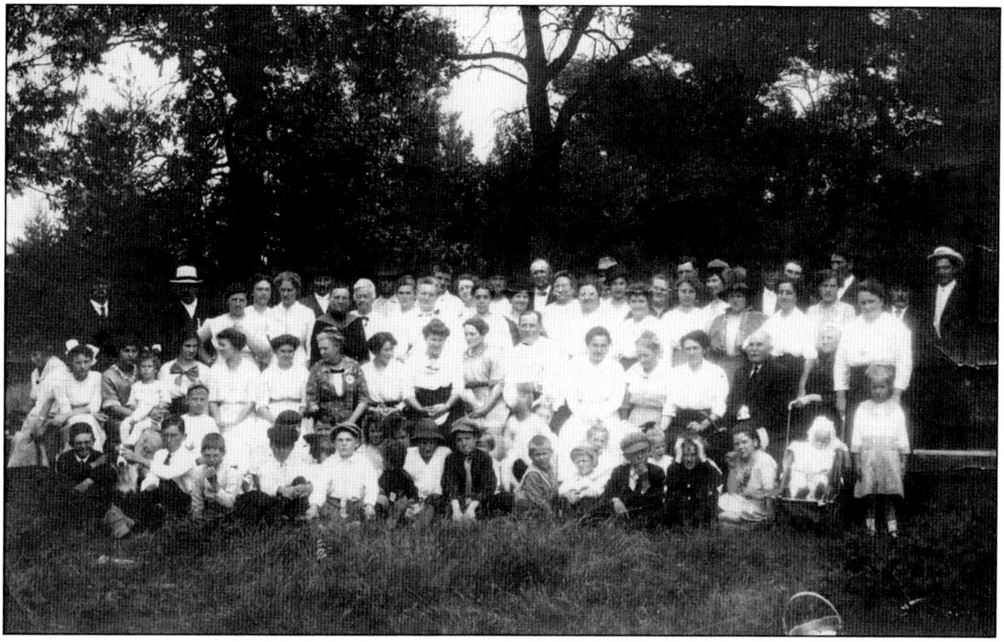

The Royal Neighbors gather for a picnic. Notice almost all the women have their hair done up on top of their heads.

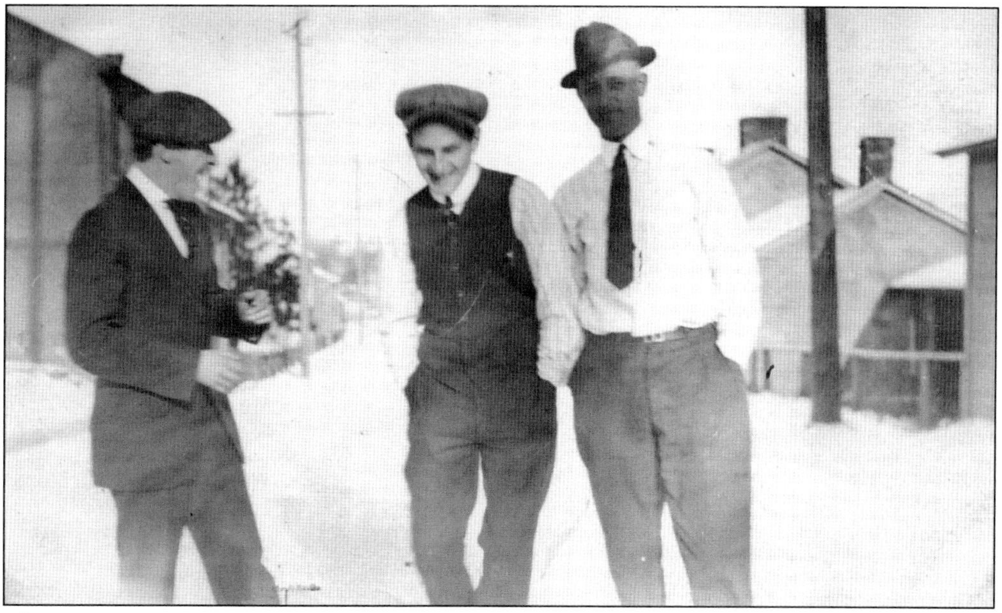

Three men share a laugh on Hoard Street, now known as Shake Rag Street. A man was rarely seen without his hat or cap on prior to the 1970s.

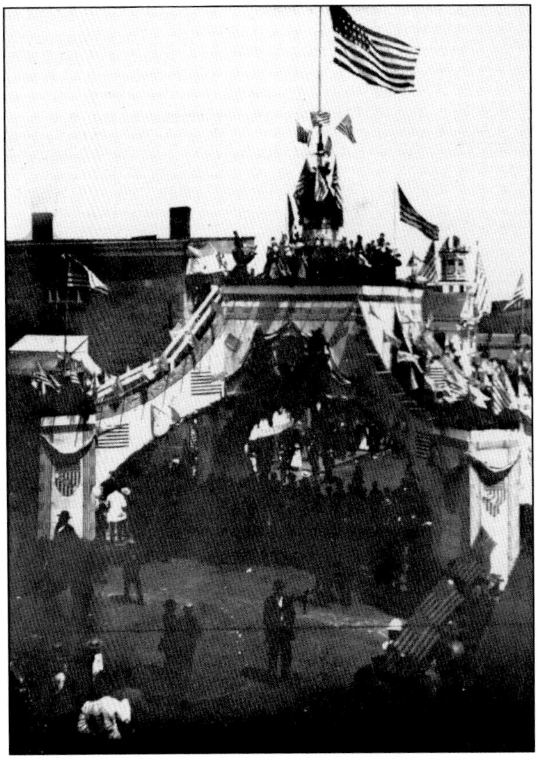

This processional arch was built over High Street for the June 10, 1886, Southwestern Wisconsin Veteran's Association reunion. It was billed as one of the grandest events in the history of Mineral Point. The crowd was estimated at 10,000, which included 600 registered veterans. The only remaining survivor of the War of 1812 was present. Dignitaries stood underneath the arch to stay out of the sun. There are layers of flags on the flagpole. (Courtesy of the Mineral Point Historical Society.)

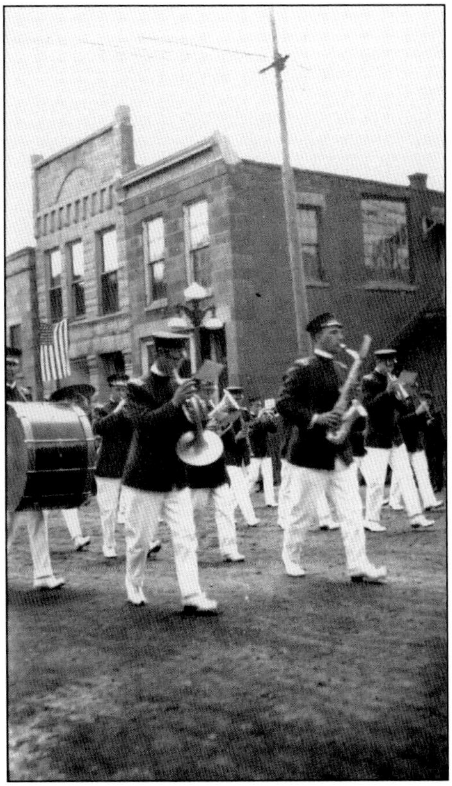

Mineral Point had a grand band for almost a century. Local bands were famous in days past. The band would lead local celebrations and parades. The band exercised patriotism and lifted pride in our democracy. This is the intersection of High and Chestnut Streets.

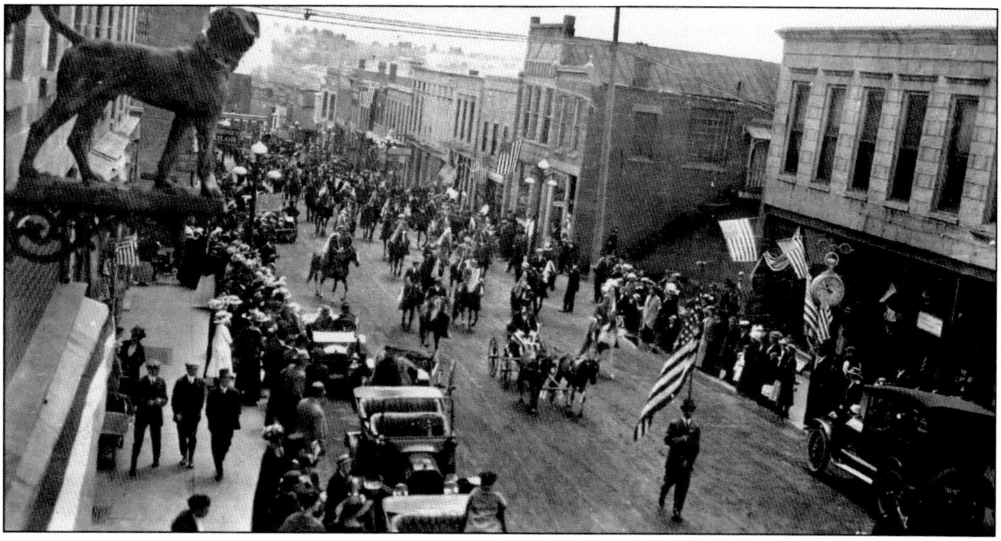

The pointer dog oversees the 17th annual picnic of the Catholic Societies of southwest Wisconsin at Mineral Point on June 9, 1911. While the main floors of most of the buildings have changed, the unique Cornish stone architecture today is much as it was then in the second-floor areas. The dog helps add to Mineral Point's distinct atmosphere.

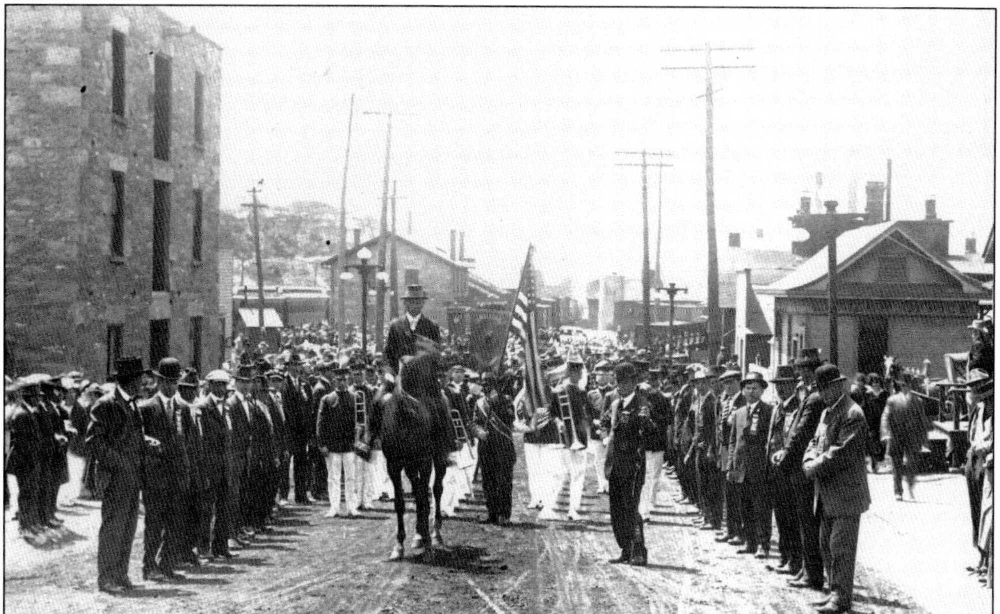

The man carrying the flag on Commerce Street was William Norman of Mineral Point. He was born here in 1885. No place better illustrates the meaning of the ideal "of, by, and for the people" than a parade.